I Believe in Music

I BELIEVE IN MUSIC

Life Experiences and Thoughts

on the Future of Electronic

Music by the Founder of the

Roland Corporation

IKUTARO
KAKEHASHI

with ROBERT **OLSEN**

HAL•LEONARD®

7777 W. BLUEMOUND RD. P.O. BOX 13819 MILWAUKEE, WI 53213

Published by Hal Leonard Corporation
7777 West Bluemound Road
P.O. Box 13819
Milwaukee, WI 53213, USA

Trade Book Division Editorial Offices:
151 West 46th Street, 8th Floor
New York, NY 10036
Visit Hal Leonard online at **www.halleonard.com**

Library of Congress Cataloging-in-Publication Data

Kakehashi, Ikutaro, 1930-
  I believe in music : life experiences and thoughts on the future of electronic music by the founder of the Roland Corporation / Ikutaro Kakehashi with Robert Olsen.
    p. cm.
  ISBN 0-634-03783-8
    I. Kakehashi, Ikutaro, 1930- 2. Musical instrument makers—Japan—Biography
  3. Musical instruments, Electronic—Japan—History. 4. Roland Corporation.
  I. Olsen, Robert, 1934- II. Title.

  ML424.K24 K34 2002
  784.19'092—dc21
  [B]   2001059094

Printed in the United States of America
First Edition

10 9 8 7 6 5 4 3 2 1

CONTENTS

Translator's Foreword

Taro Kakehashi and I first met in 1969. Our two companies had formed the joint venture, Hammond International Japan, and we were going to have to cooperate with each other for the business to succeed. I spoke no Japanese, and Taro appeared to have a limited vocabulary in English. It was not a reassuring basis on which to build a working relationship. But then, over a very awkward and uncomfortable lunch, I said something stupid, and Taro made a joke out of it.

Think of this in reverse: If your vocabulary in Japanese were a few hundred words, do you think you could make an understandable joke to someone who spoke no English? Would you even have the courage to try? Of course not, nor would I. But that incident still reverberates in my memory. With extremely limited words Taro Kakehashi could put together a joke, and I could understand the joke in the context of *English thought structure*. I still don't fully understand how that process worked, but our minds seemed to operate on some sort of common channel, so that communication could flow, despite limitations of vocabulary.

For several years we worked closely together, and the new venture prospered. Eventually our career paths parted. I moved on to Lowrey Organs, and Taro founded Roland. Since each of us was in the music business, we continued to communicate with some regularity. Even after I left the music industry in the mid-80s, we still found ways to stay in touch, although not nearly as frequently. And then, very late on a July evening, Taro phoned.

He invited me to participate in the preparation of his memoir as "translator." The fundamentals had not materially changed, Taro's English vocabulary, although substantially expanded, was still clearly a second language. My Japanese vocabulary, never large, had totally disappeared. How could I presume to translate him? As in so many other things, again this time he was right.

His accent may be Japanese, but Taro's voice is universal. My task has not been to *translate* word for word or thought for thought. My real job was to supplement his English language vocabulary and do the grammar thing. Just because Taro speaks haltingly does not mean he doesn't understand English. The careful scrutiny he applied to our "finished" product resulted in substantial further improvements.

The process was complicated (and at times exasperating). Taro dictated his thoughts in Japanese. Professional translators (with no special knowledge of the music trade) converted his words into strictly literal and sometimes baffling English. I then read and re-read each translation until I could get beyond the intermediate barrier of the translator and "hear" both Taro's voice and his intent.

At this point we could go to work. In referring to the translated text, I said our finished product. This translation may have its base in the long-standing association between Taro and me, but that has been an unstructured and highly intuitive form of communication. For 40 years the last step in my own writing process (whether it was an investment proposal or a short story) has been the critical review supplied by my wife, Anita. Combining logic, grammar and good sense, she has readily corrected and invariably improved the final text.

The real measure of her contribution to this effort is the fact that her handiwork cannot be seen. Without Anita, this English language manuscript could have emerged as a series of random and disconnected anecdotes. Through her efforts the text has been clarified, quantified, simplified, organized, rationalized, and altogether made a whole lot better.

Working with Taro Kakehashi on this project has been a rejuvenating experience for me. By coincidence, we each entered the world market of electronic music in 1964. The people and events he writes about are frequently people and events I have also dealt with.

By giving me the opportunity to share in this project, he has given me the chance to revisit important parts of my own past. Best of all, this time Anita has been by my side.

Robert Olsen
Northbrook, IL
January, 2002

PROLOGUE

There aren't many people still alive who participated in the entire dynamic era of electronic music development from World War II to the present. In more ways than one, it is my good fortune to be among the few survivors.

As we enter the new millennium, experts from all sorts of professions have been announcing their choices for the most significant developments of the 20th century. When it comes to culture, social development, or values, events related to music frequently figure prominently. Usually it's the Beatles or the original Woodstock. Often it's both of them. The fact is, without electronic musical instruments and power amplifiers, neither the Beatles as a group, nor Woodstock as an event, could have happened.

My entire life has been devoted to the development and manufacture of electronic musical instruments. There were times when it was simply a dogged pursuit of a field that fascinated me. Most of the time it was more than that. I believed in the vast potential that electronics offered for musical expression, and I was committed to finding and unleashing that potential. Now, in the autumn of my own years and looking back over a century of spectacular innovation, I realize I was privileged to have been part of a process that has permanently expanded the potential for artistic expression.

My life in electronic music started in the era of simple electromechanical design. Vacuum tubes were the high-tech devices of the day. They were followed by transistors, but only briefly. Then came

ICs, then CPUs, and, currently, DSPs. Not only did I experience these developments; I was closely involved in each step of the progress.

After World War II, the application of communication technology to music achieved its first serious impact. In the 1950s I was running an electrical appliance business, and I started building electronic organs as an experiment. In 1960 I established Ace Electronic Industries Inc. to strengthen my participation in the field. Acceptance of electronic music was slow at first, but I will never forget November of 1965. The Japan Electronic Musical Instruments Association sponsored a live concert. All eight Japanese manufacturers—Yamaha, Kawai, Panasonic (Technics), Ace, Teisco, Kuroda Tone, Columbia, and Korg—participated. The intensity of the audience was breathtaking. It was if they wanted the music to play on forever.

Remembering the state of that early technology, I am awed by the changes that have been wrought since then.

In 1972, with the establishment of Roland Corporation, I committed myself completely to the business of electronic musical instruments. By that time the application of electronics to music had become much broader. Traditional musical instruments—pianos, guitars, organs, wind instruments, and even violins—had also become electronic. Recorders and mixers were also being recognized as essential elements of music production. It was beginning to be understood that computer music was going to be an increasingly important element.

Many of the people who contributed to that early growth of the industry are no longer with us, and I am not necessarily an infallible witness to what occurred. Researching the past, I have found that my own memories are sometimes at odds with the facts as recalled by others. Fortunately, I still had the time to seek out the help of others' recollections in putting together this book.

My objective is not to recite the complete history of the industry. That is a task that has been well-covered by others. But there is a broader context of electronics and music and society that fascinates me.

In 1997 I had the opportunity to visit Don Leslie and speak with him about his wonderful manuscript, *The Don Leslie Story*. As the inventor of Leslie Speakers, Don was one of the pioneers in applying electronics to music. Among other important experiences, his story of battling the entrenched negativism of "traditional" manufacturers offers profound insights into the U.S. musical industry scene during the past 50 years.

Both Don and his wife Carolyn urged me write down my own thoughts and observations about the development of the music industry during that period. Don's book is at once an inspirational tale of success against adversity and an outstanding autobiography. I could not hope to equal his wonderful story, but I knew that I would like to give something back to the industry. By sharing my experiences and perspectives as a participating witness in the development of the modern industry, I could perhaps serve the people who are taking up the responsibility for continued development of the field.

Writing such a book was an interesting idea, but in 1997 I put the concept aside as something to be done "later." In the summer of 1998, thanks to the wisdom and skill of the surgeon and my own physician, I survived a serious and prolonged struggle with cancer. It was a lesson that could not be ignored, and I am grateful for the opportunity that modern medicine has given me. The enforced recovery time allowed me to take another look at the world of electronic musical instruments.

It is my hope that this book will be a useful background source for the next generation of designers, musicians, and manufacturers. I hope it will contribute to broadening their understanding of the relationships between technology and music.

It is to this next generation that I dedicate this effort.

I. Kakehashi
Hamamatsu, Japan
July, 1999

ACKNOWLEDGEMENTS

Among the many people to whom I owe gratitude and thanks for helping me write my story, there were several who were particularly significant.

Bob and Anita Olsen transformed my thoughts into English while being faithful to the spirit of my words. Bob and I have been friends and colleagues since the days of Ace Electronic, and his own understanding of some of the events in my life has made him a doubly valuable resource for this project. Without knowing that Bob was available, I'm not sure I ever would have started this project. Anita, an expert grammarian, has refined and polished my story into far more clarity than either Bob or I could have managed on our own.

Dennis Houlihan contributed his formidable skills at organization. He facilitated the acquisition of materials, arranged interviews with sources, and negotiated the publishing arrangements. When the project faltered, it was Dennis who put things right again.

Seiko Yoshimura was far more than a secretary. She helped me organize the raw material, and she was active in arranging for the translation of my original text into literal English. In one of the most complicated assignments imaginable, she was responsible for all aspects of coordination with the American writing project.

My three good friends, Remo Belli, Don Leslie, and Isao Tomita each gave generously of their time by granting me extended interviews. Transcripts of the interviews are included as appendices to this text. More than that, their comments and reminiscences were invaluable in helping me to recapture the immediacy of many of the events in my own life in music.

Most importantly, I owe thanks to my wife, Masako. Without her care and concern, it is possible that this book never would have been finished. During my hospitalization for cancer in 1998, I became increasingly interested in writing my story. Fortunately I was able to return to full time duties at Roland after my surgery, so that meant that the book had to be written as I could find time. Masako encouraged me in the effort, and in April 2000 I published the original of this book, "Music Is My Lifework" (LIFEWORK WA ONGAKU) in Japan. From the very beginning it was Masako who most frequently read my Japanese text, and she gave me many wise suggestions about my writing. No one but she could have done that. Masako has been – and continues to be – a vital partner in all aspects of my life.

Finally, I want to say how honored I am to have my book published by the Hal Leonard Corporation – the world's largest music publisher headed by the Chairman, Keith Mardak, and President, Larry Morton. Mr. Morton made a special trip to Los Angeles to publicly present the first sample copy to me before the 2002 NAMM show. The presentation took me by complete surprise and his kindness touched me to the heart.

CHAPTER ONE

BEGINNINGS

In 1964 I attended my first international music fair. That fair was my official entry into the global music market, but it was a journey that actually began 20 years earlier.

I was 15 years old in 1945. During the preceding five years virtually every aspect of my life had been organized and governed by the reality of World War II. Abruptly, everything changed: there were no more air raids; newspapers could write about anything, and even a somewhat wider range of food was available for those who could afford it. American clothing styles became the fashion, and a wide choice of music was suddenly in the air.

It was the music that gave me the most joyous sense of expanding possibilities. There were tunes and harmonic structures I had never heard in my life, and I was deeply impressed by them. During the war, virtually the only music we heard was patriotic "war songs" intended to promote military spirit. In the early postwar years, those songs conjured up unpleasant memories. Today these patriotic airs simply remind me of my youth.

There was a time, before the war imposed censorship on everyday life, when many songs and melodies from overseas (other than modern jazz) could be heard throughout the country. That was the period known as the "Taisho democracy." However, the flood of music that engulfed Japan in the immediate postwar days was something totally different from the cautious liberalism of the earlier period.

During the war, radio transmission was under strict government control. There was absolutely no way to hear foreign news or listen to overseas music. Putting together a shortwave radio or even possessing one was considered spying. I can even remember a policeman coming to my house to inspect the antenna that I had put up for my small, crystal set radio.

When the new music filled the air, the only way to hear it was via radio. Phonographs would not become available for a few more years. There were no private radio stations in Japan. We had to rely on all-wave radio receivers that could pick up both the occupation army's broadcasts to its GIs, and shortwave transmissions from distant places. Compared to today, our listening choices were terribly limited and the reception quality was poor. Still, we were delighted to be delivered from the wartime restriction in which NHK (Japan Broadcasting Corporation) was the only station allowed to broadcast.

We had no program schedules or listings of station frequencies. I just turned the dial at random, seeking any station. When I happened to come across a good one, I would write down the time and frequency for future reference. When a magazine was finally published that listed broadcast schedules, my choice of stations increased dramatically.

In my pursuit of modern music, I had to learn how radios worked. Just two years later this hobby would develop into my actually producing "new" all-band radios for profit, while simultaneously operating a repair shop for old clocks and watches. I was simply trying to get by in the world. Looking back, I suppose it was also my first venture into diversified product lines.

I had been orphaned at the age of two, and since that time I lived in Osaka with my grandparents. In mid-February 1945, the authorities evacuated us from our home as a safety precaution because we lived next door to a large chemical factory. On March 13, less than a month later, our new, "safer" location was firebombed. The house burned to ashes in a burst of flame. The blaze consumed my entire collection of railway models, including a stack of picture albums and scrapbooks of steam and electric locomotives. It was a collection I had started many years earlier and actually had been able to expand during the war years. Considering the sheer size and complexity of the lost collection, I knew I would never be able to replace it. Strangely, I didn't feel sad or angry when I came across fragments of the collection in the ashes of the house. Instead, I decided to start fresh with a new hobby. I still am interested in railway models, but never since have I thought of collecting them.

After our house burned my grandparents moved to my grandmother's hometown in rural Kyushu. I needed to stay in Osaka to finish my schooling, so I went to live with the family of Mr. Sakai, the father of one of my classmates. I stayed with the Sakai family until the end of the war. Food was very scarce and there were air raids almost every night. Each time the alarm was sounded we had to move to a shelter. Over time we became accustomed to the process, and we would stay in bed until the bombs actually began to fall. Nevertheless, we did not sleep well, and we were always hungry.

I was 14 years old then, and I can remember how hard it was to commute to the Hitachi Shipyard at the port of Osaka, where I had been mobilized as a student worker. The shipyard was producing various components for oil tankers, costal defense ships and special submarines. My assignment was in the milling machine department.

I once sneaked into a compartment where a special submarine was being assembled. It had been sealed off from the production area with a plywood barricade, but for some reason it was not guarded during lunch hour. I could see every detail of the submarine except the bomb nose, which had been removed. The construction was extremely rough. The crude rudder plate showed no evidence of having been machined. It seemed simply to have been sliced out by a welding device. There was a very small dome in the submarine that was barely big enough for one person to squeeze into. The unfortunate operator actually had to ride on top of the engine in that tiny space. The periscope was fixed to the operator's seat and could not slide up or down.

Graduation day at Nishinoda Technical School.

I knew at a glance that the submarine was made for just one sortie. The strategy of suicide attacks by a special Kamikaze corps was well known. In those days it was being glorified in newspaper reports. But seeing a real suicide attack vessel in front of my eyes gave me nothing but icy chills.

There were two classmates with me. We went straight back to work, and never again spoke of what we had seen during that lunchtime. We feared punishment if a guard found us, and, if we spoke about it, we were afraid of a rumor getting out. Beyond those immediate worries, the instant of our discovery was also intensely personal for me. I thought of some of my classmates who had joined the Junior Pilot Training Corps in the Air Force, and I wondered. . . . The sight of that suicide attack submarine was a trauma that lingered for a long, long time.

On August 14, 1945, the day before the war ended, bombers struck the arsenal located behind Osaka castle. This raid was different from the regular attacks that usually consisted of fire-bombs during the night. This time, when each bomb exploded it caused a massive compression wave to spread through the air. I vividly remember the terrifying physical impact of those invisible waves we experienced that day. They were like ripples of water when a stone is thrown in, but vastly more powerful.

Whenever I ride past the Kyobashi station on the Osaka Loop rail line, I still remember the horror of that merciless bombing attack. The nighttime attacks were bad enough. But when this raid took place, workers were at their jobs. The manager at the Hitachi Shipyard where I was working was one of the casualties. I now understand that the raid was carried out because there was a faction in the Japanese military that threatened to block the planned surrender. At the time it seemed a terribly cruel and senseless blow.

The skyline to the east of Osaka castle is now filled with skyscrapers. There is nothing to remind us of that devastating attack that took place on the last day of the war.

My First Business Venture

I stayed on in Osaka until graduation, seven months after the war ended. I also took an entrance examination for the Osaka Prefectural College of Chemical Engineering (now Osaka Prefecture University) in February of 1946. There were about 300 applicants for the Chemical Engineering department, and I was one of 53 people who passed the entrance exam. Unfortunately, I did not do as well with the required health check. Due to severe food shortages I had become seriously undernourished, and it was deemed likely that I would not be able to sustain the rigors of college-level study requirements.

Urban society was in disarray after the war, and my personal confusions reflected the instability of the time. In retrospect, I cannot understand how I thought I could afford a higher education. I had no savings for school expenses, nor did I have any livelihood to support me in the coming years. In April of 1946 I decided to join my relatives in Kyushu. I remember it was terribly difficult to even get a railway ticket.

Life in rural Kyushu was vastly better than in war-devastated Osaka. The food was good and the people were very kind to me. I had been transported from the harsh survival struggle of Osaka to an entirely different and relatively calm world. For me it was a time of regeneration. The environment healed my physical disorder and I felt alive again.

Inevitably, there was a negative factor to face. The calm of rural subsistence living meant that it was virtually impossible to find any sort of paying job. Finally, I obtained two part-time posts. For four months I was an assistant on a geographical survey of the district. It was assumed I was qualified for survey work because I had graduated from a technical school. (Actually, my studies were in mechanical engineering and had nothing to do with surveying.) The survey itself involved updating the obsolete land ledger that dated back to the Meiji era (late 19th century). During the four months of the survey, our team walked every road and spoke to almost every resident of the entire district. These contacts became an important source of customers when I opened my watch repair shop the following year.

As the survey work was rather limited, I also took a job at the construction site of a bridge over the Takachiho valley. I was an errand boy. A few years ago I visited the bridge. It was still there, but it was virtually unused. It had been retained as a sightseeing spot for tourists after the main road was moved farther upstream. Standing on the new bridge, I could see my old bridge in the distance. I thought of my younger days and felt warmly sentimental. My wage had been 15 yen per day (less than $1.00 in today's purchasing power). Three yen were needed for lunch, so I actually obtained 12 yen each day. The amount may have been small, but there was no reason to complain. Chances of getting any sort of job were so scarce that one had no choice. You were lucky if you had any job at all.

These were part-time jobs, so I knew I had to find something to do as a continuing occupation. The repair of clocks and watches drew my attention. In those postwar years, there were no new products on the market. People had no alternative but to fix what they had, so the demand for repair work was quite large. At night, after my work for the survey or the bridge construction, I would stand for hours gazing into the window of a service shop. I wanted to learn the repair process.

At last the manager of the shop took me in and offered me a position as apprentice to learn the repair business from him. He agreed to teach me at night. In just a few months I understood the inner mechanism of clocks. I learned how to disassemble and clean them. Since I had specialized in mechanical engineering in the technical junior high school, my knowledge of mechanical elements helped me greatly. Then I decided, since I had enough knowledge of clocks, I should move on and start learning about wristwatches.

I diffidently asked my master to teach me about wristwatches. Instantly he exploded into a shouting tirade of rejection. When he finally calmed down he pointed out that the term of apprenticeship was customarily seven years. He explained that the proper training period on clocks was three years, not two months. Learning shop management issues such as polishing showcases, arranging deliveries, bookkeeping, etc., followed clock training. Training on wristwatches always came last. The entire training period should take five years, and then the apprentice was expected to serve for an additional two years. Compensation during the seven years was limited to room and board plus a token wage for pocket money.

Considering that the apprentice would become a competitor of the master's shop, the seven-year term was reasonable, so I had no other choice but to leave. My master had rejected my request instantly, saying that it was impossible to teach me about wristwatches after merely a two-month training period. Looking back, I suppose it was natural for him to turn me down. From his point of view I was supposed to learn all of the fine points of traditional business manners and techniques during those five years. That wasn't what I had in mind.

I guess I was too young to understand how an apprentice was supposed to behave. I was too aggressive to be patient and wait my turn. Since I thought I had learned everything about clocks, I couldn't see staying there for the next few years repeating the same routine over and over. I decided to learn how to repair watches on my own, so I sent away for a book that promised complete instruction on the subject. The book was a shabby piece of merchandise printed on cheap paper and poorly bound, but the infor-

At age 16, I opened my first business: Kakehashi Watch Shop.

mation it contained was invaluable. I decided to open my shop immediately so that I could test my newly acquired knowledge on the repair orders that would come to me.

When I opened my shop, there already were three repair shops serving a town with a population of only 12,000. Not surprisingly, the existing shops did not welcome my arrival on the scene. Since I had only recently been a green apprentice, they were offended that I would presume to elevate myself to the position of competitor. They had nothing good to say about me. I went ahead without their approval.

Although my service shop occupied a tiny space of only 1.8 meters (about 20 square feet), the business was a success from the beginning. The fact that I knew so many people throughout the district helped, and the business was quite profitable. I enjoyed the work of repairing various types of watches, from small ones called "gnats" for ladies, to big watches on chains for men. Many people had acquired watches from overseas, especially from

Switzerland, and by that time almost all of those watches needed overhauling. In those days watches were considered status symbols of enormous significance and great value (unlike today, when inexpensive but highly accurate quartz watches are thought of as fashion accessories).

As I repaired various watches, I also learned a valuable lesson in business. The more expensive and higher-class the watch, the easier it was to service. Overhauling watches made up about 70 percent of my repair orders. In the case of higher quality watches, I only had to clean, oil, and reassemble the parts. That was all it took to fix them. On the contrary, it was extremely difficult to restore watches made in Japan during the war. Components were made of lower quality materials and fewer jewels compared to the high-quality watches: friction wore the cheaper parts down quickly, and mere cleaning did not restore accurate timekeeping. Even though it required delicate skill and patience to restore cheap units to working order, you were only allowed to charge two-thirds as much as the price for repair of the considerably easier, expensive watches.

In those days Switzerland was the only country practicing outstanding technique and skill in watch manufacturing. Almost every day my work showed me the undeniable difference in technological level between Swiss and Japanese watches. I find it fascinating that one of the products that finally led Japan's postwar entry into global commerce was quality wristwatches.

The rapid success of my watch repair business meant I no longer had to worry about making a living. This gave me the time and resources to resume my attention to radio receivers as a means of listening to music. In fact I began to seriously explore the possibilities of radios as a new area for my engineering interest. Watch repair, while satisfying, aims only to restore items to their original condition. When a watch was repaired and its complex mechanism finally restored to its proper function, I felt a certain pleasure, but it was nothing like the sense of accomplishment I felt when I created an all-new radio receiver.

Once I started to feel this way, I curtailed the time I spent on watches and began spending more time on the repair of radio receivers. There were exciting possibilities for growth in radio thanks to the increasing number of broadcast stations and the general expansion of the potential market for receivers. While living in the woods of Kyushu, the biggest problem I encountered was acquiring radio parts. Rather than send mail orders for components to Tokyo, I chose to go to the nearest large city, Kumamoto. It was two days away, but I preferred making my purchases in person.

I also needed access to old parts so I could repair obsolete radio models. I decided to purchase old radios that were no longer working. I asked acquaintances in various districts to bring in abandoned receivers. I purchased them at low prices, disassembled them and gathered the necessary components. With just a few newly purchased parts, I was able to construct a "new" receiver from five or six old ones.

In rebuilding radios I could not solve the problem of defective chemical capacitors. There was no way to repair a capacitor when it failed. It had to be replaced. Vacuum tubes were a different story. In those days radio vacuum tubes had a coat of magnesium lining their inner walls to enhance the degree of vacuum within the tube. I found that nearly half of the faulty radio tubes would work properly if the silver, glittery film were simply heated over a candle flame. That procedure caused the magnesium lining to absorb oxygen again, so that the degree of vacuum would be increased. This was a long way from high technology, but I restored many radio tubes in this way, and I could then use them in my repair work.

While my repair business was growing, I also helped with farm work during the busy harvest season and with rice planting at paddies owned by the relatives with whom I was staying. It was hard, physically demanding labor, but it offered a special kind of satisfaction. The problem was that I was not used to such work, and I would be exhausted when it was over. I had shivering fingers when we were done, and I would be unable to go back to my repair work for several days thereafter. I couldn't understand why my uncle never seemed to be tired. Then I realized that he was able to work so hard because it was his farm.

Despite the aches and pains, I am grateful that I could connect with the earth and learn the art of cultivation. I discovered much about myself and about life in general from the various agricultural projects. For one full year I gave myself completely to farming. It makes me pleasantly nostalgic to recall those days of watering the paddy before planting young rice plants, working with cows to prepare seedbeds or plowing through watery fields. A few years ago I visited the Smithsonian Museum of American History and saw exhibitions of tools used by American farmers. I felt affection for them because they reminded me of my days in the rice paddies.

Those four years in Kyushu were enormously fulfilling. My strong need to learn new things was satisfied by the continuing development of my activities with radios and amplification. In turn, those efforts were leading me into new categories of engineering. At the same time, I had regained my health, and I had found an inner peace in the rhythms of rural life, which I can recall with pleasure 50 years later.

Now it was time to move on. While I was in Kyushu, moving into major cities like Tokyo or Osaka was prohibited due to the poor food supply. One day I learned that this restriction would be lifted. Instantly I decided to close the shop and return to Osaka. Liquidating a shop is not at all an easy task, especially when you have outstanding orders. I had to complete all those backlogs, tie up every loose end, sell everything I had, and turn all assets into cash. It was hard work, but I completed the liquidation procedure in two weeks.

My reason for going back to Osaka was solely to go to a university. I had decided to specialize in electronics rather than chemical engineering. Even though I hadn't much cared about the prices I received, it was a pleasant surprise to learn that the amount I realized from liquidating my business was enough to support my tuition and living expenses for the coming four years.

In less than three weeks after I heard the news that return was possible, I had taken up residence in Osaka and started preparations for the entrance exam at the university. I was 20 years old and ready for a new beginning.

CHAPTER TWO

AN UNLIKELY EDUCATION

Until the war intervened, there were five grades in the preparatory schools. During the war the system was altered to cut the curriculum to four years so the students could be mobilized to work after early graduation. I was one of those who spent only four years in prep school under the altered system. Once the war was over, we realized that we did not meet the requirements for entering universities or taking entrance exams in accordance with the restored educational system. We had two choices: we could re-enter a high school, or we could take a qualifying exam for applying to the university.

First I had to get permission to return to Nishinoda Technical School. Their curriculum was focused on specialized knowledge rather than on subjects like English, general math or physics. I saw my time as limited, and I did not want to waste it on courses that were not necessary for university entrance exams. Initially I intended to take night courses at my old school so I could skip subjects like physical exercise. But I enrolled in a night course at Kitano High School instead because it was much more convenient for commuting.

It was 1950, but the enrollment at Kitano still reflected the dislocations of the war years. Several students in my class had studied at the Naval Academy or a Military Academy during the war. Many of the students were making up part of their high school curriculum in order to qualify for university exams. There was a variety of people of different ages in my night classes, and I really enjoyed the experience.

Just before graduation from Kitano High, I developed symptoms of lung tuberculosis. A thorough physical exam revealed that I needed immediate hospitalization. Unfortunately, in those days there were so many people suffering from TB that there were long waiting lists to enter all hospitals. It took six months before the authorities finally found a vacancy for me at a regional tuberculosis hospital called "Sengokuso." The teacher at the high school suggested that I take a temporary leave so that I could return to the school again. I decided to officially withdraw instead, because I could not realistically expect a quick recovery from the disease.

My condition was not too bad when I moved into Sengokuso. I could carry my own baggage when I entered the hospital. However, things gradually got worse during the following six months. I felt increasingly weary and exhausted. Eventually it became difficult to take care of myself. Day by day my health continued to decline until I finally required artificial pneumothorax treatment (pumping air into the chest cavity in order to force a lung to collapse). It caused considerable discomfort and pain for the patient, but in my case it was worth it, because it stabilized my condition.

I was demoralized by my condition, and I envied those who could have part or all of a diseased lung removed surgically and then expect to leave the hospital within a year. I was not eligible for such treatment because both of my lungs were infected. As things turned out, I was lucky not to have had access to the surgery at that time.

The money with which I was going to support my university life was exhausted during my extended hospitalization on things like meals and a variety of technical service charges. I needed some sort of side job to earn additional funds, but I was in no condition to handle tasks involving more than minimal exertion. In fact, most of my days were spent in passive radio listening. I had built a six-tube receiver, and with headphones I could listen to music without disturbing others in the ward.

In those days the primary treatment regimen for TB was passive. It consisted of clean air, plenty of rest, and good nutrition. There was only a limited range of active therapies available, and these were either extreme, like radical surgery, or ineffective, like calcium injections. Doctors really could do little more than observe our "progress" via periodic x-ray tests. The calcium injections had no discernable benefit, but they caused no apparent harm either. I suspect that both patients and medical staff knew the injections were pointless, but it felt better at least to be *trying* to fight the disease.

Clean air and plenty of rest could be supplied by the patients' own self-discipline. The need for balanced nutrition was much more difficult to satisfy. There were major food shortages throughout the country. I suppose the most important and challenging task for the director of the hospital was securing adequate food supplies for the nearly 700 patients in his care.

Among the patient population were members of the Japan Communist Party. They published a newsletter called *The X-Ray* and distributed it throughout the hospital. Each issue contained criticisms and complaints about the poor hospital rations. The paper contained so may demands for "improved services" and varieties of gossipy items that there was virtually no room for political content. Of course, their complaints were unrealistic in the context of the realities of conditions in the hospital and throughout the country. Most of us were sympathetic toward the director of the hospital with his frustrating and thankless tasks.

The patients themselves took some initiative. Those who had enough strength cultivated open areas within the hospital grounds and grew vegetables to provide for themselves. Those who had money bought eggs, butter, and dried fish at the hospital shop. I was able to purchase rations with earnings from repairing the watches and radios of patients and hospital staff.

My repair abilities not only assured me of the income I needed but helped other patients as well. Besides obtaining everyday nutrition, patients were worried about how to make a living after leaving the hospital. I established an informal school, teaching fellow patients how to repair watches or clocks and how to assemble radios. Some of the fellow patients I taught actually opened electrical appliance shops after leaving the hospital. Some others opened shops for clock and watch repair.

In 1951 several new commercial radio stations began broadcasting. Manufacturers of home appliances expanded their facilities to meet the increasing demand for radios. Some manufacturers even began assembling prototype TV receivers. Articles about TV began appearing in the popular press. Actual TV availability, both in hardware manufacture and image broadcasting, was still a long way off in the future, but excitement and anticipation were mounting.

I had read articles describing theories and circuit diagrams of TV receivers. The likelihood of actual TV availability in Japan seemed so remote that I scanned the articles with less than serious diligence. When I learned that a TV test broadcast was going to take place in the near future, it was exciting news. I read and re-read every article I could find on the subject of TV.

More than anything, I wanted to receive the test broadcast on my own TV receiver. The problem was that I could not purchase all of the components that were needed to assemble a working unit. Major components were available, but they were awfully expensive. I simply could not afford them. My only hope was to fabricate most of the necessary components by myself. That wouldn't be easy in my condition. Access to tools and materials was limited by the fact I would have to do all of the work beside my hospital bed.

The most expensive component of a TV set was the picture tube. In Japan it was called a Brown tube, because a Dr. Brown had invented it. Picture tubes imported from the English firm of Mullard were sold in Japan for 40,000 yen. In those days the average monthly salary for an office worker was 5,000 to 6,000 yen. The magnitude of the expense was way beyond my resources. Nevertheless, I dared to borrow the money from my aunt, even though my ability to ever repay was doubtful. There

My handmade TV set, featuring the "Brown" picture tube.

was no reason to believe I would recover from my disease, much less earn that sort of money in the future.

Still, once I had purchased the most expensive component, the project of putting together the TV receiver moved ahead swiftly. I was ready. When TV broadcasts began, they were delivered once a week for a few hours. Usually they were test patterns, but sometimes a movie would be broadcast. I would sit on my bed and wait for the test pattern, with my receiver completely assembled but not yet adjusted. Once the broadcasts began, I could make fine tunings and adjustments to the circuits. I enjoyed the fine-tuning, because I did it while I could observe the actual picture on the screen. It was a wonderful new experience.

At the time of the opening up of radio, and later TV broadcasting, I was excited because it meant greater access to choices in music and new forms of programming. It was not until a quarter century later that I realized the profound nature of what free broadcasting really meant in my life and the life of my country.

The technology to freely broadcast had existed since the 1920s. New stations in Japan were the result of freedom—not invention. In 1977 I visited the communist run East Berlin in East Germany. All sources of information including broadcasting were strictly controlled, and only official government ideas were permitted. Theoretically, the ordinary people could only know what the government allowed them to know. However, free broadcast from West Berlin reached most of East Germany and must have infuriated the communist authorities. Looking back, the fall of communism in East Germany was inevitable, because the people could know what the government was hiding.

We take freedom of information for granted, but in the history of the world, people have made enormous sacrifices to win that freedom for us. Now I realize what a priceless and significant experience I had when lying in the hospital; I could receive the first commercial radio transmission and see the very first TV test patterns.

Although it was only a static image on the screen, people would crowd into the area around my bed to observe and comment on what they saw. They rarely had a chance to see a TV receiver. Even though it was only a test pattern and the technology was in its early stage of development, it was fascinating. The crowded room became intolerable for those who shared the ward with me. Eventually the hospital staff decided that I should move to another place with my TV receiver to conduct my tuning experiments.

I tried to continue studying English, because I still planned to go to a university once I recovered from my illness. Unfortunately, after three years in the hospital, my disease showed no sign of remission. In fact, I was gradually losing what remained of my physical strength. Then word of new "miracle cures" with modern medicine brought hope to all of us patients. In fact, expectations grew so high that some patients even requested postponement of proven lung surgery that they were scheduled to receive. The problem was that the new medications

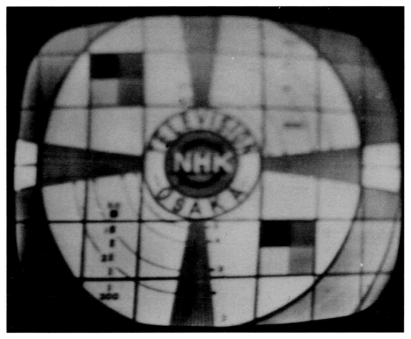

The test pattern that fascinated my fellow patients.

were extremely expensive. The black-market price of streptomycin was 10,000 yen per injection, and 40 injections were
required for recovery. It was absolutely unrealistic.

Fate intervened. Since I was in nearly failing condition, I was
chosen as a test case to verify the streptomycin treatment.
Injections began. The improvement in my condition was dramatic
and obvious from the very first day. My appetite returned immediately. Lingering fever and other symptoms disappeared. My
energy improved to the extent that I resumed my English studies,
and began to believe that everything was going to turn out all
right. By the tenth day of the treatment I was gaining weight. I
began making plans for my departure from the hospital once the
treatment was completed. Before the injections started, my weight
had fallen to 80 pounds from my original 132. I had already recovered nearly half the loss, but realistically I knew I would have to
remain in the hospital until I recovered my full strength.

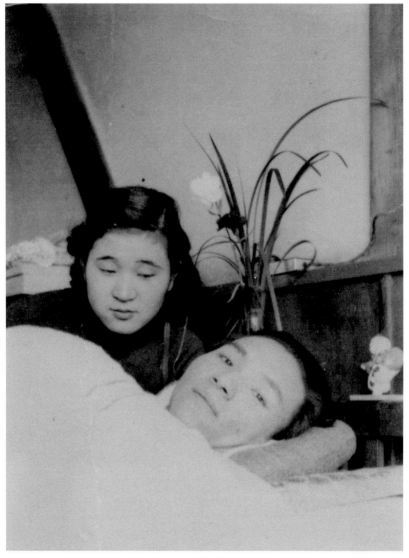

*Visits by my fiancée, Masako, were one of the few bright spots during my
stay at Sengokuso.*

I received a letter from one of my classmates at Kitano High
School in which he mentioned that he was graduating from the
university. The letter brought me back to the undeniable reality
that I had been in the hospital for four long years. I started
thinking about how I was going to lead my life after I left the

hospital, and I realized how unrealistic it would be to try again to enter a university.

I had spent four years in the hospital instead of in school. I decided I would graduate from "Sengokuso University." It would be difficult to find any other university that could provide such a comprehensive education. There were no school fees, no examinations, no final thesis, but you could still graduate. In addition you would have reunions from time to time. Therefore I proudly announced myself as a graduate of the "Electronics Department, Sengokuso University, specialized in music."

As soon as I left the hospital I married my fiancée, Masako Kondo. She continued to work at her job. But because my university was not so well-known, I could not find a job after my graduation. It was as if every employer thought such a bony guy must be useless, unable even to carry boxes. I gave up seeking employment and opened a small electric appliance shop in Osaka. I named my shop "Kakehashi Musen" (Kakehashi Radio Shop). Our first baby, my son Masayuki, was born shortly thereafter. In less than a year after leaving the hospital I had married, started a business and become a father.

I owe everything to Dr. Selman Waxman, the developer of streptomycin. His work saved my life. Fortunately, I was spared the occasional side effect of streptomycin-induced deafness, so I could continue my relationship with musical instruments.

CHAPTER THREE

MUSIC IS A VENTURE

Starting a new business requires a special kind of courage and confidence. These are not necessarily the same set of skills required to manage an established company. Operating an ongoing concern requires objectivity, prudent planning, and logical decision-making. On the contrary, most people who start truly original ventures are committed to the *newness* of their idea, and they are not inclined to restrict themselves to established business methods. Fortified by their passionate belief in their objective, these new venturers have a special ability to endure and overcome early problems and even initial failures.

If you look at the business plans of eager beginners, they are mainly descriptions of an ambition. These people already know where they want to go. They are committed to getting there, and they have little time to spare on detailed and deliberate planning. Since they focus more on their goal than on the reality of the immediate business environment, there is a high likelihood of failure. But they learn from reverses, and they come back to try again—and again. Most fail; some succeed.

If one hopes to succeed as a self-employed professional in any field, the critical first step is to acquire a thorough knowledge of that field. I am frequently surprised at how many people start their businesses without having carefully researched the entire matter. If they don't take the time to study the matter first, but rather assume they can learn as they go, they are likely to be swamped with misleading data and drowned in an ocean of irrelevant information. Even with research, success is not guaranteed; without it, success is unlikely.

There is no one set of characteristics that defines all successful entrepreneurs or that guarantees success for anyone who wants to try. However, there are certain attributes that are shared by most of those who have achieved success with a new business. I believe the most important of these attributes is the ability to learn from outsiders: the ability to listen and to be guided by the experiences of people who have prospered in all sorts of fields. Personally, I seriously doubt whether I would have been able to sustain my business if I had not had the opportunity to meet and learn from a wide variety of people.

Before we can examine the process of successfully establishing a new business, we need to define the most important terms. "Start-up" has come to refer to new businesses within traditional or established fields or categories. On the other hand, the term "ventures" tends to be used for new or emerging categories such as software or e-commerce. These rapidly developing areas tend to be dominated by younger people. Great expectations are focused on the new generation, because of its presumed ability to look at things from new perspectives and thus achieve a continuing expansion of the economy.

I believe there are three important conditions for achieving success in a new "venture."

First: You should undertake something in an absolutely new field. If the general area of business already exists, but you can do something in an entirely different way, it can still be called a new field.

Second: Any business that shows a high proportion of labor cost to total expense is not suitable. The opportunity must be something that creates high added values.

Third: It should be a business that requires minimal inventory. Good examples include the software industry, network communications, and educational applications in the music industry.

Underlying these three factors is the need for wisdom. When a new venture is initiated, its possibility for long-term success can be undermined by the lack of a sound basic structure. It is natural that when a business is started it has limited personnel, but this leaves the entrepreneur with little time to think about the future and to plan for the time after the business has been put on track. Without that time to think and plan, he is likely to be ill-equipped to run the business when it must be routinely operated on a day-to-day basis.

Indispensable considerations for continuing success after a successful beginning include coping with the subtleties of human nature and human relations. Additionally, prudent thought has to be given to establishing routines and procedures for the full range of company operations. The new venturer, lacking experience in these more traditional responsibilities, needs to rely on someone of good common sense who has been trained through company operations and previously acquired know-how. A solution is to include experienced older skills in the original team. He or she can act as an adviser and sometimes as a brake.

Music and the Entrepreneur

A significant portion of those people successful within the music industry operates according to the same principles as people starting new ventures. For example:

I. Their highest priority is put on the specific goal they have set.

II. The individual makes all decisions about steps to be taken.

III. The individual's own talent is the greatest asset.

IV. Finding a good advisor is crucial, but it is also extremely difficult.

It is a mistake to refer to the field of music as an industry in its own right. There are four distinct divisions of the general field, each with its own separate characteristics.

A. Artists, players, and composers.

B. Music publication and commercial recording.

C. Manufacturers of musical instruments.*

D. Education.

Another, perhaps more contemporary way of looking at the music business is:

1. **Hardware:** Means and equipment for playing music.

2. **Software:** Music scores and data to support the playing.

3. **Artware:** Artistic talent—the absolute core of the music business.

"Artware" is everything that supports the creator of music in his or her activities. Since the end product, actual music, is focused on appealing to the sensibilities of the public, some artists do not wish to use the term "business." This is a potentially dangerous misconception on their part. A businesslike viewpoint is vital if they are to succeed in realizing their intentions. The best solution is for the artist to retain the services of a professional manager. The manager can provide business skills in such areas as negotiation, leaving the artist free to concentrate on music and expression.

In the field of music publication (including record production) software is centered on the point where creative artists and business professionals come together to convert the artist's creation into a medium that is accessible to the public.

The manufacturing business is dependent upon Artware, Software, and also on Education. Artware is especially important,

---

* Although musical instruments and published music often share the same retail space, these are two distinctly different divisions of the music industry, requiring different skills and disciplines for success.

since it influences the evaluation of musical instruments. In the field of electronic musical instruments, it is hardware and software that are mainly interdependent. Demonstrations of instruments are needed to let the public become aware of the actual performance and expression capabilities of a new instrument. This is particularly true in the case of new concept instruments. How many people would have purchased a synthesizer based on a written description?

Those of us who design and manufacture electronic musical instruments need to be extremely careful in the matter of "new" products. The single most important consideration for a performing artist is that the instrument be reliable. Artists seek instruments that allow them to express their sensibilities, and it is true that many artists also have the desire to create unprecedented, "new" sounds. Usually it is the creative skill of the artist that develops the new sounds, but modern technology can also be used for this purpose.

It is important that the manufacturing side concentrate on providing "useful" devices to meet creative wishes. It is not the proper role of a manufacturer to demand that the artist perform totally new playing methods. That would merely be an attempt to exploit novelty devices that had been dreamed up by arrogant designers. Instead, useful advances in instrument design require the interaction of hardware, software, and artware. During the past 50 years a wide range of new sounds have been adopted. These sounds were created through collaboration, cooperation, (and sometimes battles) between manufacturers and artists. But nearly always they have been products of multiple inputs.

The development of the modern piano presents an interesting historical parallel. In Beethoven's day pianos were being experimented with and improved in a variety of ways. In the early 19th century there were as many as five or six pedals on a piano. Each was intended to offer a different type of tonal variation for the performer. As a new instrument was developed it would be offered to Beethoven and other leading artists for evaluation. Specifications were accepted or rejected according to their

One of the early experiments in multi-pedal pianos.

artistic utility. Today's pianos have three, or sometimes only two, pedals. Manufacturers acceded to the sensibilities of artists, and together they defined what a traditional piano should be.

When electronics were finally adopted, musical instruments became articulate in a new way. They were given the ability to communicate with the outside world. Later, the full range of technology of the computer age was found to have musical potential. Music is as old as the shepherd with his pan-pipes, but now it also is as new as the space age. There are tremendous new business opportunities in all three of the categories: hardware, software, and artware, as well as in those areas where the categories overlap.

Someone who enters the world of music is, in fact, undertaking a new "venture" in the entrepreneurial sense of the word. A musician may not think of himself as a business manager, but the joy he feels is the joy of creating an enterprise as well as the joy of creating a song or rendition. Many people who are active in the music business think of themselves as being on their own—alone, so to speak. This is true not only of artists, but also designers and even manufacturers. The truth is that there is a complex web of interaction and support involving a substantial number of people. As I said at the beginning, to start a new venture in any aspect of the music business, one needs not only a good advisor, but one must listen to opinions of others as well in order to avoid the trap of isolated thinking.

There is no reason to overlook the huge array of business opportunities that are available. The world of music is a treasure house of possibilities for new business ventures.

CHAPTER FOUR

CHOOSING MY PATH

EXPLORING THE OPPORTUNITIES

Kakehashi Musen may have begun as a small retail business but, over the following two decades, it grew and evolved into an efficient manufacturing business and also a partner in a highly successful joint venture with the Hammond Organ Company. Looking back on the relatively brief history of Western music in Japan, I can now see that that path of growth was a logical development. However, when I ventured into the field of electronic music, it was a major decision with very little precedent to follow.

Since their introduction in the late 19th century, reed organs and related wind-operated instruments like accordions and harmonicas steadily gained acceptance in Japan. In 1928, Tombo Musical Instrument Company Ltd. began making and marketing accordions, and sales grew every year. Even in 1943, in the middle of World War II, 38,000 accordions were manufactured.

For the first half of the 20th century, singing rather than instrumental performance had played the key role in elementary music education in Japan. After the war a program was started to equip every classroom in the country with a reed organ. Music lessons at school were so effective that many families of elementary school children began to purchase organs for their homes. The production of motor-operated blower organs replaced treadle ones, and the business became attractive not only to traditional instrument makers, but also to appliance manufacturers that were supplying the motors. It wasn't long before the appliance manufacturers began directing their attention to producing electrically powered reed organs.

I couldn't ignore this since retail shops had also begun to handle electrical appliances. However, when I looked closely at the products that were being manufactured, I realized there was a great gulf in the technical strengths of general appliance makers as opposed to companies specializing in musical instruments. On the one hand, it seemed almost impossible for appliance makers to acquire the music expertise needed to produce satisfactory instruments. On the other hand, it was equally difficult for musical instrument manufacturers to master electronic technologies. The path to success seemed to lie in a niche somewhere between the two existing disciplines. It was 1958. I was 28 years old, and I decided I would find a way to make electronic musical instruments my life's work.

My original Kakehashi Musen, which opened in August, 1954, began in a space of about 54 square feet. Essentially it was a storefront business that assembled and repaired radios and TVs. Soon it also began to serve as a retail supplier of appliances such as washing machines and electric rice cookers, which started coming onto the postwar market. As the retail business expanded beyond its initial focus on radios, I changed the name of the company to Ace Electric. Even though the business was growing, I still nurtured a strong interest and enthusiasm regarding the potential of electronic musical instruments. Eventually I had to decide whether I would continue as a retailer or commit myself to manufacturing.

For several years I had been experimenting with the manufacture of musical instruments as a hobby. In 1955 my first goal was straightforward. Rather than trying to make a polyphonic instrument that could produce harmonies, I simply wanted to make an electronic unit capable of playing a single-note melody freely. I pursued that idea for several years. Initially, I experimented with the Theremin. It was a relatively simple circuit arrangement. My instrument consisted of an aluminum box

Special double-fold packaging includes an illustrated history of the theremin written by Robert Moog, together with a biography and photographs of Clara Rockmore.

SIDE ONE
(25:18)
Band One — Rachmaninoff: Vocalise — 3:46
Band Two — Rachmaninoff: Song of Grusia — 4:16
Band Three — Saint-Saëns: The Swan — 2:56
Band Four — De Falla: Pantomime — 3:45
Band Five — Achron; Hebrew Melody — 5:23
Band Six — Wieniawski: Romance — 4:47

SIDE TWO
(24:12)
Band One — Stravinsky: Berceuse — 3:08
Band Two — Ravel: Habanera — 2:42
Band Three — Tschaikowsky: Berceuse — 4:14
Band Four — Tschaikowsky: Valse Sentimentale — 2:06
Band Five — Tschaikowsky: Sérénade Mélancolique — 7:39
Band Six — Glazunov: Chant du Ménestrel — 3:58

The thermin itself is housed in a wood cabinet app
eighteen inches wide and a foot deep. With its legs
about three and a half feet high. The front is slanted
convenient music stand. A vertical pitch antenna rod
in the upper right hand corner of the cabinet. A tubu
controlling volume emerges from the cabinet's left
Tuning knobs and control switches are located on
part of the front of the cabinet.
To play the theremin, the performer stands in fror
strument, a little left of center. The feet are spread
keep the body as motionless as possible. To dete
pitch of the instrument's tone, the player varies the d
tween his right hand and the pitch antenna. When
ment is properly tuned, the pitch goes from lower
octaves below middle C when the player's right hand
his shoulder, to approximately 2½ octaves above

Album cover featuring Clara Rockmore, the world's foremost Theremin player.

containing circuits and two antennas, one on either side. To play it, one simply moved the right hand either nearer to or farther from the adjacent antenna to determine the musical pitch and the left hand to or from the other antenna to control the volume. Unfortunately for me, the circuits were easier to master than the playing technique. I decided I would be wise to move on to other forms of monophonic instruments.

Some years later I was impressed by a monophonic keyboard instrument the Soviet Union displayed at the Osaka International Trade Fair. It was called "Ekvodin," and it offered pleasant string and reed instrument voices. No one on the display stand could discuss it with me, but two days later a Soviet trade representative visited our office. He quoted a price in rubles, which meant nothing to me. But when I translated it to U.S. dollars, I was stunned. In the exchange rates of those days, he was asking for approximately $28,000! Not surprisingly, negotiations were unsuccessful. The next day the same official phoned with an offer to reduce the prices to $1,350. Although he had cut the price by 95 percent in less than 24 hours, I turned down the offer. It was clear that this sort of illogical "negotiation" did not bode well for a constructive relationship.

Probably the best monophonic instrument of that era was the Ondes Martenot, produced in France after World War I. Although complicated in design and difficult to play, there continue to be professional musicians who perform on the instrument. The foremost Japanese artist to use the Ondes Martenot was my friend, Wataru Saito. It was a great pity that Mr. Saito died young. He had achieved great popularity and probably would have gone on to major stardom. It was while helping him with tuning and adjusting the instrument that I became convinced that keyboard instruments were the best format for developing electronic music.

The very first stimulus for making me interested in electronic music was hearing an early electronic organ at a church. The live sounds from that small-sized electronic organ impressed me more than any recordings of pipe organs I had ever heard. Even if I had had the opportunity to hear a pipe organ in person, I doubt that it would have motivated me to think of trying to manufacture one. I made up my mind to pursue the electronic musical instrument business because of the combination of two factors. Of course, I was impressed by the wonderful sounds being generated, but what excited my enthusiasm was the knowledge that the instrument was made of parts and materials that were relatively close at hand.

Achieving a synthesis of those two factors—authentically wonderful sounds produced by readily available technology— would result in a splendid instrument at a fraction of the price of a traditional pipe organ. There was no precise moment of epiphany when I committed myself to the task. Instead, it was a goal that grew and became clearer in my thinking as I gradually made progress in my research and experiments.

While retail business doesn't have a precise schedule, there is the advantage that one can take time off to pursue other interests. It was thanks to the intermittent demands of the retail trade that I could follow my early interest in developing electronic music. In the very first years I never conceived of building an instrument as large as an organ, but time and experience had substantially widened my vision.

Back in 1955 I had heard recordings of organ music but I had never seen an actual instrument until I saw the pipe organ at Doshisha University Eiko-kan in Kyoto. I was amazed at the

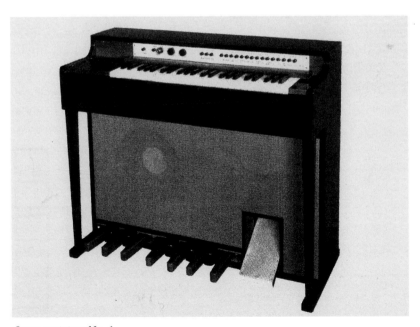

Organ prototype No. 1.

complexity of the console of the instrument, but it was easy to see that the mechanism for actually making sounds was rather simple. I figured that by substituting an electric oscillator for pipes and using headphones, I could produce a compact instrument. Although admittedly primitive, the instrument did work. I used a reed organ keyboard, relay contacts taken from telephones, and a transistor for the sound source. In terms of circuits, I simply lined up a number of monotone instruments for the required number of keys. *Voila!* I had produced a 49-note, single-manual, 12-pedal instrument, which I labeled "Prototype No. 1." Unfortunately, it didn't sound a bit like an organ, but it was a start.

When I decided to go into manufacturing, the best place to start seemed to be by learning from the experience of others. I gained valuable knowledge by looking up information about the history of existing manufacturers such as Pioneer, Sansui, and Akai, all of whom supplied parts to radio and TV manufacturers and who had originally operated on a scale that I could understand.

Kakehashi Musen had grown into Ace Electrical Co., Ltd., and was now a mid-scale retailer of home appliances with more than 20 employees. Now that I had decided to work at electronic music on a full-time basis, I brought in Mr. Yoshinori Harada to take over the retail company. Initially, I borrowed space inside an independent research laboratory managed by my friend, Hidemitsu Kanesada, and in 1960 I established Ace Electronic Industries, Inc. We developed a two-manual keyboard spinet-type organ, but an electronic organ with a blower motor would not sell unless it was a one-manual keyboard at an inexpensive price. I made a prototype, but I could not prompt any interest from the independent wholesale trade. Mr. Sakata, my friend and later a major investor in Ace Electronic, mentioned my project to an associate who was a senior executive at a company affiliated with the Matsushita (Panasonic) Group. Matsushita offered to market it under their National brand name (overseas known as Technics).

Ace itself was too small and under-financed to produce an organ under the Ace Brand, so I accepted. I asked Mr. Sakata to

The very first Technics organ. In truth, it was designed by me and manufactured by Ace.

become president of Ace. The production factory was set up in a National pre-fabricated house, and our production of electronic organs began. The very first National (Technics) electronic organ model SX601 was designed by me and born in Osaka.

In those early years of experimenting and developing prototypes, the only way to proceed was by trial and error. There was virtually no technical information available regarding developments in the field of electronic musical instruments. To the extent that research was being conducted in Japan, it was individual amateurs operating in relative isolation who were doing it. Technical data from foreign sources was not generally available locally. If a book were to be published, I would place an order and wait for up to half a year before it arrived. It wasn't until 1962 that I was able to obtain a text that had been published in the U.S. in 1958.

In those early days one of the only sources of information on emerging technology was to look inside samples of foreign products such as the Organo and the Minshall instruments. Another source was to study U.S. patents. Unfortunately, Japanese law allowed local importers to obtain patents on technology as they imported it—even if the data was already widely known and used in other countries. This created an enormous advantage for established importers, while giving Japan a negative reputation in the eyes of Western manufacturers.

When I look back on my early adventures with what were primitive designs in the field of electronic keyboards, I realize that the sounds those instruments produced probably were not particularly good. The fact that I perceived the sounds I originally heard in that church as splendid organ sounds was only partially due to the sounds themselves. Part of the credit should be given to the resonance of the church building itself, and another factor was the personal feeling I brought to the experience of listening.

I now understand that the images created by sound can be almost mysteriously complex. Due to the structure of the hall, the intensity of the performer, the mood of the audience, and the total environment in which the performance takes place, there are cases in which sounds that are not and cannot be produced physically are actually heard in people's impressions. In this connection there is a wonderful quotation from Dr. E. Lieb who addressed the Euro-Piano Kongresso in 1965. He said:

> Roughly speaking, the effects of piano sounds are 25 percent dependent on pianos, 25 percent on halls, 25 percent on performers and the remaining (at least) 25 percent on listeners' feelings. In other words, problems regarding piano sounds are not easy from the purely physical viewpoint, and when accompanying psychological phenomena are added, they become as limitlessly complicated as human beings themselves are.

Notwithstanding the success of Kakehashi Musen as a retail business, when a future course for the business had to be chosen, I commited to the manufacturing side of electronic music. With Ace Electronic Industries Inc. the first proprietary products we sought to develop were accessory units that would produce rhythm patterns to accompany musicians on their instruments. Business started slowly at first, but we began to achieve international notice with rhythm units in 1964, and a few years later we began producing our own keyboard instruments.

SEEKING THE PERFECT RHYTHM

Ethnic music, increasingly being shared around the world, is wonderfully rich in variety. My enjoyment of it has doubled since I began dealing with rhythm instruments.

The "classical" music that developed in Europe focuses on the overall composition, melodies and harmonies, and an element of rhythm has a special meaning within that context. However, traditional music and the music brought in from colonies have a taste of their own. There are a large number of musical styles in South America and Asia that are solely for percussion instruments. From an historical viewpoint, American music is heavily influenced by the music of Africans, Native Americans and South Americans. In the late 19th century a unique musical melting pot was created there, by the arrival of immigrants from all over Europe. That marvelous combination now has been further enriched by the effects of the global migrations of the 20th century.

In Japan, by way of contrast, the way of keeping time by clapping hands at banquets is similar throughout the country, probably because of the influence of the traditional farming culture. This is also true of Japanese folk music, which is chiefly for singing. However, the rhythms of Japanese drums are different from one region to another, and the total variety of rhythms is astonishing.

In the 1960s electronic percussion instruments began to appear in the electronic instrument market. "Side Man," a device installed beside a piano or organ for rhythm accompaniment, was marketed by the Wurlitzer Company. The device was designed to rotate a disk, using a motor and switch to determine the timing of the instrument

Rhythm Ace Model R-1. The unit that began the Ace Electronic product line.

played, and it employed vacuum tubes to produce the percussion sounds. Judged by today's more sophisticated technology, "Side Man" was crudely made of first-generation parts, namely a combination of the mechanical and electronic components. Still, the product took the lead in automatic rhythm machines, even though its performance was not completely reliable.

The application of transistors to electronic organs opened wonderful new avenues of technical possibilities. The transistor was particularly attractive for the development of smaller yet more versatile rhythm instruments. Ace Electronic led the way with the Rhythm Ace model R-1, the world's first transistorized, non-automatic, percussion instrument.

Now it was time to show it to the international market.

CHAPTER FIVE

ENTERING THE WORLD OF MUSIC

In the 1960s there were two focal points for the world music industry. The most important of these was the American convention of the National Association of Music Merchants (NAMM) held each June in Chicago. The other major event was the Frankfurt Spring Fair in Germany each February. Unlike NAMM, the Frankfurt Fair was a general exposition of all sorts of consumer goods, even including things like ceramics and rugs. The "Musikmesse" occupied one building at the back of the fair grounds. At NAMM the show was only about music.

Another important difference between the two events was that traditional European products and old-fashioned attitudes about "proper" music dominated the music part of the Frankfurt Fair, while the American NAMM show was much more attuned to new ideas in electronics and eager about the development of consumer interest in new product concepts. If my products were going to succeed in the world market, the obvious place to start would be NAMM.

Only a few weeks before the 1964 show was due to open, I received news that my application for space had been accepted. There was no time to make proper arrangements. But this was an opportunity I could not miss. Accompanying me, as I boarded my first international flight, were a small Japanese-American phrase book, large hopes for the future, and samples of the two portable products I intended to display.

The 1964 NAMM show was held in the Conrad Hilton (the world's largest hotel).

In those days, there was no direct air service from Tokyo to Chicago. It was customary to fly via Anchorage, Alaska. Even though it was summer in Alaska, while waiting for the flight to continue to Chicago I could look out of the windows of the air-conditioned terminal and see huge, snow-capped mountains all around. A few hours later the plane landed in Chicago. Walking to the terminal, I was greeted by a blast of hot humid air that almost blew me off my feet. I was in Chicago! I was going to the NAMM show; Ace Electronic was going to meet the world!

Without knowing any of the ropes, I somehow managed to check into the Conrad Hilton, the place of the show. In fact, my lodging room was my exhibiting booth.... Everything was so large. Even the door was big and heavy, so that I had to push it with all my body weight to open it. Visiting the show itself was quite a business. It was my first experience of exhibition, and I had no idea of how to go about displaying and making product presentations. On the bus from the airport, I even realized that I couldn't make myself understood in English, although I had practiced before my departure.

A proud but nervous exhibitor at the 1964 NAMM show.

Not only my booth, but every booth was using a guest room as an exhibiting space. Entering into each room required a sort of boldness for someone like me, who had no intention of purchasing and only a limited ability at speaking English. To make things tougher, I, as an exhibitor, had to wait on visitors and explain to them the specifications of the products. It was such a big deal for me then. As I had designed the products, I knew about them well, but explaining them to visitors was a totally different thing. I brought only two items—"Rhythm Ace," a manually operated rhythm box, and "Canary," a musical instrument for solo play. These were the instruments I had brought with me on the plane. My exhibition room was one of the smallest available, but still those two products were dwarfed by the size of the room.

The first day of the show went by and then the second day. Only two parties came to my booth. The first was a couple, who, upon entering the room, asked me something like, "What are you making?" I straightened myself up, pointed to the first transistorized rhythm box and answered them: "This is Rhythm Ace!" They

Mystery couple, sign in please.

seemed to understand what I said, but they were still not sure what it was. I showed them a photo displaying the Rhythm Ace installed on an organ, and then they finally understood ... but that was the end of it! They began leaving the room, smiling and saying "Good luck." In any event, they were my first guests: "I've got to take a picture!" I clicked the shutter of my camera. I still have that very picture. Being so anxious, I had forgotten to ask them their names. (I would like to be able to contact those very nice people shown in the picture above. If anyone can tell me how I can reach them, please write to me c/o Hal Leonard Corporation.) I have to admit that I was then totally unqualified as a salesperson.

The second guest was a Japanese gentleman. Looking at his business card, I was astonished. He was Mr. Kisaka, a head of the central laboratory of Panasonic. I also took a picture of him. Along with another picture of myself, the three snapshots are highlights of my photo album.

I needed more visitors, so I decided to tout. I added a hand-written message to my business card that read: "Transistor

Rhythm Machine & Melody Keyboard." After the exhibition hours were over, I inserted the modified card in the closed doors of display rooms that seemed to house manufacturers or wholesalers of organs.

The third day saw a drastic change. People from more than ten American companies came to my booth, including ones from companies that I had never heard of. The touting tactics had worked, but waiting on the visitors was rather complicated. From a certain company, a president and an engineer came along together . . . it was hardly practical for Japanese companies in those days to send more than one person. Names of some companies that I received included Baldwin, Conn, Minshall, Wuritzer, Hammond, Lowrey, Estey, Thomas, Kimball, Gulbransen, and Magnavox. I received orders for eight sets of samples from eight companies. It might sound trivial now, but it was more than enough to give me confidence to keep going.

In fact, those sample orders did not lead to further opportunities for continued business. The greatest fruit of that exhibition

Second and third from left are Michael Levine and Joe Saltzman of Sorkin Music (Multivox), on a visit to the ACE factory immediately after the NAMM show.

was that a wholesaler called Sorkin Music was appointed as our U.S. representative.

Attending the NAMM shows over the next several years, I gradually came to understand that Chicago was a city of great significance to the history of American jazz music. In central Chicago, there is the Wrigley Building, housing the company famous for its chewing gum; on the other side of the Chicago River, there was a nightclub called *The London House*. It was famous for offering live concerts by noted jazz players, and I visited there whenever I was in Chicago for subsequent NAMM shows.

Now the NAMM show has moved away from the summertime in Chicago. The organization is now known as the International Music Products Association, and the show is held in Southern California in January. Because of the tradition associated with the name, it is known as "Winter NAMM." The exhibition has grown substantially each year, and it is now the world's premier trade show for musical instruments. Unlike hotel rooms at the Hilton, display booths are now made in an open style so that anyone can see products easily. The Winter NAMM has become a concentrated scene of new products and a source of up-to-date information. As such it is a paradise for dealers and music artists.

Since the time I was 16, when I began to discover the rich variety available in the world of music, my yearning to become involved in the overseas world of music had been growing. In 1955 when I started to produce sample organs, I had already realized that there was no other way than to go to the States to get to know more about organs. On the other hand, I was then running a small electric appliances shop, and under such circumstances it was hardly possible to realize such a dream.

After ten years, the 1964 NAMM that I attended turned out to be an important turning point in my life. During the week of the NAMM show, I got a chance to appreciate the breadth of challenges and problems I would have to deal with if I were to successfully enter the world market. Some of the issues included the differences between the musical instruments industries of the

States and of Japan; the rapid progress being made by American electronic musical instruments and their accelerating development efforts; and the scale of American wholesalers compared to the level at which I was operating.

MEMORABLE MANUFACTURERS

After I had gotten over jet lag and depression, I felt comfortable enough to think about other exhibitors. The room next to mine was showing a "machine" to playback sounds recorded in audiotapes. A keyboard was connected in order to play the "machine," and by pressing the keys, the tapes would start running. You were not allowed to depress any key for more than eight seconds. In spite of such limitations, the machine was capable of generating superb sounds including a chorus of human voices, an ensemble of stringed instruments, various kinds of sound effects, and so on. After listening to it repeatedly, I could gradually tell shortcomings as well—things like noises of tapes, tremors, or echoes when pressing chords. It was also necessary to exchange sets of tapes installed in sort of picture-frame units. At any rate, it was bewilderingly troublesome to install so many tapes . . . as many as keys . . . and to play all of them steadily.

Furthermore, I felt dizzy trying to imagine the complexity of the mechanism necessary to have every tape rewound whenever individual keys were released, or to record every sound in correct intervals. As many as thirty-five keys were installed in two rows, for which groups of tapes in different colors were allocated, lessening the number of tape exchanges. Words just failed me in front of the machine. The company did not seem so large as an organization, but their power to design such a mechanism and to implement it as a musical instrument was so astonishing . . . it was utterly beyond my imagination at that time. The name of the machine was "Chamberlin," and it was later transferred to England and was renovated as "Mellotron." Sixteen years later, I found out that the former president of Roland (U.K.) Ltd., Brian

Nunney, had been the head of the Mellotron factory, and that the former sales manager of Roland (U.K.), Fred Mead, used to be the production controller of Mellotron as well.

The booth on the other side of the Chamberlin display was showing various items for pipe organs, from components to even cabinets. It was absolutely impossible to obtain such items in Japan. I was impressed with the size of the American market in which specialization was so widespread. Every component was attractive to me. I immediately asked them if I could visit their factory, and they readily gave me their consent. The company was called Klan, Inc., in Waynesboro, Virginia. They gave me a note indicating the location, telling me that it would be easier to come via Washington, D.C. There were only a few names of places on the note; Chicago, Washington, D.C., and Staunton, VA (Piedmont Airlines), and that was all. For me, as a first-time visitor to the States, it was impossible to make a trip alone with such little information. I recalled that one of my colleagues at junior high, Mr. Tsukishima, was stationed at the National Bureau of Standards in Washington, D.C. Believing that there was no other way, I asked him to travel with me. As I recall, I still haven't gotten around to remunerating him for his translation help.

Other exhibits were also tempting, but I couldn't wait on customers in my booth and see other displays at the same time. Therefore, I decided to lock my door after three o'clock and spend the rest of each day visiting all the other booths. Every company was using talented demonstrators. It was by no means possible just to simply glance at them. I had to stop and listen carefully. All the songs played were familiar to me. Although the progress of Japanese electronic music instruments was lagging behind, there was no time lag between Japan and the States in popular music trends.

I found a "Theremin" exhibited in one of the booths. The "Theremin" appears in every story of electronic musical instruments. In 1920, at the Eighth Soviet Electric Convention, Leon Theremin played melodies in public for the first time. He understood music well, as he played the cello himself. With his new instrument, the motion of his playing was more like a conductor than an instrumentalist—waving both hands back and forth towards the box as he performed various melodies. The "Theremin" I saw at the NAMM was not a prototype for demonstration, but a finished commodity. I learned only later that Dr. Robert Moog was the demonstrator. We didn't know each other then; it was before the development of his famous, module-type synthesizers.

I encountered a sort of strangely negative atmosphere in the booth of each organ manufacturer, and I wasn't allowed to get a good look at their display models. In later years I learned more about the technological secrecy of the American manufacturers— in particular as it related to possible Japanese competitors. What I specially remember was that there were many accordions exhibited, and at some of the leading importers a great array of different brands was shown. Most of these accordions were made in Italy, carrying buyers' brands. Some were made in Germany or in France, but I did not see any made in the U.S.A.

Although I only had time to see a part of the music industry, I felt as if thrown into a totally unknown world. My first NAMM show had finished in the twinkling of my bedazzled eyes.

"HOLLYWOOD BOWL"

That 1964 NAMM show was my first participation in the American market, and I literally had no time to spare. I was not able to visit the attractions of downtown Chicago or the many museums and other famous sites of the city. Instead, I spent most of the time in the hotel booth. Every evening in the hotel lobby I could attend live concerts sponsored by various manufacturers. I enjoyed the superior entertainment performed by excellent artists. These were in fact demonstrations of the latest products.

Without having seen much of Chicago, I left for Waynesboro via Washington, D.C., and then to New York City, and finally to Los Angeles. When the airplane was close to New York City, the pilot circled over the city, before landing at LaGuardia airport. I still remember my excitement at seeing the world-famous city.

In New York City, I stayed at a hotel only one block away from the street lined with various musical merchandisers, but I didn't realize the fact and thus missed visiting there. At that time, there were no friends to advise me of such things.

By the time I arrived in Los Angeles, I had learned a little more about American ways. Checking in at the hotel was a bit more comfortable as well. I had found out that walking on your own was the fastest way to learn about local things. It was also economically shrewd. At that time, there was a Japanese governmental restriction on amounts of money that you could take with you on overseas trips, and only $500 was allowed for one person for one trip. The money that I had was running short, forcing me to consider how I could get back to Japan with so little money remaining. One of my work colleagues had advised me that if you choose the most economical hotel room available among the well-known hotel names, you would still be able to enjoy comfortable accommodations. Therefore, I decided to stay at the Biltmore Hotel in Los Angeles. The most reasonable room that they could offer was $16 per night. Considering the fact that I was going to make a stop over at Honolulu, even a couple of dollars was important. I negotiated with the hotel and finally got a room at $12.

Through the negotiations, I realized that speaking English in Osaka-style was much easier for me than if I tried to speak in a textbook style. By that I mean the structure of conversation rather than anything to do with accent. I realized that blunt Osaka-style conversation was effective even in English.

Once settled in my room, I searched in a newspaper for places to go to spend the next day constructively. I was lucky enough to find an advertisement for a concert featuring a variety of famous artists that included Duke Ellington, Oscar Peterson and Ella Fitzgerald. I decided to go there.

It was hardly possible to find such a superb combination of artists in one concert in Japan, and I again said to myself: "This is

America!" Changing several buses, I got to the Hollywood Bowl before sunset. Since I didn't have an advance ticket, I had to buy one at the gate. There was a wide range of seats available, and prices varied greatly. The affordable one for me was a seat at four dollars, equivalent to the money that I had saved at the hotel. Most of the four-dollar seats were placed in the last row, and you could hardly see the players' faces on the stage. Still, the acoustics were reasonably good. Based on the distance from the stage, there must have been a considerable sound delay if you tried to listen from the back row. Thanks to the quality of the P.A. system, I didn't have to be disturbed by the gap between the sound and the actual performances. Still, when you listen to a concert from such a great distance, you cannot really enjoy the true meaning. Nevertheless, I felt content just to be able to actually listen to them in live performance.

As suggested by its name, the Hollywood Bowl is a vast open-air theater making the most use of its valley-shaped land and taking advantage of the wonderful climate of Southern California. The concert was wonderfully exciting. As a souvenir, I bought a printed brochure. Twenty years later, I invited Oscar Peterson to my house after a tour of the Roland factories in Hamamatsu. He was in Japan on a concert tour. I asked him to write his autograph on that very brochure I had saved. He told me stories about his working with Duke Ellington and other episodes involving Ella Fitzgerald. I felt, after twenty years time, as if I had finally reached a seat near the stage. It was one of the most memorable evenings of my life.

In 1999 I received happy news about Oscar Peterson. He was awarded the 11th Praemium Imperiale. This award was established in 1987 to commemorate the 100th anniversary of the Japan Art Association and follows the last wish of H.I.H. Nobuhito Takamatsu. That year's laureates are as follows, all of them highly distinguished in their own fields.

My program from the Hollywood Bowl concert.

Music:	Oscar Peterson
Painting:	Anselm Kiefer
Sculpture:	Louise Bourgeois
Architecture:	Fumihiko Maki
Theater/Film:	Pina Bausch

The awards ceremony was held at the Meiji Memorial Hall in Tokyo on October 28, 1999 and my wife and I were invited as two of Oscar's friends. Many Japanese jazz musicians were also in attendance. On behalf of the recipients, Oscar played the piano at the reception that followed the ceremony. Everyone there enjoyed his excellent performance, and applauded him enthusiastically. It was a wonderful night.

CHAPTER SIX

THE SMALL UNIVERSE OF TRADE SHOWS

The scale of the NAMM show had been growing each year, and its show place was changed from the hotel to a major exhibition hall, the McCormick Place Convention Center. Every morning during the show, a special paper called *Up Beat Daily* was distributed to each room. It was (and still is) a free newsletter of the industry issued by a major trade magazine. It reports all events and schedules during the run of the show. On the second day of the 1976 NAMM, one of my friends told me that I had appeared in the *Daily* of that day. I was shocked when I saw the copy of that day's paper when it was delivered to my room.

My eyes were caught by the word "Invader." "Why?" was my first thought. Exports of pianos from Japan had been a major issue, and my first guess was that the same arguments now were being made about electronic musical instruments. The exchange rate of yen to U.S. dollar was around 270 to 280 yen per one dollar then, so that Japanese products were still affordable compared to nowadays. Later in 1978, the rate was drastically raised to 180 yen per dollar or even higher. (When I started the business in 1972, it was at 360 yen per dollar.) In 1976 it was still at 270 yen, and there shouldn't have been any fair reason for being blamed about pricing.

During that time in Japan, a video game called "Invader" was dominant in game centers. "Invader" had been exported to the States also, so I wondered if it had become a catch phrase for the latest trends. I finally understood after reading the paper carefully again and again, that the word was in fact "Innovator." The article was quite favorable to me, and I was relieved at the same time that I was embarrassed for having misunderstood even for a moment.

What is most important for product evaluations in the States is whether the product is usable as a musical instrument or not, with matters of pricing and non-performance shortcomings of secondary importance. Therefore the evaluation standards are very severe, and if this priority is not met, the debut of any product will be difficult or even unsuccessful. This is especially true for electronic musical instruments. It sometimes happens that product reviews written by musical journalists will compare two different instruments of totally different price ranges, which can be rather embarrassing. However, as long as they talk about musical instruments, one should put up with such contradictions. Especially in the field of electronic musical instruments, owing to advancements of semi-conductor technology and cost reductions, concepts of price ranges can sometimes be meaningless.

In my entire life I have performed product demonstrations in front of an audience only two times. The first occasion was at a private fair in Japan given by Mr. Murai, the president of Naniwa Musical Instruments, one of our dealers at that time. He had gathered nearly 40 retail people at a demonstration place in Takarazuka City in order to introduce the SH-1000. We were totally involved in making adjustments to the machine for the fair and had no time for training demonstrators. The task of explaining the first synthesizer in Japan to players was quite complicated and there was no other choice but to do it by myself. The SH-1000 was a monophonic instrument with ten kinds of tones. It also had the capacity to create new sounds using sawtooth and pulse waveforms. Having memorized only two-bar-long melodies for each tone, I scarcely managed to find my way out of the demonstration, but everything was recorded! I am still profoundly grateful that the tape of that "performance" was lost.

ローランドがシンセサイザーに《新しい生命》をあたえた本格派！ (本体価格) ￥150,000

ROLAND SYNTHESIZER SH-1000 NEW TYPE

1＝演奏が極めて容易なのです。
2＝簡単に素晴しい音色が創りだせます。
3＝10種類のカラフルな楽器音もプリセットされています。
4＝特殊な効果音も意のままにOKです。

The Roland SH-1000. The first synthesizer built in Japan, and the only one demonstrated by me.

The second time was in Sydney during the first trade show in Australia. It was an opportunity to introduce "Revo," which was equipped with an electronic circuit to add rotational ambience to organs. Organs were indispensable for the demonstration. In order to let audiences feel the rotational touch, it was necessary to change music speeds during the demo play. A two-bar melody was not long enough, so I had to play at least six bars and operate the speed switcher at the same time. During the three days of the show, I consistently played "Yesterday," the only tune I felt confident performing. The product did not sell very well, probably owing to my poor demonstrations.

In any event, the trade show turned out to be an important opportunity for establishing Roland Corporation Australia Pty. Ltd., Roland's first joint venture company. At least in that respect, I can take some satisfaction in believing that the demonstrations were successful. It was a painful lesson, but I have learned that it is difficult to be a good demonstrator. Enough years have passed that the experience has become one of those good old days. Although I wish to remain an innovator for the rest of my life, I have decided to leave demonstrating to the professionals.

TRADE SHOWS— SOURCES OF VALUABLE INFORMATION

For people involved in the creation of musical instruments, attending trade shows is indispensable. In Japan, most trade fairs or business shows have a certain style . . . with a small box for receiving business cards and beautiful young ladies making presentations. The NAMM shows, back at the time they were held at that Chicago hotel, had a totally a different atmosphere. You could directly discuss business with the heads of companies. Current NAMM shows are closer to entertainment shows rather than trading businesses. But it is owing to the growth of the industry itself, and I have no reason to regret it. Still, I cannot forget those special atmospheres of the old days.

Since first attending in 1964, I have been at every NAMM show as well as every Frankfurt Musikmesse during the past 38 years. Occasionally there were obstacles such as health problems or other scheduling conflicts, but I gave the highest priority to attending NAMM and adjusted other schedules accordingly. I also tried to be in the best shape for every NAMM. Thanks to those efforts, I never missed a show.

Besides the latest information about competitors or other music companies, I can get a feeling for the human side of the business and sense the atmosphere of the entire industry at the NAMM show. It is generally customary to arrive a few days before the opening of the show, in order to make adjustments to equipment and to check on all aspects of the display arrangements. After such preparation work was over, it was always possible to see friends or acquaintances at the hotel. There was a certain "family feeling" in those preparation days, perhaps because of the relatively small size of the industry. At any rate, such gatherings are one of the exciting aspects of the NAMM show.

NAMM 1997. Chris Bristol of Roland US and I recall past trade shows in front of the Roland History wall.

In the field of electronic musical instruments, I can find many people of my generation. In fact, most competitors are also my friends. I can share information with them about trends in the latest technologies. I would say it is more difficult to do the same thing with people from Japanese manufacturers, although conversations with Japanese technical engineers can be conducted rather openly. It could be due to the special atmosphere of NAMM.

Trade shows are also places for recruiting people, and there is considerable movement within the music trade. It is such a fast-moving industry that, when meeting acquaintances, it is wise to check their name badges, even though you already know them in order to confirm the companies that they are presently working for. It was also a surprise for me that one never encounters the gloomy atmosphere that would be seen in Japan if someone changed his or her job within the same industry. In Japan, it is hardly possible to hire someone directly from a competitor. First, there must be an interval, a "cooling-off period," before such recruiting can possibly be done. But with patience it can be accomplished. At Roland you can find people from various manufacturers in the industry, including Lowrey, Technics, JVC Victor, Yamaha, and Kawai. Such a thing is still unusual in Japan.

At the 1964 NAMM, my first experience, electronic organs were dominant while accordions were still selling quite well. With a cycle of approximately five years, leading star products would change, but none of them has disappeared. The only thing that I regret nowadays is the fact that the number of American piano manufacturers is decreasing, just as it is in Japan. However, exhibitions of European piano manufacturers at Frankfurt Musikmesse are still very prominent.

The display of products at the Frankfurt Musikmesse reflects the continuing diversification of the music trade. New software companies sell their products on CD-ROMs right alongside traditional manufacturers of pianos as well as stringed, wind, and percussion instruments. It is one of the remarkable phenomena of this industry, which might not be found in other fields.

CHAPTER SEVEN

COMMENCEMENT

The transistorized rhythm device that I took to the 1964 NAMM show was a simple manual instrument that produced percussion sounds when buttons were pressed. The response to the instrument was favorable, but sales were not good. Its performance without automated rhythms was not effective, and the device was not adopted by manufacturers of electronic organs.

What the market really wanted was an automatic unit that would produce percussion sounds in regular rhythmic patterns. This presented a serious technical challenge. No fewer than two bars (a bar being a unit such as 1-2-3 in a waltz) were needed to produce a discernable pattern. Even then, if a single pattern was repeated over and over, the rhythm would be dull and monotonous.

To make basic rhythm patterns with electronic circuits, it was necessary to produce pulses that could interact with a sound source electrically at a pace where one bar of music was divided into *no fewer* than 24 segments. Even at that level of complexity, the results would not have been particularly satisfactory. In truth, a 48-part division was needed to approximate more complex rhythm patterns, such as the Viennese waltz. Although a 48-part division was not truly sufficient to produce technically accurate sounds, it was not economically feasible to go further. In those days to produce a 96-part division of each bar would have required doubling the number of parts that were used, and

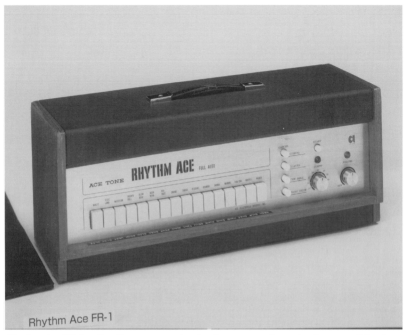

Rhythm Ace FR-1

Rhythm Ace FR-1 – Our first automated unit. It was a turning point for me and for Ace.

product costs would have skyrocketed.

In Rhythm Ace, we developed a circuit that was called a diode matrix. It produced rows of pulses that would determine the sound-making position for each instrument. After a circuit was set and designed, it was extremely difficult to change it. In 1967, Ace Electronic managed to market the "Rhythm Ace FR-1," an automatic rhythm instrument. Immediately before putting it on the market, Bossa Nova became popular, and I wanted to incorporate that rhythm into the new product. Answers to my questions about what was a proper Bossa Nova rhythm pattern differed from person to person. As time was running out, I made the last-minute decision to insert the rhythm used in the popular tune, "Girl From Ipanema." I hate to think what the result would have been if we had chosen the wrong Bossa Nova pattern.

Technology has continued to develop, and now it is possible to produce and change rhythms at a pace in which *one-quarter* of a bar is divided into 128 parts. The days when the R-1 and FR-1 were marketed now seem to belong to a different age, but the FR-1 was clearly a turning point for me and for the business.

We took the FR-1 to an exhibition in Hamburg, Germany, and a young sales manager of a local distribution company immediately saw its potential. His name was Erik Gramkow, and if it were not for his foresight, it is entirely possible that the future of Ace Electronic products in Europe would have been considerably less successful. Mr. Gramkow has continued his leadership in the European music market, and he is now the president of Roland Scandinavia. With respect to the FR-1, it was adopted by the Hammond Organ Company for its newest instruments, and that step eventually led to the development of a strong alliance between our companies serving most of the world's markets.

EXPERIENCE CAN BE A COSTLY TEACHER

Some years ago I visited the city of Assisi in Italy and learned about the famous St. Francis who was born there. His *Serenity Prayer* is good advice for all people, but it is specially true for an entrepreneur.

Lord, give me the serenity to accept what I cannot change,
The courage to change what I cannot accept,
And the wisdom to know the difference.

After taking the first step towards launching Ace Electronic on the international market, events moved quickly. There were a few setbacks and many successes. In the end a very difficult and painful decision had to be made between what I could accept and what I would have to change.

In 1967, the Hammond Company began importing our rhythm units for incorporation into their product line, including the revolutionary new instrument, the "Piper." Also, Hammond International, the overseas arm of Hammond, was seeking a way to enter the Japanese domestic market and to develop a production source for its other international markets. From our point of view, Ace needed three things: to secure a strong position in the U.S. market; to maintain its role as the Hammond agent in the Japanese market; and to strengthen its participation in European markets. In 1968 we jointly formed Hammond International Japan. Ace would continue to market its own brand, and the Ace factory could increase its total production by serving as the production source for the requirements of both Hammond International Japan and Hammond International.

Prototype of the revolutionary Hammond Piper and the Ace Electronic engineers who participated in the project.

Because the Osaka plant was too small for the increased levels of production, I decided to move to Hamamatsu with the intention of acquiring a new plant. Through the help of the Kyowa Bank, I decided to take over a company called Zenon Gakki Seizou, which had manufactured pianos and reed organs. Zenon had been a participant in the reed organ market for many years. However, starting in 1964, Zenon found it progressively more difficult to keep up with changing marketing techniques. By 1969, despite growth in the unit sales of reed organs, the Zenon company had gone out of the reed organ business. In November of 1969, Bob Olsen, vice president of Hammond International, came to Japan to discuss plans and strategies for Hammond International Japan, and I took him to Hamamatsu to look at the Zenon plant.

The factory was almost hopelessly rundown. There were holes here and there in the office floor, and the building and facilities of the plant had been seriously neglected. The situation was worse than I expected, and I was very concerned regarding what impression the plant gave Mr. Olsen. I recently had an opportunity to ask him about the impression. His comments were:

> It was a disaster area. From the outside, the building was not impressive. It appeared to be abandoned and uncared for. Inside it was even worse. If I hadn't known it was 1969, I would have assumed it was residual damage from WWII. It was terrible. My recollection is of an echoing (and poorly illuminated) vista of scattered junk, discarded equipment, and puddles of water. It was a total mess, and I found it hard to imagine it being turned into a useful production facility.

Anyway, Mr. Olsen raised no objection to the purchase. I found out later that his silence did not necessarily indicate agreement. He felt that the decision ought to be made by me as managing director of Hammond International Japan, and that it would be impolite for him to express his own negative view of the facility. We proceeded with the deal, and for the next two years I spent three days a week in Hamamatsu overseeing the reconstruction of the plant.

My original Ace Electronic Industries Inc. grew throughout the 60s. To fund that growth we took in an investing partner, Sakata Shokai, which was run by Mr. Kazuo Sakata. Mr. Sakata had a good understanding of organs, and he was valuable as a shareholder and as an investor. Over time his capital infusions actually made Sakata Shokai the majority owner of Ace. It was a solid relationship built on trust and respect. When the Hammond joint venture became a reality, it was formed as an equal partnership among the three companies. Thanks to periodic infusions of capital, Ace continued to prosper. Things were going so well, and we were so busy, that I did not pay attention to the fact that my personal ownership of Ace had been reduced to a minority of the total shares. Serious problems arose three years later, when Sakata Shokai was taken over by Sumitomo Chemical Co., Ltd. Sumitomo was mainly interested in the chemical side of Sakata Shokai, but an unintentional aspect of the acquisition of Sakata was that

Sumitomo Chemical had also become the majority owner of Ace Electronic.

It was terrible to have to work with employees dispatched by Sumitomo Chemical. They did not understand music or the music business, and they were not interested in learning. There was no point in complaining that people from a chemical company like Dupont focused on the acquisition and application of industrial raw materials, did not know about music. I tried to make the best of it.

The development and sale of our product lines was proceeding nicely, and exports were becoming more and more attractive. As long as I was developing overseas markets in cooperation with Mr. Shiro Murai, manager of overseas sales for Sakata, results were excellent, and we were able to proceed from one success to another. For most of the preceding 15 years I had focused only on technology and the domestic market. Now, thanks to the guidance of Mr. Murai, I was able to learn the intricacies of international marketing from a world-class expert.

Corporate earnings for Ace and Hammond International Japan improved and grew steadily. However, due to the increasing intrusion and utter insensitivity of Sumitomo personnel, it finally became impossible to cooperatively develop future plans. Eventually I had no option but to walk away from Ace Electronic, the company I had personally started in a storefront 20 years before, and the company to which I had devoted virtually my entire professional career.

In 1972 I resigned and said farewell to Ace Electronic and Hammond organs. If I had not committed myself to a life's work in electronic music, I probably would have gone into an entirely different field of business. But now I was in my early 40s, and it seemed to me that it would be wiser to start up a completely new firm in the electronic music field than to try to start at the bottom in some unrelated sector.

*Here are the Ace factory complex and some of the key
staff members I had to leave behind.*

LESSONS LEARNED

Creating the Roland Corporation was a whole new experience. It was as if I were starting my business life all over again. However, this time I understood the nature of the market and the challenges that lay ahead.

The first step was to select a name for the new company that could be recognized and pronounced throughout the world. I decided that it should have two syllables and that it should include voiced (rather than hard) consonants, in order to be most pleasing to the ear. The letter R was chosen because it was not used by many music companies; therefore it would stand out clearly in industry listings or trade show indexes. It was only later that I learned of THE SONG OF ROLAND and the image of strength and courage it conveyed.

As I prepared to start over, I paused to look back and marvel at the coincidences that had brought me to the field of music and to the beginning of what was virtually an entirely new industry.

When we decided to acquire the Zenon factory and begin manufacturing in Hamamatsu, I became interested in the history of the area and why it had become the center of keyboard manufacturing in Japan. The first manufacturing plant in the district was established by Torakusu Yamaha, the founder of Nippon Gakki, whose brand name, Yamaha, became so famous throughout the world that the company ultimately changed its name to Yamaha Corporation. Mr. Yamaha actually started out as a watchmaker's apprentice and studied the trade for a total of seven years. He started a watch repair business in the Osaka area, but when that didn't prosper he transferred his attention to making musical instruments and chose Hamamatsu as the best location.

I too had operated a watch store in Kyusyu for four years, so I began to look further for information about other pioneers in our business.

In Germany, Matthias Hohner started out in the clock and watch business and only later achieved world fame as the maker of Hohner Harmonicas. Laurens Hammond also began his business

A Hammond clock. It is driven by the same synchronous motor that started the home organ industry.

success as a maker of fine clocks. In fact, the organ business actually was a division of the Hammond Clock Company until the 1950s.

I did not become aware of the similar background of these famous men until much later, but I think I can understand why we all followed the same path. Traditional timepieces embodied the quintessence of machinery. The precision of the mechanism held a fascination for virtually anyone with an interest in engineering.

In my youthful self-confidence, I decided that I had learned all there was to know about the science of time, and that repairing watches was nothing more than returning them to their original condition. I am embarrassed to recall how superficial my thought process was. Watches have a profound and mysterious charm, but I noticed this only after I left the business. Even after I started Ace Electric, the very first product I designed was intended for the watch repair industry. There was an excellent Swiss time adjustment device called Vibrograph. It was too expensive for a small repair shop to import, so I set out to create a more affordable version for the Japanese market. What I developed was a portable electronic device with which any watch repairman could quickly measure and adjust the accuracy of any watch. Unfortunately, my device, WATCH MASTER, required more precision than most watches could achieve, so nothing concrete came of the effort. However, I could not have understood the circuits of organs if I had not studied frequency division circuits at the same time I was running a shop for electric appliances.

The relationship between time pieces and organs was different for me than for the previously mentioned three great men. However, I think that the coincidence of our career paths clearly demonstrates that there is a parallel between the attractions of time and music that links all humanity at a fundamental level.

But now I was looking ahead to new challenges, beyond the world of electric organs. The new generation of electronic musical instruments was just coming into existence in the early 70s. When Roland began developing electronic musical instruments, I had to explain what the commercial applications were whenever a new branch manager was installed at Roland's main bank. There was no precedent for the concepts. Each new model could be a departure from what had preceded it.

In those days a commodity tax was levied on any product manufactured in Japan. However, synthesizer type products were so radically new that there was no definition for them in the taxation manual. This left the taxing authorities in the frustrating position of not being able to apply a tax to the new products. When I was with Ace, a tax inspector actually suggested that we were intentionally designing products simply so that we could avoid the tax laws. His bureaucratic mind found it difficult to understand that these totally new instruments were being developed to enable musicians to find new ways to express their creativity.

This was the direction that I set for Roland. We would not be a company that followed trends. Rather, we would seek to discover and define new market sectors with creative products that gave musicians wonderful new avenues of expression. It has been almost 30 years now, and the journey continues.

CHAPTER EIGHT

JAPAN, AN IMPORTER OF SOFTWARE

A TRADITION OF SEEKING

In considering the development of Japan as a unique culture, one should not overlook the important contributions made by foreign sources, thanks to the Japanese willingness to seek out and adopt valuable intellectual achievements. Of course, the importation of mechanical advances, such as products of the industrial revolution, have been economically significant, but the introduction of philosophical and other abstract concepts have probably had a more profound effect on influencing how Japanese culture functions. In order to differentiate between the two types of imports, it might help to think of manufactured items as hardware, and intellectual achievements as software.

The first record of an official Japanese embassy to China appears when the Kenzuishi mission journeyed to the Sui dynasty. Shortly after the Tang dynasty came to power in 618, a new Japanese mission, the Kentoshi, was sent. Although very few detailed records survive, it is known that the majority of the Kentoshi was made up of Buddhist monks and bureaucratic officials. It is reasonable to assume that a variety of people from different occupations were also included in the mission.

The very existence of those early missions illustrates the interest of the Japanese people in opportunities for outside contact and in the acquisition of new information. It was a courageous effort to undertake such a dangerous and arduous trip to a virtually unknown land. On their return journey the people of the mission would be further burdened with the need to safely convey documents, scrolls, and artifacts. Nevertheless, they dared to go, despite knowing they would not return for many years—if ever.

Among other accomplishments, the Kentoshi brought back a large number of Buddhist scriptures. The *Analects of Confucius* is one of those scriptures imported nearly 1,500 years ago, and it remains to this day a fundamental influence on Japanese ethics and morals.

In addition, the Kentoshi ambassadors returned with a complete set of Chinese legal codes and a variety of scholarly manuals dealing with war tactics. Perhaps the most important of the Chinese writings on tactics was *The Art of War* by Sun Tzu. Warriors in the age of civil wars in Japan carefully studied all of the Chinese writings on war tactics. They also made a point of employing as senior staff officers and strategic planners military professionals who were well versed in *The Art of War* and other Chinese literature. As we begin the 21st century, *The Art of War* continues to be published and studied throughout the world, although now it has evolved into a basic reference text for business strategy studies.

A thousand years after the Kentoshi, the governing structure in Japan had changed. The Imperial family continued to be the nominal rulers, but a powerful hereditary official, the *Shogun*, exercised power in the name of the Emperor, who had been reduced to serving as a figurehead. It was essentially a feudal structure. Local barons (*Daimyos*) autocratically ruled each region of the country, with the *Shogun* ruling the *Daimyos* as first among equals.

In the 16th century, the Edo Shogunate restricted contact with alien commercial and cultural influence by using two methods. A license, authenticated with the *Shogun*'s own vermilion seal, was required in order to leave Japan on a trading mission. Voyagers with the license were known as vermilion seal ships, and they managed to carry a substantial number of Japanese merchants to

Southeast Asian and Pacific countries. The other restriction dealt with foreign visitors. Access to the Japanese market by foreign traders was limited to the isolated port of Nagasaki. As an added safeguard for the *Shoguns*, the *Daimyos* were largely prohibited from engaging in any sort of foreign commerce, in order to restrict them from increasing their individual economic power.

In the mid-16th century, European firearms (hardware of the latest technology) and the Western concepts associated with Christianity were introduced to Japan. Previously Japan had imported Chinese culture and the concepts of the Chinese legal system from 6th-century China and had also accepted Buddhism. Now European culture was being introduced to Japan by the vermilion seal trading ships. Through those two conduits of transfer, large amounts of intellectual software were imported in exchange for large amounts of silver and gold.

In 1868, the centuries-old feudal system of the Shogunate finally collapsed. The national period of intentional seclusion was brought to an end, and Japan saw the dawn of a new era, known as the Meiji Restoration. Information-gathering missions were sent off throughout the industrialized world. The knowledge that was brought back was used by the Meiji Government to establish a new constitution, which would lead to the rapid modernization of the country and the further enrichment of Japanese culture.

World War II was an economic and civil catastrophe for Japan, which might well have resulted in civil anarchy. Some of the credit for averting that situation rightfully belongs to the courage of the citizens who struggled through the postwar period. It should also be recognized that the social strength and resilience required to achieve that recovery was a result of Japanese society's absorption of the intellectual software that had been imported over the previous 1,500 years.

U.S. occupation forces quietly but drastically revolutionized the social life of the Japanese people. Some of the changes they introduced included the breakup of the *Zaibatsu* (large business trusts) and the redistribution of ownership of farmlands. The unquestionable power of the occupiers was so overwhelming that, in today's world, it is difficult to imagine what the situation was like. The changes were called the peaceful "revolution from above" but that only meant that there was no civil war or bloody battle involved in imposing the changes. As a boy of 15, I was very much aware of being in the midst of a radical revolution taking place all around me.

It was fortunate for Japanese society that this new start was allowed to take place within the context of Japan's own, centuries-old cultural background. In a style similar to the *Shoguns* of medieval times, the U.S. military government held absolute power but was prudent enough to act through and with the traditional Japanese state to implement its various social reforms. Had the occupiers simply imposed their will by right of conquest, it is likely that the changes would have been endured during the occupation and subsequently rejected.

The beginning was bleak. The economy was virtually paralyzed from wartime destruction, and severe food shortages gripped the cities. While the necessities of daily life were slowly reconstituted, fashion trends, music, movies and new technologies also came flooding in. As I recall, I was enthusiastic about virtually all aspects of the new culture except fashion, which wasn't one of my personal priorities. I was much more interested in radio since that was a potentially exciting source of music.

The introduction of the new technologies and the adoption of patent licensing encouraged the reconstruction of Japanese industries and the national economy. In fact, the country soon entered a period of remarkable growth. In addition to the manufacturers of home appliances who continued from the prewar days, including Matsushita (Panasonic) and the present Sharp Corporation, heavy electric machinery manufacturers such as Toshiba, Hitachi, and Mitsubishi also entered the consumer electronics field of radios, TVs and home appliances.

An American manufacturing expert, Walter Deming, created a system of quality management which was largely ignored in the

United States, but which became the basis for the Japanese theory of achieving sustained quality in manufacturing. The Annual Deming Prizes were given to Japanese manufacturers who developed highly sophisticated quality control techniques. The quality control standards of the honored companies were not merely improvements; they were closer to revolutionary concepts.

The Deming experience, and its positive impact on the nation, is a contemporary example of the ongoing Japanese willingness to accept intellectual creativity from overseas and then adapt it to the unique needs of the domestic Japanese environment. In this respect it can be seen as carrying on the tradition of the "Kentoshi" embassies and the Vermilion seal trading ships.

The achievements of the Meiji Restoration and the flowering of postwar Japanese industry could not have been realized without the tradition of openness to new information. It is a tradition that goes far beyond mere imitation. Only a fraction of the fine arts or crafts imported by those early cultural exchanges still exist. But the introduction and acceptance of new forms of philosophical and intellectual vitality have had a far greater and more permanent influence on us.

Buddhism, for example, had its origins in India about 2,500 years ago, and Zen Buddhism was imported into Japan via China around the time of the Kentoshi mission, a thousand years later. In Japan, as well as in many other countries where it is freely practiced, Zen remains a widely observed form of religious worship. Buddhist priests and Buddhist temples are the prime conservators and instructors in the disciplines of Zen belief. However, in addition to its theological status, Zen principles have gradually been adapted and absorbed by the larger Japanese society as well. Those principles have been molded into a philosophical system that guides aspects of everyday life for large sections of the population, even though they do not consider themselves to be followers of the Buddhist religion.

The word *software* carries a clear-cut image in the world of computers, in which both application and operational software have been developed. It may be possible to call classics imported from the outside world, such as Buddhist scriptures, "software," since they contributed to the formation of ideologies and behavioral norms of the Japanese people. Japanese philosophers evolved those concepts further and handed them down to subsequent generations. That continuous process has contributed to shaping the entire Japanese culture.

When we view various cultural introductions as a sort of "software," we can better see the significance of their influence on the overall mechanisms of our social structure. We Japanese may be seen as lagging behind in the construction of some forms of systematic organization, such as the formation of new networks for highway traffic. But, on the contrary, we study and digest imported information in our own, Japanese way, and then new "software" is created which is unique to the needs of the Japanese culture. This willingness of Japanese society to absorb foreign concepts can be seen in virtually all aspects of Japanese life.

Through the introduction of Chinese culture and Buddhism, Chinese written characters (*Kanji*) were introduced to Japan and have become the most widespread form of writing. Later, when Western technology was introduced, Arabic numerals and Greek scripts were also accepted and adapted to local needs. For example, we often use internationally recognized Greek letters such as "beta version" or "alpha cost." In the field of machine drilling, X, Y and Z are used to specify coordinates. Prior to English, Portuguese and Dutch were introduced to Japan, and their specialized terms have also been absorbed directly into the relevant fields. This Japanese process of incorporation is in direct contrast to the French, who insist on restating even the most basic foreign concepts, such as "TV" or even "computer" in their own language.

In the field of music, cross-cultural adaptation was more difficult. Along with the introduction of Buddhism, the native music of the Asian continent was brought to Japan. This music later fused with the traditional Japanese culture and, eventually, a unique, Japanese style of music and musical instruments evolved. Although there must have been some indirect commercial exchanges with Europe during the days of the Silk Road, music would not have been part of that process. It would have been virtually impossible for European music to cross Arabia or India. European musical concepts probably did not arrive in Japan until the second half of the 16th century, when Jesuit missionaries brought their religious music along with their organs and harpsichords. With the subsequent decision of the Tokugawa Shogunate to impose a policy of national seclusion and absolute suppression of Christianity, the introduction of European music was terminated without having had any lasting influence on the local music culture.

When the Meiji Government came to power, it placed major emphasis on developing all educational policies in an international context, and early in the regime musical education was included as a part of the new curriculum. Initially, music education was started in the same way as other school courses, but Japanese music and Japanese instruments had evolved using a pentatonic scale, while, more than a century earlier, the Western world had evolved to the scale of seven whole notes, which, with the addition of flats and sharps, became the diatonic scale of 12 equally tempered notes—also known as the chromatic scale.

The process of trying to adopt the diatonic scale in Japan must have been extremely difficult. During the centuries of the Shogunate, Japanese musical theory had evolved its own unique and complex configuration. Music professionals raised within that closed musical culture were abruptly assigned the task of first learning and then teaching an utterly alien concept of musical structure and sound.

At first attempts at adjusting to the chromatic scale ended in failure. Some of the best musical minds of the nation were sent overseas to study the Western method of musical notation, but despite the most conscientious and sincere efforts of these established professionals, it seemed that the intellectual gulf between the two systems was simply too vast. There are even records of suicides because of the frustration inherent in the task.

The eventual breakthrough came about through a more patient approach. Young musical scholars were sent as virtually permanent residents to study at the best American and British music schools. Although already versed in their own culture, they were still young enough to be open to alternative musical concepts, and it was they who successfully developed techniques to bridge the gap and introduce Western music to the national curriculum.

So it was that Japan would have to go through two different musical revolutions in fewer than 100 years. It took several generations for Japan to fully absorb the concepts of Western musical notation. While that was taking place, the experimental development of electronic musical instruments was already under way in other parts of the world.

As they had done over the centuries, Japanese commercial interests set out to learn about these new developments and then to create new concepts. By the 1960s many Japanese manufacturers began developing electronic organs. By the early 1970s innovation was coming at a rapid rate, and only forward-thinking companies could hope to survive and succeed in this dynamic new field.

Suzuki Teaches the World

The "Suzuki Method" of musical instruction is an excellent example of the creativity that can be brought to bear, once Japan has imported software from other lands. In this case the interaction of several important elements was involved. The wonderful result was the invention of a truly revolutionary approach to musical education.

The increasing appreciation for Western musical notation and instrumentation meant that a domestic manufacturing industry was needed to serve the local markets. Mr. Suzuki's father became a successful manufacturer of violins. His son, Mr. Shinichi Suzuki, was raised within the culture of violins and, as a young man, he was able to travel to Germany to study proper playing techniques.

About eighteen years after his studies abroad, Mr. Suzuki returned to settle in Matsumoto, the primary city in a district that is widely famed for its production of stringed instruments and other precision machinery. The unique climate of the region offers very clear air and exceptionally low humidity—perfect conditions for working with fine wood and exacting specifications. Perhaps because of the high esthetic content in the local economy, the city of Matsumoto also developed a strong civic identification with music appreciation, instruction, and related cultural pursuits.

I frequently visit Matsumoto to conduct business at the Roland ED Corporation that is located in the area. Whenever I arrive at the Matsumoto train station, I can expect to see mothers and children carrying violin cases, and I know where they are headed. The head office of the Suzuki Method is officially named, "The Talent Education Research Institute," and is located in Matsumoto City.

One can clearly identify the process by which Japan imported Western musical theory, and the background and travels of Mr. Suzuki are a matter of record. History is not so clear with respect to the origins of the violin itself. Of course, the desire to make music is inherent in the human soul (or is it more politically correct to say *genome*?) In any event, residual evidence of stringed instruments and flutes can be found in the physical relics of virtually every cultural history. I like the theory that bowed instruments were pioneered in Mongolia and introduced to the West by the warriors of the Golden Horde. After all, the Morin Khuur (Mongolian Fiddle) bears a resemblance to the Western cello, and the horsehair bow seems likely to have evolved in an equestrian society such as that of the Mongols.

Whatever its origins, the violin continued its European evolution until the late 17th or early 18th century when it finally took its current shape. In Japan, stringed instruments that had originated on the Asian mainland became central to the musical culture. In particular the Shamisen came to represent refined beauty, with its being played in a stylized setting and the player elaborately dressed in Kimono. The Shamisen is plucked or strummed with a plectrum, and it remains culturally prized throughout Japan. However, it cannot compare with the sophisticated playing style of the violin. Because the violin is a bowed instrument, it is capable of producing a continuous sound.

The versatility of the instrument also means that mastering the complex playing technique can be excruciatingly difficult. Unless started at a very young age, it is virtually impossible to become fully proficient with the violin. There are several special challenges. Beyond the issue of bowing technique, there is the unavoidable fact that the violin is fretless. Unlike the guitar, whose frets inform the fingertip of the player that she has moved up or down a step, violinists must learn to create the precisely correct pitch by themselves. They have to rely on their ear. Although this attribute makes the violin the ultimate in virtuosity, it is easy to understand why keyboard instruments were selected as the fundamental teaching tool in Japan. Thanks to their relative ease of playing and their self-determined pitch, keyboards were the natural choice for every elementary school in the country.

And then came Dr. Suzuki. Having committed his life to the violin, he searched for the best way to teach the instrument he loved. It was already well understood that the best violinists had begun studying as children. But the form and structure of instruction was costly and highly personal. Dr. Suzuki wanted to bring the expressive potential of the violin to a much wider world. His research included frequent visits to the zoo to observe the physical behavior of monkeys. It was there he discovered that the primates were neither right- nor left-handed.

In public lectures about the development of his method, he explained the heart of his theory. "It is not appropriate to force a left-handed child to be right-handed. We can train children to be able to use both hands instinctively.... This is the basis of my educational methodology."

In the early 1960s, Dr. Suzuki went to America with ten children and a message. The demonstrations were not just dramatic, they were also charming. The audience could see small children enjoying themselves while playing. This was not the traditional image of "lessons" and "practice."

The Suzuki method starts with toddlers and involves letting the child figure out how to "copy" a song, just as he copies the words he is learning from his mother. By teaching music as a natural function during that crucial time that the brain is maturing, the Suzuki Method has enabled tens of thousands of children—throughout the world —to learn

photo courtesy of Talent Education Research Institute

Dr. Shinichi Suzuki, Founder of the Suzuki Method of teaching.

the violin. Some of those children are now close to retirement age, and some are three years old. It is a glorious accomplishment and a wonderful gift to humanity.

During the 1980s I learned that Dr. Suzuki had included piano lessons in his education programs. Roland was by then a pioneer in the field of electronic pianos, so I decided to try to visit him. Although Roland had achieved a certain success, we were nowhere near the stature of Dr. Suzuki, so I was uncertain as to whether my request for an appointment would be granted. I decided it would be prudent to recruit an ally.

Fujigen is a guitar manufacturer located in Matsumoto, and its president, Mr. Yokouchi, was not only my friend, he also was well-acquainted with Dr. Suzuki. Through his kind intercession a meeting was set. Emboldened by the fact that Mr. Yokouchi agreed to accompany me, I brought along our newest electronic piano and explained all the advantages of the instrument: volume controls, headphones, and authentic actions. Dr. Suzuki expressed great interest. He said, "the children will like this very much," and called in one of the piano teachers.

The teacher examined it carefully and expressed reservations about the "touch," but Dr. Suzuki was focused on the future. He ignored the teacher's comment and asked a nearby staff person, "Can we use this in our concerts? When is the next concert scheduled?" Then he turned to me and asked, "How much is it for the piano including a headphone set and a bench?"

Dr. Suzuki bought our HP-70 Piano. Oscar Peterson starred in a TV commercial announcing the new product.

I was taken aback by the speed with which the conversation had turned to money, but the world of business can sometimes be like that. Preparing to leave, I asked him if he could use the electronic piano in his classrooms. He smiled and replied, "Since I am pleased with this piano, I would like to purchase it from you. I wish to pay you at the list price, since the president of the manufacturer took the trouble to come all the way to our office and make a kind presentation."

He handed me a check for the full list price. I was thunderstruck! Yokouchi and I looked at each other uncertainly. The Roland factories only sell to dealers and distributors, so all of our business is conducted at wholesale price levels. I may be the first, last, and only person at Roland who sold our product at list price.

Dr. Suzuki lived for 99 years. In all of those years he gave his life to music and enriched the world with the fruits of his labors. When he started his work, there were virtually no Japanese experts in Western music. Upon his death in 1998, tributes were published in leading papers throughout Asia, Europe and the United States. The world was grateful for his efforts at exporting such a brilliant new method of teaching. The most lasting tribute will continue to be the generations of individuals who are able to acquire the gift of music, thanks to the genius of Shinichi Suzuki.

As for me, it is one of the joys of my personal life that I had the great good fortune to meet and speak with Dr. Suzuki several times.

CHAPTER NINE

REACHING OUT

I earned my college degree at Sengokuso Sanitarium. My subsequent experiences with Ace Electronic and the Hammond joint venture were my post-graduate education.

Looking back on that history, I can see that there was a haphazard pattern to the growth and development of Ace Electronic. From the very beginning my primary ambition was to explore the application of electronics to the field of music. Those had been exciting years, with rapidly unfolding opportunities of all sorts, and I had subordinated all other company considerations to concentrating on issues of product and market opportunities. Eventually, events beyond my control (and my own inattention to the details of ownership percentages) led to the loss of my first company.

By the time I realized that I no longer held ultimate management control of Ace Electronic, it was too late to salvage the situation. Nevertheless, that did not mean I had "lost" or that my ambitions were defeated. It was true that I no longer had a company, but I had acquired a world of experience, and that would be the hidden capital for building Roland Corporation.

With some regret but with high hopes for the future, I left Ace Electronic and Hammond International in March of 1972. I understood it was going to be a long and sometimes bumpy road on the way to achieving a new position of leadership. It was the continuation of a journey I had initiated nearly 20 years earlier with the establishment of Kakehashi Musen. Back then I had only my enthusiasm and optimism to guide me. This time I was well aware of what problems might lie ahead, and I was eager for the challenge.

Academicians and other students of business have generally agreed that there are four stages in the life of a successful enterprise:

Getting Ready: Much work needs to be done before business transactions with third parties can begin. This is a period fueled by hard work, high hopes, and declining capital.

Start-up: The initial, high-risk period when the company tries to balance obligations and opportunities, while seeking to establish a recognized presence in the marketplace.

Breakthrough: If all has gone well, at a certain point the opportunities and obligations come into balance. The market accepts and appreciates the products of the new company, and a period of very rapid, but potentially expensive, growth occurs. During this stage the company is extremely vulnerable to run-away costs and interest expenses, as it seeks to rapidly expand.

Maturity: The company has survived its period of explosive growth, and it can now confidently operate in a much less risky environment.

There is an *optional* fifth stage: **Decline:** Decline (and disaster) occur when a company decides it is successfully mature, and that it is no longer necessary or wise to take risks or be "too" innovative. The history of the musical instrument industry is littered with tales of once successful, pioneering companies, that now exist only as memories, or possibly as brand names owned by other companies.

The Roland Corporation was officially established on April 18, 1972—one month after my departure from Ace and Hammond. Along with a few employees, I started Roland in a rented shed, not far from my original company. Although my intention was for Roland to become a major player in the music industry and a worldwide force in innovation, the day we opened for business we had neither a product line nor a customer network.

A major challenge facing any new business is the requirement for cash to support operations while it is getting started. To be in business, a manufacturing company has to be able to pay its employees and its suppliers. At the same time it must maintain adequate inventories of parts and materials and extend credit to its customers. With a total capitalization of only $100,000, Roland urgently needed to begin manufacturing and selling products.

Immediate prospects in our home market were not very promising. In general, the problems of distribution present similar structural challenges anywhere in the world. However, the Japanese music market, with its high population density, had unique characteristics. In the specific case of new electronic instruments, the domestic market had a radically different character from the American market. I use the past tense today, because the business structure of the Japanese market has matured and become similar to the American and the North Atlantic markets.

In 1972, one challenge faced by Roland was the unique structure of the Japanese market for keyboard products. That situation had evolved due to the fierce competition between the two main piano manufacturers, Yamaha and Kawai, which took place in the postwar period. Not many people know that more pianos are sold in the Japanese domestic market than in the entire United States market, even though the U.S. population is twice as large as Japan's.

There was an almost unrestrained competitive fierceness between the two leading companies. The result was that Nippon Gakki Co., Ltd. (now Yamaha Corporation) adopted a dealership system, while Kawai Musical Instruments Mfg. Co., Ltd. created its own directly managed sales outlets. The outcome was a highly effective division of Japanese marketing channels. Even worldwide, it is not easy to find a parallel to the distribution dominance that resulted from the battle for the Japanese piano market. In 1972, the substantially fragmented "independent" music retail trade was thoroughly intimidated by the two piano giants, leaving virtually no room for market penetration by a newly formed company. For Roland, the only path available was to develop new kinds of electronic musical instruments not presently offered by the two established giants. With the advantage of unique products, we might be able to convince the domestic retail trade that it was safe to begin carrying our line. However, that strategy required an investment of time and capital that we simply could not afford.

Our only hope was to first create a foothold in the overseas markets, which had already begun to mature, and then gradually work our way back into the domestic market. There was an additional financial attraction inherent in this approach. Export payments were collected by letters of credit, which we could redeem simultaneously with the shipment of the product to the overseas customer. Since cash was the only lubricant that could keep the developing Roland organization in operation, immediate payment was crucial.

Realistically, in the domestic market it would have been impossible to obtain large orders for product on the basis of cash on delivery. Since Roland was starting with limited capital and we had not had time to develop a record of creditworthy performance, bank financing simply wasn't available. Our only alternative was to limit our sales to those markets and customers that provided cash payment at the time of shipment. Of course, in order to do even that, we first had to create a product to sell.

Our parts suppliers agreed to accept 90-day notes as payment. Their wonderful trust allowed us three months to manufacture a product, deliver it, and obtain cash payment. It would not be an easy way to operate, but there was no alternative.

I recall it as a time of continuous tension. In retrospect it was also a valuable learning experience. It was during those early years that I learned about the constraints of cash management. Mostly

I am deeply grateful to the suppliers and the other cooperating companies that, relying on my personal history, granted those 90 days of precious time to Roland, a company with no track record. All of them were companies that had dealt with me in the days of Ace Electronic Industries Inc. Their willingness to accept the risk shows how important it was that Ace Electronic had maintained a strong reputation for competence and integrity.

In order for Roland to stay alive and prosper, the key was to make effective use of that 90-day credit window by developing products that we were *sure* would sell abroad, and that also had *potential* for acceptance in Japan. This was not so much a strategic decision, as an acceptance of reality. Even in the best scenario, we were well aware that we would have to operate using our suppliers' credit for at least four or five years. As matters turned out, it actually required eight years until we reached a continuing positive balance between our receipts and payments.

There was an additional challenge in developing an effective way to reach the retail trade—both foreign and domestic. Historically, a three-step form of distribution had served the musical instrument markets. Products made by small manufacturers or individual craftsmen were sold to independent wholesalers who handled distribution and offered financing to the under-capitalized retail trade. There was a rich array of products, and the activities of the wholesaler as middleman, whether operating solely with local manufacturers, or acting as an importer as well, made it possible for both small producers and independent retailers to operate efficiently.

By the late 1960s a discernable trend was emerging in America and the North Atlantic markets. As the market for electronic musical instruments continued to grow, it was attracting the interest of major sources of capital in the form of corporate acquisitions. This development, and the capital investment it brought with it, contributed to the accelerated development of new products and marketing expertise for the established brands. It also overwhelmed efforts by unrelated electronics manufacturing firms to diversiy through developing competitive strength in the music trade. Too, it adversely affected the role of wholesalers in the area of electronic music.

The independent wholesaler system that had been so essential for the distribution of traditional acoustic instruments was inappropriate for the more capital-intensive, electronic musical instrument trade. Among other problems, the three-step system was not structured to meet the needs for technical service.

Nevertheless, Roland had neither the product line nor the financial resources to take on the complexity of doing business directly with the retail trade. Despite the limitations inherent in three-step selling, our initial development of the overseas markets would have to be via the existing wholesale trade. As we succeeded in adding additional products to the Roland line, we knew that the need for direct interaction with the retail level would rapidly increase. What we had to develop was a distribution approach that could satisfy both our immediate needs while also being adaptable to our longer-term strategic goals.

Less than two weeks after the establishment of Roland Corporation, I flew to Canada on the first stop of an intended visit to the crucial North Atlantic markets. Roland Corporation was so new that I didn't have anything tangible to sell. I carried with me simple hand drawings and specification sheets for the rhythm machine we were preparing to build. In effect, all that I had to offer was a picture and a promise. Nevertheless, if I failed to write orders for the unit, there would be little hope that Roland would survive long enough to become a manufacturer.

My first sales call was to Mr. Eugene Trademan of Great West Imports Ltd., located in Vancouver. I fully understood that it was probably the most important sales presentation I would ever make. When it was over, Mr. Trademan applied for an exclusive for the Canadian market and gave me a sizeable order along with a forecast of requirements for a further three months. In the entire world, this was the very first order for a Roland product.

I was truly delighted. Now it was no longer me and my

colleagues in Japan talking to each other; I had received objective validation from an independent expert, who actually was willing to commit his own resources to our success. I immediately called Japan with instructions to rent a factory and place orders for production materials.

Not only had Mr. Trademan's order given me the factual basis to begin making financial commitments (as a new venture start-up, there was

Mr. Eugene Trademan, Roland's very first customer.

no other way to initiate business than to first get orders, and only then actually start building products), it also had given me a terrific boost in confidence for the presentations I would be making in the U.S. and Europe during the days ahead.

Our business relationship with Great West Imports developed so well that we eventually went on to form a joint venture company with them. However, that was for the future. On that first sales trip Roland's crucial need was to get initial orders for substantial quantities. We needed those orders as the basis of our beginning production. That meant that the objective of that first trip was to recruit major wholesale distributors who could serve large market areas. Of course, we hoped that there would be sufficient compatibility that the potential for a future partnership was not out of the question, but our first priority had to be short-term survival.

I went on from Vancouver to New York to meet with an importer-distributor named Multivox Corporation of America. This was the company that, under its prior name of Sorkin Music,

Laurie Gillespie, Chairman of Roland Canada with me and Mr. Dan.
We are marking the start of a new venture, a "Edirol North America."

had served as a distributor for the products of Ace Electronic. They also were enthusiastic about the prospects for the new Roland rhythm unit, and they became the second member of the Roland distribution network.

In 1972, the accumulated markets of Western Europe presented a different sort of challenge. Because of multiple cultures, differing regulations, and uneven levels of development potential, the region could not be approached as a single entity. The new Roland was a struggling small business. We did not have the resources to simultaneously cultivate and administer a range of smaller markets, but we urgently needed to tap into the substantial order potential of the area as a whole.

A practical solution to our urgent need presented itself in the form of a Danish-owned company, Brodr Jorgensen ("BJ"), which was the existing distributor for Ace Electronic throughout Europe. The company was owned and controlled by Mr. Alfred Jorgensen. Mr. Jorgensen and I always had enjoyed a constructive business relationship, and the BJ organization wanted the Roland franchise.

Erik Gramkow in front of the Brodr Jorgensen office.

Roland urgently needed broad-based market coverage. BJ had well-established distribution subsidiaries in the U.K., Germany, Switzerland, and all of Scandinavia. These were the best-developed European markets for electronic music products. In addition, the BJ companies already held excellent distribution franchises for compatible music products. Perhaps the deciding factor was that, in Erik Gramkow, Jorgensen had an outstanding general manager in whom I could place high confidence. Cooperation between our two firms was a logical step, and so an agreement was reached.

I visited other markets on that first sales trip, but the primary strategic goal had been achieved in the structuring of those first three major appointments. Roland now had competent, well-established representation serving North America and the major European markets. We had assured the stability of our initial production volumes, and, with payment by letters of credit, the way was now clear to focus on product development.

I began this chapter by summarizing the development phases of a new business venture. My general thoughts on music as a business opportunity were covered in Chapter Three, *Music is a Venture*. However, I think it may be instructive to examine the specific experience of Roland with respect to survival and adaptation.

Getting Ready: Although it only required a month for Roland to be established, it should be remembered that all aspects of the business were already fully understood, and all necessary contacts already existed. In effect, we could "hit the ground running."

Start-up: Establishing financial arrangements, lining up the first customers, producing the first rhythm units, and expanding on that first, tenuous arrangement was a time of hectic activity.

Breakthrough: By 1977 we were well on our way, but a variety of problems were beginning to surface. When a business is rapidly growing, control becomes increasingly difficult. It's almost as if the company starts to wander off in its own direction. In our first year sales had been about 100 million yen (US $300 thousand). By the end of our fifth year, sales had reached approximately five billion yen (US $28 million). Roland revenues were already greater than Ace Electronic's had been, and the future looked excellent. We set the goal for our tenth anniversary (five years hence) at ten billion yen, and then set out to conduct a thorough review of company operations in order to identify changes that would need to be made to achieve that objective.

In terms of marketing many products overseas, developing a domestic market, building factories, recruiting employees, planning new products and managing our funds, the capacity of our management group was stretched dangerously thin. All of the founding management-level employees were committed to helping the company succeed, but there was no time to rest, and problems continued to surface. To maintain marketing momentum I needed to travel overseas frequently. However, I needed to increase my efforts in product design, in order to stay competitive in the rapidly evolving market place. Not only was technology shifting from transistors to integrated circuits, but we had made the strategic decision to be pioneers in the field of guitar synthesis. I somehow managed to do both by working overtime. Time and perspective tended to blur. It seemed as though work was being accomplished by rushing from task to task, but the actual condition of the business was unclear.

It came as a shock when I realized that the company had begun walking on its own, without regard for our actual capabilities. Like a runaway train, the momentum developed by the company exceeded any rational speed limit. The question that confronted me was how to deal with the situation in a constructive manner. Ultimately I decided that, instead of lowering the company's speed, it would be more beneficial to bring in experienced drivers. I reorganized the company into various separate functions, and set out to find experts for each responsibility.

Of course, making the plan could be done a lot faster than finding the people to make the plan work. But over the next several years we did get it done. I stopped designing on my own. I had a management specialist come in to cover finance fields in which I was inexperienced, and I divided marketing into overseas and domestic divisions.

In Japan it is not customary for skilled people to change jobs on short notice, so it took some time before Mr. Tadao Kikumoto joined us to take over the research and development department. Later, Mr. Itsuji Miyake joined us as managing director of administration. This took place three years after I asked Mr. Sumio Abekawa, vice president of the Daiwa Bank, to arrange for Mr. Miyake (who had been in charge of Roland while he was a branch manager of the Daiwa Bank) to come on board.

Visibly, our company began to take form. With these and related changes, Roland edged out of the breakthrough problems that confront all venture companies. For Roland, success continued to come at an accelerating rate.

CHAPTER TEN

A LONGER VIEW

We understood that when the new products we envisioned finally became realities, serving major markets via independent, multi-line wholesalers would be too limiting a distribution channel. Even as wholesalers were being appointed, we tried to view each inter-company relationship in the context of its potential for a successful joint venture.

I already had had considerable experience with joint venturing as partner and as managing director of Hammond International Japan. I knew joint ventures could work, and I also understood what some of the ownership problems might be. Since the Roland distribution strategy was going to aim at developing joint ventures around the world, I decided that we needed to put in place a fixed set of criteria that would be applied uniformly to each and every relationship. The alternative of having differing arrangements with various partners was simply out of the question. If each venture were structured differently, it would be impossible to develop a global family of companies that could operate as a single, cooperative group in an open and harmonious manner.

Using my earlier experience as a guide, the following four basic policies were established to govern arrangements for our initial joint ventures:

At the time of the HIJ joint venture, Hammond Corporation was the global leader in electronic organs. Their willingness to

accept a 50/50 partnership created elements of trust and dedication that were invaluable for the growth of the local business.
Therefore:

1. The ratio of the amount of investment should be equal
   among Roland Japan and the joint venture partner(s).
   When three or more partners are involved, the combined
   local ownership should be no less than fifty percent.

Thanks to my understanding of the Japanese business environment, and the autonomy I enjoyed as director of HIJ, I was
able to deal swiftly and efficiently with problems as they arose:
Accordingly:

2. The person heading a joint venture company should be a
   native of that country and an investor in the business. He
   will be responsible for the entire management, including
   daily tasks, personnel, and all business transactions.

   (Now that the Roland group is 30 years old, and regional
   operations are staffed by teams of qualified business
   people, the initial need for unique local expertise and
   shareholding at the level of general manager is no longer
   an absolute. Accordingly, we have revised the policy to:
   "The person heading a joint venture company should be
   the most suitable person. He will be responsible for the
   entire management, including daily tasks, personnel and
   all business transactions in his territory.")

For an equally owned joint venture company to operate in
the best interest of *all* partners, there must be a clear separation
of responsibility between the venture itself and its separate
owners, so as to assure that the individual venture survives or fails
on its own merits.

3. The joint venture company should operate independently, including all matters of finance.

At its inception, a joint venture will be a union of partners
who share an understanding and an objective related to a specific

market. Personnel involved in the partnership will change over time, but it is vital that the local sense of purpose be sustained.

4. The initial local, managing partner should be younger than I am. (Sad to say, at my age, that is not a requirement, it is a fact of life!)

Legal advisors cautioned me that equal ownership would inevitably lead to a form of gridlock in which critical decisions could not be made. They strongly urged that Roland Japan hold a majority of equity, even if it were only 51 percent to 49 percent. I saw it differently. In view of the numerous problems that could result from a one-percent difference, I believed that the ratio needed to be 50/50. Each partner had to see his role as true owner. It has been 25 years since the first joint venture was established. In that time we have had to work our way through problems such as changes in the exchange rate, relations with competitors, and industrial property rights. Solutions have always been found, and the relationship of equality among partners continues unchanged.

As this book is being written, the number of Roland joint venture companies around the world has risen to 23. Getting to this point was not always a smooth journey, but that is true of any major strategy, including that of the history of our product development. The fact is the two activities—product development and distribution strategy—are irrevocably linked to one another.

The process of creating products and developing markets is more like navigating a river than climbing a stairway to success. Technology, competition, and continually changing tastes dictate the need for a steady flow of new products and the equivalent need for innovative approaches to the perpetually evolving marketplace. Roland Japan dedicated itself to becoming a leader in product. However, without the passionate commitment of Roland partners throughout the world, it is not at all certain that Roland would have been able to achieve its growth. In consistently adapting to the ever-changing marketplace, and in generously sharing insights with the global Roland family for the reciprocal benefit of all, the joint venture partners are at the heart of the Roland philosophy.

In those formative years we needed an adjustment in operating philosophy that was enormously difficult for me to implement. By being involved in virtually every aspect of the business, I had personally built Ace Electronic from zero into a $40 million dollar business. It was hard work, but it was fun and very satisfying. The 1972 sales of Roland were only one million dollars, but the potential was clearly there and my prior experience was invaluable. Within ten years we had reached $100 million, and our target for 1990 was to achieve $200 million. Growth of that magnitude required much more top-level attention to financial and administrative control if we were to succeed. It meant that I would have to surrender my intense involvement in the technical side of the business, and focus more of my time on issues of general management.

First and foremost, I am an engineer. The idea of lessening my involvement with the design and development function was at first unthinkable. I finally (regretfully) concluded that my fascination with product development was really a part of my larger dream of leadership in the music industry. My responsibility to the family of Roland employees, customers, and shareholders was to see that Roland continued to grow and prosper. Of course, I stayed closely in touch with the engineering side of the business, as it is at the heart of our success. But I sometimes wistfully recall those relatively less successful old times, when the days were long but the excitement never seemed to stop.

ASSEMBLING THE ELEMENTS

With initial access to major markets established, and a longer-term distribution strategy defined, Roland now needed to begin the process of producing products and broadening its product lines. As we progressed with those activities, we could also build a distribution presence in the domestic Japanese market and seek to broaden our access to additional export markets.

As indicated earlier, the distribution situation in Japan presented its own set of challenges. The first Roland products would be rhythm machines, for which domestic demand was well established. However, the best distribution channels were already carrying that category of product made by other manufacturers. No matter who we appointed to be our regional distributors, we would encounter the problem of being a "second" line in their product category. Due to that situation, our sales results would inevitably be limited.

Basically, we had two choices. The network of six regional wholesalers that I had previously established for Ace Electronic was probably the best-positioned relative to the market. However, those six wholesalers also depended on the Ace product lines for a significant part of their sales volumes. To avoid jeopardizing their relationship with Ace, the distributors would necessarily have to restrict their sales efforts on behalf of the initially limited product line of Roland. On the other hand, independent whole-salers, aware of the special antagonism that Ace might hold towards Roland, actively sought the line. They promised larger initial orders, but they were not as well established in the specific market segment as the Ace distributors.

While I was managing Ace Electronic I used to fret about the vulnerability of our distribution situation in the domestic market. It irritated me that our defenses against competitive actions were inadequate. However, when I began struggling to establish the new Roland line, I saw things from a very different perspective. Compared to Roland with its scant capital, Ace Electronic was huge! It loomed so large in the market that it simply was not open to attack.

Since we had major overseas distribution arrangements in place, it was possible for us to take the longer view, and give the Roland line to the six regional distributors I had previously worked with when I owned Ace. It proved to be a very valuable trade-off. By being able to accept initially low order volumes, we acquired a proven and trustworthy distribution network that was willing to work with us on the basis of cash on delivery.

The other potential impediment to getting established in the domestic market channels could have been Yamaha and Kawai. Had either of them chosen to aggressively deny us access to their retail customers, it would have been considerably more difficult for us to gain a foothold. However, neither major company was then interested in the comparatively tiny niche of the domestic music market that we served, so we were not perceived as a potential threat. Ironically, when Yamaha finally did enter the growing synthesizer market in the later 70s, several years after first our synthesizer products were introduced, the local trade saw it as an endorsement of the product concept, and the Yamaha entry actually helped to accelerate our own growth.

We had started business in April of 1972. Before the end of our first year, Ace Electronic decided we were a threat to their product line and officially informed their entire export distribution network that cooperation with the little Roland Company would be grounds for termination of the (then much more valuable) franchise for Ace products. The same message was also verbally transmitted to the Japanese domestic trade.

In the case of local retailers and foreign importers doing business in small markets, that ultimatum was a real threat to their survival, and many of them had no choice but to terminate or strictly limit their connection to Roland. It was extremely gratifying to me that both Mr. Trademan in Canada, and the Brodr Jorgensen organization that was serving Western Europe, unequivocally rejected this demand and pledged their loyalty to Roland. Doing my best was all I could do to reward them for their trust. Multivox in America was in a more precarious position, but a compromise was reached that allowed them to continue with the major portion of our product line.

A special situation existed in Australia. The Brash Organization had been the Ace Electronic distributor for many years, and Geoff Brash and I were close personal friends. Geoff is

Our formal wedding photo.
The future was about to begin.

My wife, Masako, and me on the first anniversary of Kakehashi Musen.

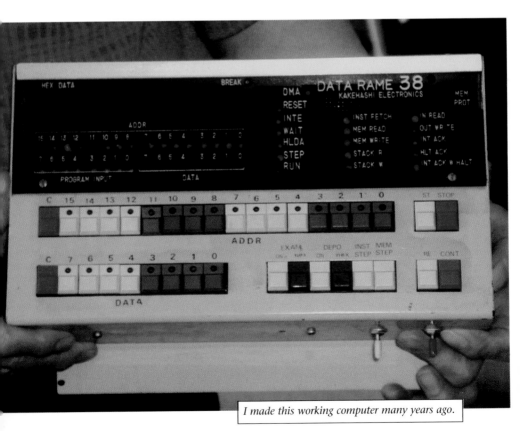

I made this working computer many years ago.

My first NAMM show was small by today's standards. (What grew to be the Consumer Electronics Industry was then a very small part of NAMM. It was relegated to display space in the basement.)

My friend and collegue, Alfred Dronge. Because of his untimely death I never did get to tour the Guild guitar factories.

With Alan Young, senior engineer with Hammond. We are holding a "reverb unit" that Hammond supplied to the audio industry.

Beginner's Luck: Ready for the salmon to jump into the boat.

With Oscar Peterson in his studio.

Roland's Hosoe factory established in 1987 as our primary manufacturing location.

Harold Rhodes and Henry Steinway at their induction into Hollywood's Rockwalk, January 17, 1990.

At the 1996 NAMM show. Stevie Wonder spent several enthusiastic hours exploring the features of the Roland Digital Recorder model VS880 – the first portable digital recorder in the industry.

With Bob Moog relaxing on the porch of his North Carolina home.

Oscar Peterson being honored at the Imperium awards.

Jeff Baxter of the Doobie Brothers; longtime friend of Roland and premier demonstrator of the GR500 guitar synthesizer.

The dedication of the Rodgers composite organ at the Bel Air Presbyterian Church. These are some of the people who helped to make the project a success.

Geoff and Jenny Brash. Good friends from the early days of Ace and destined to become Roland's first partners.

a wonderfully ethical man. If I had offered the Roland line to him at the very beginning, he would have been put in a most difficult position. Even though I preferred to have the Brash Organization represent us, I decided to give the Roland line to one of his major local competitors. We discussed my decision, and I made it clear to him that I saw the future of Roland in Australia as one that would eventually be shared with Brash. We both agreed that we looked forward to a time that we could join our fortunes in the Australian market, but this opportunity would have to wait for future developments.

* * * * *

In the early years of our operations, Roland concentrated on two priorities: being a reliable supplier to its primary markets, and developing new products. We understood that, so long as our line was limited to relatively low-unit-cost accessories, we would be restricted to doing business through multi-line wholesalers. Starting with rhythm units, we gradually extended the line of accessories to include amplifiers, speakers, and—in 1974—our first electronic piano, as well as a synthesizer keyboard attachment that could be connected to an electronic organ as a third keyboard, lying atop the instrument.

It wasn't yet a complete product line, but it was enough to start moving us ahead.

CHAPTER ELEVEN

FOUNDING A FAMILY

STARTING UP DOWN UNDER

It had taken four years of struggle before we finally had enough of a product line to begin thinking seriously about implementing our long-term distribution strategy of locally managed, joint venture companies. After considering the alternatives, I decided Australia would be the ideal place to start. A year or so earlier the Brash Organization had acquired the original Roland distributor, so there was no impediment to our finally joining forces.

Australia is special in a variety of ways, and I believed it had singular characteristics that would be particularly valuable to Roland.

Because of its vast size and remote location, the country is virtually a world unto itself. Even the seasons of the year are the reverse of the northern hemisphere. Although it is continental in size, distribution can be efficient, because most of the Australian population is crowded along the eastern and southern edges of the country. Four of the five major cities, from Brisbane on the north through Sydney and Melbourne to Adelaide on the south, lie on the eastern side of the continent. The city of Perth is on the west coast, facing the Indian Ocean, but there is a vast desert effectively separating that population center from the rest of the country. In fact, Perth is closer to Singapore than it is to Sydney.

The climate of Melbourne is most similar to that of the major commercial cities of Japan, and for that reason many Japanese find Melbourne to be a comfortable place to live.

The settlement of what eventually became the country of Australia was originally done by Britain. One of its first uses was as a penal colony, but the attractions of climate and economic opportunities soon turned it into a thriving population. For many years the country enforced a "White Australia" policy, which prohibited immigrants from Asia and Africa. This allowed Australia to avoid some of the racial problems that developed in the United States and Europe, but it left it with a population so limited in numbers that it was insufficient for the task of exploiting the industrial potential of the vast land.

The resulting market for consumer products is unique. In most product categories there are no more than a few local manufacturers, and in some fields there are no manufacturers at all. This limited domestic competition, along with the fact that all imports are on a substantially equal footing in terms of shipping costs and import fees, creates a market with an unusually level playing field. The best of the world's products are offered in direct competition with one another.

To make the Australian market even more inviting for our purposes, the consuming public has a highly developed taste and interest in commodity selection. It is a refined and, in light of the comparatively limited population, a relatively high-volume market.

In addition to being an attractive market in its own right, Australia also held the potential of being a natural place for Roland to perform test marketing and other forms of consumer research.

My own experience with the Australian market dated back more than ten years. I first came to know Mr. Geoffrey M. Brash as a distributing agent during the days when I was operating Ace Electronic. Over the years of working together, we became the best of friends, and in 1976 we agreed on the idea of establishing a joint venture. Since both of us were busy running our own busi-

Roland Australia's first dealer meeting: April 2, 1976.

nesses, we also agreed to recruit a third person to run the new company, with each of us owning one-third of the shares. In those early years Roland had a rather limited product line, and it required real courage to commit to such a fragile undertaking. I am still deeply grateful to Mr. Brash for his willingness to become my Australian partner.

To get the venture started with a proper celebration, it was decided to host a reception party at the Sydney Opera House on the first of April. This world-famous structure commands a splendid view of Sydney harbor and its ever-changing panorama of merchant ships, brilliantly colored sail boats, and even warships moving about on the broad expanse of water. There was no better place in the entire country for announcing the establishment of a new company. However, when we stopped to consider the still very limited product line that Roland Corporation Australia, Pty. Ltd. would be starting with, we worried that dealers might look at the date on the invitation and think that it was an April Fools' joke—or at least draw comparisons to its being a joke. Only half in jest, we changed the reception date to the second of April.

From the very beginning the company did well enough that it was able to host annual dealer meetings. I don't think I will ever forget the third meeting. It was held in the Sydney suburb of Newport, and all the personnel stayed late the night before the meeting in order to rehearse for the next day's show. The show would feature the introduction of the new, GR series guitar synthesizer that was to be the focal point and highlight of the entire event. Somehow, in all the commotion and confusion of the late-night preparations, the guitar-shaped controller of the GR synthesizer was stolen.

The loss of this controller could only be called a catastrophe. The stolen item was the only one of its kind in existence. That meant that we would have nothing to show to our dealers, who had journeyed to Sydney from all over the country just for this event. We immediately informed the police, and we also asked a local newspaper to help by writing about the fact that the stolen guitar was not really a musical instrument. It was merely a controller of a synthesizer system. It was solely designed for

The "million dollar" guitar synthesizer.

It doesn't work—you can have it back...

THIS is the $1 million guitar (left) plucked from Newport during the weekend.

The guitar was stolen from a national music dealers' convention where it was the star of the show.

The only one of its kind in the world, the instrument can produce the sound of a human voice, whistle, make bird calls and even rude noises.

But for the thief, it stayed silent.

Without a "little black box" the guitar cannot strike a single note.

After spending a day trying to play the instrument, the thief decided to return it to the owners, the Roland Corporation of Japan.

"It doesn't work—you can have it back," he told the relieved owners.

The thief phoned the Newport Inn and spoke to Roland Corporation officials after reading of the guitar in The Sun-Herald.

They went to a nearby home and recovered the instrument after promising not to take further action.

The guitar is now back with its inventor, Mr Taro Kakehashi, who spent $1 million and more than two years making it.

CESSNOCK JAIL 'A JOKE'

By MURRAY TREMBATH

POLICE today described Cessnock Jail as "a joke" following the escape of another five prisoners on Saturday.

The prisoners did not return after running in a 16km race from Cessnock Town Hall, around Mount View and

Mr Taro Kakehashi with the $1 million guitar.

Thanks to the power of the press, things turned out all right.

control, and although it looked like a guitar, it was useless for any other purpose. The article also strongly urged anyone who found the guitar controller to inform us immediately.

All of our frantic efforts paid off. After various negotiations the guitar was returned to us intact and in time for the dealer meeting. A local newspaper, the *Sun*, wrote a detailed account of the entire incident. Possibly because of the fact that the guitar was recovered unharmed, the story became even larger, and a local TV station picked it up as well. A newspaper journalist asked me about the value of the guitar. I told him, considering its development costs, it was worth a million dollars. The subsequent story described the controller as a dream-like product worth a million dollars!

The entire incident demonstrated the immense power of the media. What originally had seemed like a catastrophe, turned out to be a powerful advertising and public relations tool.

* * * * *

The Australian music market is host to a wide variety of imported products. In another of his business interests, Mr. Brash was importing pianos from China under the Lisner brand name. Although the prices out of China were extremely attractive, quality control techniques there were not yet reliable. This forced Mr. Brash's company to perform an inordinate amount of extra work in adjusting the imported pianos before actual delivery to customers. He once asked me to personally undertake the task of training the Chinese piano factory in matters of quality. I had no first-hand experience in China, and I was not an expert in the technology of acoustic pianos, but I felt I ought to be able to make a worthwhile contribution to the spheres of factory operation and quality control.

In those days every factory in China was government managed. Accordingly, investment priorities were determined within the context of national economic policy. During my first visit to China, I asked to see a factory producing TV sets. The factory looked similar to Japanese factories of only four or five years earlier. While not on the cutting edge of technology, the manufacturing lines were well organized and they operated smoothly as they produced TV products for export to Germany. But it was clear when I got to the piano factory that it was not dear to the heart of the current national economic policy. The facility was so out of date that there was virtually no basis for discussing quality controls.

Another nearly insurmountable problem was language. Direct conversation with the factory staff was extremely difficult and of limited utility. I tried with all my might to convey what needed to be said by writing every Chinese character I knew on a blackboard. They saw what I wrote, and they listened to me very carefully. Each year I returned and tried to instruct them about various aspects of quality control. I struggled, and they listened politely, and the quality of the pianos did not improve at all.

Mr. Brash was not about to give up. In 1983 he decided to send an Australian jazz quartet to Beijing and present the first jazz concert in China. He wasn't doing this solely in the context of an importing business matter; rather, he was exploring and trying to develop more subtle channels of cultural communication with China. It was an act of broad vision that accorded well with the Chinese culture, in which human relations are held in particularly high value.

At that time in China, you could not know the name of your hotel in advance. Government travel officers allocated hotels to visitors and informed them of the specific arrangements after they had arrived. We hoped to stay in central Beijing, but instead we spent our two-day visit assigned to a place called the Bei Wei Hotel, out in the suburbs. It seemed to be exclusively for local Chinese people to use. The rooms were plainly decorated. Other than a TV set, which occasionally showed Japanese language cartoons, "extras" were sparse.

On the next day we decided to have an early lunch before heading for the downtown auditorium to set up for the concert. The menu was exclusively in Chinese, and only I had the slightest idea of what the words might mean. Because simplified Chinese characters are different from the Japanese Kanji characters, I told my companions that my guesses might be only 30 percent accurate. They promised to eat whatever was served, and we decided that each one of us would order a different dish. The waiter spoke no English, so I simply pointed to each meal on the menu. And then the wait began.

Thirty or 40 minutes passed, but no meal was served. Everyone began to become irritated, but we managed to turn it into a humorous situation by theorizing that this must be a traditional Chinese style of serving. After more than an hour had passed, they finally started serving dishes of food. We were overwhelmed by the number of dishes being brought to our table. It seemed that in a blink of an eye our table was full of dishes, and even more dishes were being stacked on adjacent tables. It only required a few minutes to figure out what was happening, but the relentless parade of dishes went on while we were puzzling out the answer.

Current President of Roland Australia, Glenn Dodson, his wife, and my wife on a Sydney Harbor excursion.

Immediately I dashed into the kitchen and made exaggerated gestures to stop the process. The staff figured out my message pretty quickly, and I slumped with relief when they stopped cooking. Still there already were more than 40 dishes on the tables. We were a party of eleven. Instead of a separate dish for each of us, the restaurant people thought that each of us wanted 11 different dishes. If it had taken us any longer to figure it out, we would have had 121 dishes to consume instead of a mere 40. All the excitement must have whetted our appetites. Looking at the 40 dishes, we first burst out laughing and then thoroughly enjoyed eating the entire array.

The concert itself was a great success. Mr. Brash had selected a first-class jazz ensemble of four skilled professionals, led by Don Burrows on flute and clarinet, with James Morrison playing trumpet. The performance was very well received, and was also written up by the *Beijing Evening News*.

Visiting China several times in the 1980s, before the crackdown on pro-democracy demonstrators in Tiananmen Square, helped me gain a better perspective on Chinese industry and its domestic market.

In this new millennium China is becoming a worldwide production base for electronic products, and Shanghai and Shenzhen are demonstrating remarkable growth. Knowing their past condition and the disposition of local people helps me evaluate the present China in a more meaningful context. This is another gift I received from my long collaboration with Geoff Brash.

* * * * *

In 2001 we celebrated the 25th anniversary of Roland Australia. To mark the occasion we returned to the beautiful Sydney harbor and entertained staff and key dealers. It was April first, and everyone knew we were not fooling.

John Egan, Chairman of Roland Australia, me, and Geoff Brash toasting the 25th anniversary of Roland Australia.

GOOD NEIGHBORS MAKE GOOD PARTNERS

Worldwide, there are 23 joint venture companies making up the Roland Group. Among them are only three countries that are host to more than one venture: Italy, Taiwan, and the United States.

Not long after I started Roland, our Canadian distributor, Gene Trademan, introduced me to a Taiwanese associate of his, Mr. Yin-Shang Shaw. The company that Mr. Shaw owned was called Audision Electronic Industrial Corp. Its business then was microphones and microphone stands. In addition, it had just started to produce musical input equipment including pre-amplifiers.

The factory owned by Mr. Shaw reminded me of the early days of Roland, and the two of us seemed to look at the world in a similar way. That early rapport and mutual respect contributed to the start of a supply relationship between our two companies. Initially, I purchased microphone stands. As time went on and we grew to understand each other better, I began to think of creating a joint venture company in Taiwan that would produce commodities concentrated in analog technology. We soon agreed to the idea of creating a new factory and starting a new company.

Mr. Shaw and I searched all over Taiwan, looking for the best location for the new company. We visited possible sites from Kaohsiung in the south to Hshichi at the far northern end of the island, and many potential locations in between. Finally, we decided on a location in Nankang, a town close to Hshichi. (I remember that the real estate agent was a woman. Compared to Japan, women are considerably more active in the Taiwanese business scene.) We attempted to negotiate but made no progress. They would not accept any price reduction. Ultimately, we surrendered and acquired the site at the prices asked for by the landowner.

As soon as the signing of the contract was completed, splendid fireworks started to explode outside. I asked what was going on. The agent explained to me that they had prepared the fireworks to celebrate the conclusion of the business agreement. Listening to the loud sound of the fireworks, I felt relaxed

The team that put together the Taiwan joint ventures.

thinking that the negotiation was finally over. Yet at the same time I couldn't help but feel that the success was theirs.

Thanks to the tenacious efforts of Mr. Shaw for quality improvements and the collaboration of Mr. Katsumi Yamamoto, who was the president of BOSS Corporation at that time, the Taiwanese factory plays a very important role as the chief source of supply for Roland and BOSS commodities. That was how Roland Taiwan Electronic Music Corp. began.

Besides the relationship between Mr. Shaw and me, I regularly visited a certain company in Taiwan that supplied video display monitors for computers. Personal computers were just beginning to sell on the market, and we started to sell the display monitors under a brand name Amdek. Mr. Go Sugiura, a son-in-law of Mr. Sakata, the president of Sakata Shokai, Ltd., was mainly in charge of that display monitor business for us.

The name Amdek was created by combining the first letters of five different words including Analog, Music, Digital, Electronics and Kits. Kits were packs of unassembled parts and cases of sound effecting devices for electric guitars.

In addition to the kits, the newly started company dealt with display monitors, drafting plotters for CAD (computer aided designing) and sound source equipment for computer-aided music. Sales of Amdek monitors were tremendous. At one time in the United States, the name Amdek was regarded as a generic name for all the display monitors on the market. On the other hand, price competition for display monitors became increasingly severe. In 1983 I decided to withdraw from the business of display monitors and to transfer the Amdek brand to Mr. Sugiura. It was also a little too early for the sound source equipment for computer-aided music to achieve much of a market. To complete the strategic shift, we decided to cease supplying the kits of parts as well.

The company was renamed Roland DG Corporation, and its development was mainly centered on CAD plotters. Thus the Roland Group started undertaking the business of computer peripheral equipment.

In connection with searching for a good source of display monitors, I was introduced to Mr. Shin-Fa Ho. We appointed Mr. Ho as our representative for distributing Roland products in Taiwan. His business partner, Mr. Shin-Shun Tu, was doing business in Japan as a representative for procuring components for Taiwan Sanyo. The business for the sale of Roland products in Taiwan started with the collaboration of Mr. Tu and Mr. Ho. When pronounced in Japanese, the name "Mr. Tu" may be heard as *father*, while "Mr. Ho" can be *mother*, and I felt that the combined image of a father and mother as partners was perfect.

The Taiwanese joint venture of the Roland Group, Roland Taiwan Enterprise Co., Ltd. started operation as the distributor of Roland products. Mr. Ho is of course one of the shareholders of Roland Taiwan Electronic Music Corp., the Taiwan-based manufacturing company of Roland products.

In the early days labor wages in Taiwan were considerably lower than those of Japan, so quite a few Japanese enterprises made their way into manufacturing in Taiwan. Sooner or later most of them shifted their production facilities to Malaysia or

Thailand, seeking even lower wages. On the other hand, as the wages in Taiwan rose, engineering skills were improved as well, and the country eventually produced the lion's share of motherboard technology, which is essential for personal computers. Taiwan has also been an increasingly important factor in the industry of semiconductors. Operating within this thriving industrial environment, Roland Taiwan Electronic Music Corp. has assumed a very important role for the Roland Group as a supplier of commodities with high added values.

As this book is being written, the next scheduled joint venture is being prepared to open in mainland China, under the direction of Mr. Shaw, President of Roland Taiwan Electronic Music Corp.

AMERICA: NEW PRECEDENT, NEW GROWTH

From the special characteristics of the Australian market, it would be a major advance to bring the joint venture concept to North America.

The Canadian situation was developing nicely. The volume of business had not yet reached the point where a joint venture company would be appropriate, but Mr. Trademan and his team were doing a thoroughly professional job of developing the entire market for Roland products. However, results were not as satisfactory south of the border.

Although the United States was the largest potential export market for our products, we were not experiencing the rate of growth that we expected or that we believed the product line deserved. Sales in the eastern part of the country were doing reasonably well, but market development in the western states was clearly lagging. After discussions with Multi-Vox, we decided to appoint a second importer in order to achieve more complete market coverage.

About the same time that Roland Australia was being launched, we entered into an arrangement with Beckmen Musical Instruments (BMI) in Los Angeles, making it the distributor of Roland products for the western part of America. The energy and

Thomas Beckmen, Alfred Jorgensen and me at a trade show 1975.

effectiveness of BMI quickly showed positive results, and just a few years later the U.S. became the second market ready to be converted to a joint venture arrangement.

In line with the four strategic principles that we originally had developed for creating the joint venture family, we negotiated an agreement with Mr. Tom Beckman, with each of us owning 50 percent of the new company, and with him becoming the president of Roland U.S. During the first decade of Roland U.S. operations, Mr. Beckmen's management made excellent progress in developing a leadership position in the U.S. market. However, near the end of the 80s, currency exchange rates and global political and economic conditions all began moving in unfavorable directions relative to American imports from Japan.

I personally continued to believe in the future of Roland in America, but it was also possible to interpret these trends as limiting the prospects for the continued strong performance of Roland U.S. If one accepted the more negative assessment, then

The official opening of the new Roland US offices (L. to R.: Dennis Houlihan, me, Katsuyoshi Dan and Mark Malbon) in 2000.

the company should adopt a defensive posture, rather than seeking growth. I worried that a decision of that sort would be perilously close to the "decline" phase of a business that I discussed earlier. Nevertheless, local decisions were the responsibility of local management, and, for the next several years, the sales growth achieved by Roland U.S. slowed precipitously.

Because of my strong belief that a policy of aggressive growth should continue to be pursued, a strategic disagreement began to develop within the partnership. After jointly considering the matter, we agreed to purchase Mr. Beckman's 50 percent share of the business, and Roland U.S. became the first wholly owned distribution subsidiary of Roland Corporation.

We were extremely fortunate to have Dennis Houlihan agree to become the new president of Roland U.S. Notwithstanding its wholly owned status, for operational purposes the marketing programs and decisions of Roland U.S. continue to be handled locally, within the same conceptual guidelines as if it were a joint venture. It should be noted that, during the first eight years of Mr. Houlihan's stewardship, Roland U.S. has more than doubled its annual sales rate.

TAKING A PASS ON EUROPE

The other major overseas market area, Europe, was growing rapidly, but we were making no progress in implementing our long-term strategy of developing joint ventures to serve the region. The Brodr Jorgensen organization had its own distribution companies in Germany, England, and the Scandinavian countries, and it also had well-established trade connections in most other European countries. That had made BJ an ideal wholesale distributor when Roland was getting started. Now that the Roland product line was more complete (and complex), it was becoming more desirable for Roland to become directly involved in national distribution. Unfortunately, Alfred Jorgensen, politely but firmly, declined our repeated invitations to discuss any partnership arrangements. He had his businesses organized as solely owned proprietorships, and he was not interested in sharing access to "his" markets. This was my first serious encounter with the inflexibility of which I had previously heard. I mistakenly assumed that time and further negotiations would eventually yield a mutually satisfactory result.

Had I been able to anticipate the terrible damage his position soon would inflict upon Roland, I would have moved more aggressively. But Roland's business was developing nicely, and we literally were working with a world of opportunities. I decided to let European arrangements remain as they were for the moment and to focus my efforts on more readily accessible prospects.

CHAPTER TWELVE

MOVING TO HAMAMATSU

Putting together a global distribution system presumed the existence of a reliable source of supply for competitive products. In fact, our growth on the manufacturing side was considerably less structured than the customer network it was intended to supply.

After I founded the company in Osaka, we grew rapidly. A major problem was space for expansion. Unable to operate in just our original building, the number of small Roland factories increased one after another, until finally work was going on simultaneously in five or six dispersed locations. Eventually we had to confront and deal with this situation. The result was an eight-year program during which we moved the factories, one at a time, to the city of Hamamastu.

During previous business dealings I had been greatly impressed by the nature of the people in Hamamatsu and by the open warmth with which they accepted people who could have been treated as "outsiders." That was an important factor, since our workforce would have to relocate. I was also reassured by the sophisticated, industrial development plan that the city had in place. I had no hesitation about deciding to move there.

My first encounter with Hamamatsu took place around 1956, when I visited in search of keyboards for the organ I was trying to develop while operating Kakehashi Musen. It was logical to look for components there, since 100 percent of all pianos and the majority of all electronic musical instruments are produced in

Hamamatsu. (The other dominant industry is motorcycles, which accounts for more than 90 percent of all national production. Locals like to joke that "Hamamatsu has two great industries. They have one thing in common: they both make noise!")

In order to save time and money, I would take a night train from Osaka that brought me to Hamamatsu station around 3 A.M. This enabled me to start working first thing in the morning and return to Osaka that same day. Twelve years later, in conjunction with the founding of Hammond International Japan, I purchased the Zenon piano factory there and started to produce the two brands of electronic organs, Hammond and Ace Tone.

Converting the Zenon operation to electronic organs had its own special challenges. To impart the knowledge of electric musical instruments to piano craftsmen was a difficult job. Each of them had a big toolbox and didn't want to leave it. For a piano craftsman working with his hands, his toolbox was essential. Although major piano makers had already introduced mass production and no longer needed the skills of such craftsmen on their production line, the old-fashioned production system still remained in medium- and small-sized manufacturers. As indicated earlier, the factory required substantial remodeling (we even had to replace the floor). We threw out all of the old factory equipment, and then installed the production line for organs. To do this, we had to forbid the craftsmen from bringing any of their belongings, *including* their toolboxes, into the factory. Although the toolboxes belonged to the company, we allowed each of the craftsmen to take theirs home to keep, which satisfied them.

Every week I stayed in Hamamatsu for around three days and spent the balance of the week in Osaka. I maintained that commuting schedule for two years. Through this experience, I became convinced that Hamamatsu was a suitable place for production. When I founded Roland Corporation in Osaka in 1972, I rented a small factory in Hamamatsu as well and we started production in both cities.

There was a time during the development of the Japanese economy after World War II in which city planning was vigorously debated. The industrial base was turning from hardware to software. To improve city functions, big city factories moved to the suburbs while city redevelopment and design were being discussed. In Osaka City large companies, rather than medium and small enterprises, led the exodus. They did not simply relocate just outside the city, but went to other prefectures, whence they spread all over the country. Medium- and small-sized enterprises that needed to stay close to their supplier infrastructure could not move as far, but before long the medium-sized enterprises did depart, leaving only the small companies in the city. Eventually the companies remaining in Osaka found themselves unable to compete with Southeast Asian countries in term of wages. They too disappeared—one after another—until only those companies that had their own proprietary technology remained in the city area.

In Osaka, the decline of the Kansai district has been strongly criticized over the last dozen years. It came about because of errors in the original city planning, and thus it can be said that the decline happened just as it was planned. Furthermore, many heavy industry plants such as Nippon Steel Corporation and large oil refining companies had established themselves on the south Osaka coast. No part of the beautiful sandy shore of the past was left. It was gone. Pollution was such that swimming around Osaka Bay was not recommended. The view of the seashore as well as of the sandy beaches had disappeared. Under such circumstances, I started to think about moving all of Roland Corporation's manufacturing operations to Hamamatsu. I had started a small factory there at the same time that I founded Roland, and over time the number of Roland operations increased and expanded.

The total move took quite a long time, approximately eight years from start to finish. Constructing new factories and shifting equipment was a hard task, made even more difficult because of the responsibility involved in moving employees. It was indeed fortunate that most of the employees could adjust to such a major shift. Regrettably, there were some people who, for family reasons, could not leave.

The big move was completed successfully on the whole, thanks to the generous and even optimistic nature of Hamamatsu, which imbues the region with a spirit of acceptance of new ideas.

Roland Corporation was originally established in Osaka. I myself was born in Osaka and I maintained my "permanent" residence there until the age of 50. However, the time had come to leave Osaka. The rising property costs made it difficult to secure property. At this stage, it was a big assignment for us to find a really promising location to develop. We looked around for land throughout the entire prefecture. Finally, we concluded that Hamamatsu was the best place for a production base because of the existence of infrastructure associated with exporting from both the Shimizu and Nagoya ports.

Hamamatsu has more start-up ventures than other regions. It is ranked sixth in Japan in the number of "over-the-counter" public companies, which is higher than both Kyoto and Kobe, where start-up ventures are popular. I believe that this can be attributed to an understanding of Hamamatsu City and other nearby towns and villages. The smooth move by Roland Corporation and myself would not have been realized without the opportunity of collaborating with the regional development plan in the Hamamatsu area promoted by the Ministry of International Trade and Industry, and the cooperation of Mr. Hayato, the town mayor of Hosoe-cho at the time.

In 1980, I sold my house in Osaka and moved to Hosoe-cho, where I currently live. I have been living in Hamamatsu City for the last 22 years, 33 years if I include the time when I refurbished the old Zenon factory and rented a small house there. Perhaps I liked Hamamatsu too much, but I think it is only natural because I have been there longer than in Osaka where I was born and raised. After 1945, I moved 17 times, but my current address is where I have lived longest.

CHAPTER THIRTEEN

CRISIS

The decade of the 70s involved hard work and the usual range of stresses associated with starting a new business. There were customers to be satisfied, suppliers to be paid, payrolls to be met, competitors to be dealt with, and banks to be convinced. Nevertheless, it was a constructive time of creativity and progress.

From the schematic and the drawing of a rhythm unit that started the business, Roland now offered substantial product lines of keyboard products, amplification and sound modification accessories (including such items as the guitar synthesizer that was worth a million dollars in publicity, when it was briefly stolen from its Australian introduction).

In 1980, the value of the yen surged upward relative to European currencies, putting severe financial strain on firms engaged in the import of Japanese products. When the firm of Brodr Jorgensen reacted by declaring bankruptcy, it was a shock to the European music trade. For Roland Corporation, it was a potential catastrophe.

In the autumn of 1980, I was on a routine, but important visit to Gene Trademan in Vancouver, when I received a message from our Osaka headquarters that Brodr Jorgensen was experiencing financial difficulties. While serious news, it was a fact that virtually the entire music trade was chronically under-financed. I was confident that an established firm like BJ would manage to work its way through whatever the problems were. I completed my

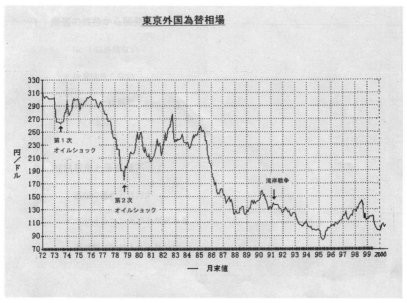

東京外国為替相場

Although the captions are in Japanese, the graph of the rising yen value is easy to understand. In 1970 one dollar could buy 290 yen. By 1980 a dollar could only buy 210 yen.

business in Canada and went on to Australia in accordance with my pre-established schedule. In some ways my lack of immediate reaction to the European crisis proved to be valuable. In Australia I met with my good friend and partner, Geoff Brash. His words of advice were to prove invaluable during the difficult times that lay ahead.

It wasn't until I got back to the head office that I learned the full extent of the impending disaster. The BJ organization, which for practical purposes controlled a third of the entire world market for Roland products, was effectively out of business. At that time Roland shipments to Europe were averaging $1.5 million per month. The value of inventory actually held by BJ, but now in the hands of the bankruptcy creditors, could not be estimated accurately. It was more than one million dollars in his central warehouse, with untold additional quantities at subsidiary warehouses. In the meantime, three different crises were exploding in front of us:

In the midst of the Christmas selling season, the European retail trade was not assured of getting deliveries of Roland products from the BJ organization. This would open opportunities for our competition.

About $1.5 million in new product was already on the ocean, in transit to BJ. This stock would become the property of the bankruptcy creditors the moment it landed at the port of Hamburg. Because the creditors were only interested in getting their money back, they were free to dispose of the inventory without concern for the stability of our future market position.

In Japan, existing Roland production schedules had been set to supply the world market, and we were now in the process of producing far more than we could reasonably expect to sell in the near term. Since our customer for the entire European market was on the verge of going out of business, we might be unable to sell those products. Lack of payment for that excess inventory would effectively cause the financial ruin of Roland.

Not only had we lost our distribution channel for a significant portion of our global market, we also had to worry about what would be the disposition of the existing inventory of Roland products that was now in the control of the receivers. For Roland Corporation, successfully resolving the crisis was literally a matter of life and death. To make matters even more difficult, Erik Gramkow had left the BJ organization a year earlier, so I could not count on the open and cooperative communication that had been one of the strengths of our distribution relationship.

The most obvious first step was to reduce production as quickly as possible. That would not solve any of the three crises, but it would at least keep things from getting worse. The real dilemma was how to stabilize the European situation in such a way that Roland could avoid the inevitable fate of being sucked into the financial vacuum created by the failure of the BJ organization.

The situation for Roland in Europe was not unlike a passenger involved in a terrible collision. Roland was trapped in the wreckage of the BJ collapse. An ambulance must be called, first aid must be administered, and then the patient must receive treatment to assure long-term health.

For Roland the equivalent of the ambulance was its ability to immediately terminate any increase in the inventory problem. The existing European inventory was a huge, unstable mountain of product, which, if upset, could bury Roland's future in the market. I immediately ordered a temporary shutdown of production at our factory. In addition, I negotiated an arrangement with the steamship lines to refuse to deliver our goods to the consignee in Hamburg, but rather return the goods to us in Japan. These steps were vital, because they kept the problem from becoming even larger. However, cutting off product flow would not be enough to save Roland. The entire situation had to be brought under control and profitable access to the European market quickly restored.

The only first aid that might stabilize the situation was a generous application of money. For most of the eight years since Roland started, it had been a precarious balancing act of operating in the narrow window of supplier's credit and customer payments. By 1979 we had finally achieved a positive, sustainable cash flow, but there had not been anywhere near enough time to create reserves against the magnitude of the looming BJ default.

The task before me could be stated more simply than it could be accomplished. I had the gloomy assignment of negotiating with the bankruptcy receivers to minimize the damage caused by the Jorgensen collapse. At the same time I had the urgent need to restructure and replace European market distribution coverage. Both of these complex projects had to be completely accomplished before the next Frankfurt Musikmesse, scheduled for early February—only three months away!

For help I turned to the three banks that had been working with Roland ever since our beginning. Each bank was familiar with our operations and knew our history and the caliber of our management. Both of the first two banks I approached refused to give us any help. After examining the facts and the numbers, neither bank felt it was prudent to increase their risk by advancing more credit to a company they had decided was likely to fail.

My last hope—Roland's last hope—was the Daiwa bank. The local branch manager who supervised our account did not have the authority to extend further credit, but he was sufficiently interested that he arranged for me to make a presentation at the head office. With him at my side, I was given one hour to present my case.

Since I did not know what exact circumstances I would encounter in Europe, I could not offer a detailed plan. I described the situation as I knew it, including the steps we had already taken, and I stressed the critical importance of gaining control of the existing inventory. Other than that, I spoke of our strategic objectives for Europe in the context of our overall distribution planning. We then discussed details of the problem and what steps I might be able to take to resolve the situation. Their immediate decision was to grant to Roland a special line of credit for two million dollars. That would enable me to enter into credible negotiations with BJ creditors, and perhaps start the process of rebuilding our distribution.

It was a brave decision by the bankers. Without the support of the Daiwa Bank at that critical point, it is unlikely that Roland would have been able to survive. The speed of their decision was at least as important as their willingness to help. The situation on the ground in Europe had not changed, and as time passed it would become progressively more dangerous. As it turned out, we only needed to use about one-third of that special line of credit. But the strength of the financial commitment gave me the composure I needed at the negotiating table.

Armed with the pledge of support by the Daiwa Bank and a variety of provisional ideas on how to proceed, I boarded a plane for what I expected to be a three- or four-week trip. Except for the week between Christmas and New Year's—when I could go home for a brief visit, because it was impossible to get the attention of the European financial community—I spent the next three months alone, crisscrossing Europe in search of solutions.

Alfred Jorgensen at the Brodr Jorgensen headquarters in Copenhagen.

The situation that greeted me was extremely tense. Due to the financial difficulties of BJ, local creditors had appointed an independent attorney, Mr. Moltke, to act in their interest. It was he who would determine the ultimate disposition of assets, including that ominous mountain of Roland inventory. Of course, his primary interest was in securing recovery for his clients, so he brought maximum pressure on major suppliers such as Roland to cooperate in "saving" the BJ organization.

It was not out of the question to participate in a rescue effort, but before agreeing to such an arrangement, I needed to see and understand the complete financial position of the BJ organization. Regrettably, Mr. Jorgensen took the position that his word ought to be enough of a guarantee to satisfy my curiosity, and he refused to open the books of the business for examination by qualified outsiders. I decided I should learn more about the situation in the various national markets before going any further with "rescue" discussions, so we adjourned for the moment.

In the next weeks I visited every Jorgensen outlet and Roland distributor in Europe, talking to the individual managers, assessing the local conditions, and exploring with them the possibility of future cooperation. I was greeted by widespread uncertainty and considerable anxiety. The Jorgensen organization had never been forthcoming with information about its activities, and this time was no exception. Local managers knew that some sort of crisis existed, but they had no idea of the specifics. All of them were deeply worried about their own job security and eager to consider future collaboration.

When Christmas Eve came, I happened to be in Paris. Late in the afternoon I finished discussions with the local Roland distributor and took a cab back to my room at the airport Holiday Inn. Due to the impending holiday, there was very little traffic. At the hotel the situation was even more desolate. I couldn't be sure, but it was quite possible that I was the only registered guest that night; clearly the management wasn't expecting much business. The lobby, including the reception desk, was completely empty.

After leaving my coat and business papers in my room, I went downstairs to have dinner. The restaurant was closed. Airport hotels are isolated from one another, so there was no "neighborhood" in which to find food of any sort. I explored the deserted main floor of the Holiday Inn until I finally located the usual array of coin-operated vending machines. These are the megalithic devices that customarily offer a wide range of amenities including small, overpriced packets of snacks and candy.

By this time I was sufficiently hungry that price was no longer a consideration. However, although the machines offered a lavish selection of toothbrushes, combs and a few soft drinks, all of the candy and food slots were empty.

There I was. It was Christmas Eve in Paris. I was alone in an airport motel. My only dinner turned out to be a single can of Coca Cola.

It was definitely time to go home.

CHAPTER FOURTEEN

OUT OF THE ASHES

After my brief visit to Japan, I went to Hamburg to see Jorgensen's main bank and then returned to Copenhagen to resume discussions with Jorgensen and the creditors' attorney. The meeting was extremely difficult. The lawyer sat at the head of the table; Alfred and I faced each other. We had worked together for many years. When Ace Electronic tried to strangle Roland in its early years, Alfred stood by us with his full support. Now I wanted to support BJ as much as I possibly could.

The subject of a "rescue" by the creditors was raised again. While Roland was a major supplier to BJ, our financial relationship was dwarfed in importance by his relationship with Hammond Organ Company and with his primary bank, both of which had been working with him on an unsecured basis. In contrast, Roland was only worried about control of its own inventory and the retention of the Roland distribution network. Thanks to our letter of credit terms, there was no debt to be worried about as well. When I learned that Hammond, which was said to be owed about $3 million, had written the BJ account off entirely and had even refused to attend any "rescue" meeting, I knew there was no hope.

With Alfred watching me intently, the attorney looked me in the eye and asked me whether I was prepared to help save the Jorgensen organization. I had come to Europe to try to save Roland. If there were anyway I could help Jorgensen at the same

Kim Nunney (Pres. Roland Canada), Brian Nunney (first Pres. Roland UK), John Booth (Pres. Roland UK), and me.

Michael Heuser of Roland Switzerland and Wolfgang Lachnit, founding director of Roland Germany.

The founding of Roland Scandinavia (Erik Gramkow is on the ladder).

time, I would gladly have participated. The attorney phrased the question as if some sort of rescue were possible, but by this time I knew better. The accumulated debts of the BJ organization were simply too huge to be satisfied. I had no choice but to refuse. The meeting ended shortly afterward, and I left to return to my hotel.

It was a typical midwinter day in Denmark, where the sun rises weakly above the horizon for only a few hours each day. Slate gray skies and lightly falling snow did nothing to improve my mood as I made my way to a cabstand near the opera house. Seeing my signal, the cab pulled away from the curb and waited. I had opened the rear door when Alfred came hurrying up and stopped me. With the cab waiting in the street, he stood rigidly before me, and urged me to reconsider. The scene remains vivid in my memory. He was a tall Dane, widely

127

known for his proud and erect bearing. I can still remember the unprecedented sight of his pleading face, framed by the ornate façade of the towering opera house behind him. All I could do was sadly repeat my position, as drifting snowflakes accumulated on the slumping shoulders of his black overcoat.

I have seen Alfred in public places once or twice since then. We exchange nods, but there is not much left to say.

The next month was a flurry of frantic activity. Negotiations with the creditors were complex, but I did manage to secure control of the Roland inventory. Then it became a race to put together joint venture distribution companies, in order to assure continuity of supply to the various national markets. Actual incorporation dates for those new companies were:

United Kingdom: *Roland (U.K.) Ltd.*: January 19, 1981

Germany: *Roland Elektronische Musikinstrumente GmbH*: January 27, 1981

Switzerland: *Musitronic AG*: March 15, 1981

Scandinavia: *Electronic Musical Instruments Roland Scandinavia A/S*: March 16, 1981

We also confirmed supply relationships with the various national customers of the former BJ organization.

A little more than three months earlier, not just our European situation but Roland's own prospects for survival had looked uncertain at best. Instead of the calamity feared by the first two banks I approached back then, we were able to go to the 1981 Frankfurt Fair with newly invigorated distribution and assured continuity of product supply. In subsequent years, eight additional distribution joint ventures for Roland products have been established throughout Europe, and the potential for additional growth continues to be attractive.

* * * * *

The courageous support of the Daiwa bank helped us weather the inventory crisis brought on by the first appreciation of the yen. However, in reconstructing our European distribution, I knew that further steps had to be taken, because it was highly likely that the value of the yen would go up again.

Within the European market, each national importer had purchased his products from Jorgensen based on European currency exchange rates. This was fine for the buyer, because it insulated him from any abrupt shifts in the value of the yen. One of the reasons for the BJ collapse had been Jorgensen's untenable position of buying in the increasingly more expensive yen, but then having to resell in European currencies.

From the very beginning Roland had followed a basic policy regarding international trading. That policy was to conduct all of its exports on a yen basis. The yen is now accepted as a major trading currency, but, back in the early 70s, that sort of policy was virtually unheard of. At times it was difficult to insist on doing business solely in yen transactions, but we had to adhere to our rules, in order to live in that 90-day window of supplier credit and cash payment.

We had developed a strategic distribution policy even before Roland wrote its first order. On the day we started in business, it was already our long-term intention to serve most markets via locally based, joint venture distribution companies. We knew that eventually as much as 70 percent of the value of our exports could be due to our joint venture companies.

That meant that, if our Japanese manufacturing resource sold its exports on the basis of U.S. dollars, the U.S. partner would have been guaranteed a stable price, but all the other partners would have been exposed to constant variation in their individual landed costs. By trading in yen, all partners paid the same prices. In turn, all of the partners applied constant pressure on the factories to cut costs to the bare bone, by continuing development of sophisticated production processes.

The Roland policy divided responsibility between the manufacturing and the marketing companies, with no special or privileged arrangements given to joint venture customers. The manufacturing and design functions in Japan had to make their absolute best efforts to maintain appropriate price margins by cutting as much cost as was practical. They also had to concentrate their engineering efforts toward offering products at the lowest possible prices. In return, the overseas marketing function (primarily joint venture companies) was required to carry the risks involved in possible exchange fluctuations. That policy worked reasonably well for ten years. We had no way of anticipating the upward surges in value that eventually would begin to take place.

Every time the value of the yen shot up, the overseas customers (partners) would have to make extensive modifications in their selling prices. Price modification can be extremely difficult in individual markets, because fluctuations in currency values do not affect all global competitors equally. Maintaining a strong position in a local market under such unequal conditions requires tough decisions.

Although yen-based exporting had worked well, the chaos and near catastrophe attendant upon the Jorgensen collapse made it obvious that we had to find ways to minimize the loss from currency fluctuations. The natural conclusion was to look to the establishment of overseas manufacturing facilities. Such an arrangement would substantially mitigate risks associated with exchange movements. I immediately started to search for suitable locations.

For the western hemisphere the general decision wasn't very difficult. Production facilities in either the U.S. or Mexico would suffice. But Europe presented a much thornier set of issues. Culture, languages, tariffs and even commercial laws varied throughout the Continent. As it turned out, the search for the perfect location would take five years. Our first step was to draw up a list of conditions that had to exist before a location could be considered suitable for our needs.

There needed to be daily flights to Japan, and there also had to be convenient access to a major ocean port. The port facility was necessary for importation of parts from Japan and other supply locations, and for export of the finished merchandise. Traditions and regulations regarding labor relations had to be compatible with our own experience. It was also important that there be an attractive quality of life available for Japanese staff and their families who would be working at overseas production facilities. Language also became an important criterion. English had become the common language of world commerce, so there had to be a general proficiency in English for a location to be suitable.

Roland wasn't alone with its need to develop offshore production; many Japanese industries were confronted with a similar challenge. For a great majority of them, East Asian countries were seen as being the best location because of their low labor costs. Establishing factories in Thailand, Singapore, Malaysia, Indonesia, or South Korea became a major trend, and for most companies, this worked out very well.

We had two ways to proceed. One was to take advantage of low labor costs in the Southeast Asian countries, the other to establish our plants in the center of the markets for electronic musical instruments in North America and Europe. Both options contained advantages and disadvantages. We had the alternative of selecting a highly skilled production environment, or one with attractively low labor costs. One could almost say it was a choice between culture and cost.

The situation for Roland was different from that of the majority of Japanese manufacturers. We were confronted with the same exchange problems and cost pressures, but there are very few electronic musical instruments with an actual market large enough to economically justify full-scale mass production. Typically, the production process for musical instruments is intermittent, with short production runs allowing multiple products to be produced in smaller individual quantities. This type of process relies on a highly skilled work force.

Apart from the attractive labor costs, there were drawbacks associated with an Asian production base. In East Asia we would have to train and develop inexperienced workers from the very beginning. Additionally, the economics of our production meant that our facilities needed to be supported by a reasonable level of local demand, but the Southeast Asian countries were not significant markets for us.

Our conclusion was to establish our manufacturing facilities in the U.S. and in Europe. It was a decision based on giving priority to the longer-term needs of marketing and manufacturing, as opposed to the near-term savings that were available if we built our plant in Southeast Asia.

Although our decision had been made, Taiwan still drew my attention because of its special characteristics. The Taiwan dollar was linked to the U.S. dollar, minimizing exchange problems. The electronics industry in Taiwan was thriving. Various technologies had already been transplanted from Japan, and the Taiwan consumer market was already filled with locally produced products carrying Japanese brands. Although Taiwanese labor costs were higher than those offered by the rest of Southeast Asia, they were still attractive compared with labor costs in Japan. Finally, even though it lacked a large consumer market, Taiwan did have a well-developed technical base.

Eventually I decided to establish three overseas operating bases. I would build plants in the U. S. and Europe in order to be inside our major markets. This way I could be confident that the needs and opportunities of the markets would be reflected directly onto the production resource. I also decided to establish a distribution center in Taiwan as a means of controlling parts supplied to other countries, serving as a supply source of semi-finished product, and local distribution of completed units.

I still believe I made the right decision for Roland. In the industry today, manufacturing for most portable keyboards has been shifted to Indonesia and Malaysia. One of our competitors has established its plant in China, and the plant is operating with great success. On the other hand, in the context of our business strategy Roland dared not expand manufacturing operations into those areas. Our best chance to outperform the competition has always been to concentrate our efforts on research and development. Our strategy is always to be the leader in product quality and in innovating opportunities to create new sounds. For us, research and development is emphasized not simply as a device to compete with other manufacturers. We were, and still are, committed to research and development as a comprehensive and positive program to enable us to lead the musical instrument industry.

Choosing a site for our European plant was a complicated process. With the benefit of hindsight, I must admit that it was more complicated than necessary. Although the topic was very much in the news, I underestimated the rate of integration of the European Community. My own view was that it would not take shape until early in the next century. In reality the process of integration was already well underway.

When it came to selecting a national home for our operation, we first had to go through a process of elimination. First I eliminated the Scandinavian countries because of high labor costs and shipping distance from other continental markets. Germany also had to be excluded because of its exceptionally costly labor.

Spain presented a more attractive cost structure, but there were concerns regarding reliable local supply of basic materials to support a manufacturing operation of our type. Mr. Antonio Punti, the president of Vieta Audio Electronica, our Spanish sales agent at that time, provided me with comprehensive information on Spain. However, we could not be confident that local suppliers could meet the requirements for manufacturing sophisticated musical instruments.

France was the country of fashion *a la mode* and wine *extraordinaire*, but there was not much history of success in manufacturing electronic musical instruments other than the Onde Martinot. In addition, a general facility with the English language was a requirement, so France was also excluded from the list of potential sites. This left us with the United Kingdom or the

Benelux countries, where English was widely spoken and manufacturing operations were feasible. We already had an established affiliate, Roland (U.K.) Ltd., in the United Kingdom. However, based on difficulties we experienced assembling amplifiers in that country, I could foresee serious problems in starting a new manufacturing facility there.

It seemed pretty clear that the Benelux countries would be the best choice.

During the several years that we spent looking for a suitable location for our new plant, Mr. Bruno Barbini, president of our joint-venture company, Roland Italy S.p.A, repeatedly asked me to meet with a friend of his who was producing synthesizers and who wanted to explore the possibility of dealing with Roland. I was not at all interested in pursuing the subject; I had the preconceived certainty that manufacturing in Italy was not feasible. Like most prejudices, my misconceptions about Italy were based on ignorance. I simply didn't know enough about the manufacturing environment in the country.

Two years after our search for a European production location started, Mr. Barbini brought his friend to the Roland booth at the annual Chicago NAMM show. I had not changed my mind about Italy, so Mr. Barbini did not try to make an advance appointment for his friend. We did talk for a while, though, and I began to see the opportunities in a different light. The story told by Carlo Lucarelli, Barbini's friend, was very attractive.

Among a wide range of related subjects, Mr. Lucarelli spoke persuasively about the current situation of his business and his vision of the future of the manufacturing industry in Italy. I was not immediately convinced, but I began to re-think my earlier exclusion of the country from any consideration. After all, one's image of a country can be highly subjective. Most of my impressions of Italy were based on news stories from earlier times. I had thought of Italy as a place where the trains didn't run on time, the mail was never delivered properly, and the Mafia was involved in everything.

The four directors of Roland Europe: Francesco Rauchi (deceased), me, Carlo Lucarelli, and Giuseppe Vecchietti.

I suppose there are still quite a few people whose image of Japan is an early postwar one of *"Fujiyama, Geisha-girl,* and the *Yakuza."* Even if his perspective is more up to date, someone who has never looked closely at Japan might have a dark impression limited to visions of the Yakuza (gangsters) being involved in everything and of virulent religious cults setting off nerve gas in public places.

Mr. Lucarelli's words profoundly altered my view of Italy. The warmth of his convictions melted my previously frozen attitude. Now I could understand the logic for putting an operation there. I could envision the specific facility, the geographic conditions and the benefits for Roland. After two years of not being able to find any single location that pulled together all the aspects we needed, I realized that Italy was the very place I had been seeking.

Almost exactly one year later we completed the diversification of our manufacturing sourcing by acquiring the Rodgers Organ Company in the United States. It is interesting to note that Rodgers

Organ Company was incorporated in Oregon at the same time that I was establishing Ace Electronic Industries Inc. in Japan. In fact, shortly after Ace entered the export market, I called on Rodgers to try to interest them in the FR-1 Rhythm Ace for their theater organ. My sales visit was not successful, but it did give me the opportunity to meet senior management and to appreciate the technological skill of the organization.

That visit was in 1968. Twenty years later I learned that the current owner of Rodgers, Steinway Musical Properties of Boston, Massachusetts, was interested in selling the company. I immediately opened negotiations. The subsequent process of acquisition was unusually rapid, because both parties were interested in completing the transaction fairly and promptly.

On behalf of Roland I was seeking to implement several more steps in our long-range strategy. As mentioned earlier, I wanted a technically qualified manufacturing base in North America. In addition, by the late 1980s, Roland had begun to focus on the development of electronic organs, and I was interested in a broad approach to the market that would include both classic and home models.

I toured the Rodgers factory in February of 1988, and was pleased with what I found. Although the physical plant would need some renovation, the base of human technology and product commitment was first rate. I knew it could be a good fit for the two of us. Roland would acquire well-developed skills and knowledge in the field of classical organs—particularly with respect to the critical area of voicing. On the other side of the equation, Rodgers would gain access to our state-of-the-art digital technology which would have a positive impact on their product development capabilities.

The investment group named Steinway Musical Properties wanted to sell Rodgers simply because it was a business that was not of interest to them. They had acquired a package of companies from CBS when CBS withdrew from the instrument business, but their real interest was in the Steinway brand. By selling the Rodgers Company at a fair price, they could free up their own capital and concentrate on Steinway.

My 1968 sales call at Rodgers Organ. Mr. Fred Tinker, co-founder of the company is third from right.

The third party in this transaction was Rodgers itself. Steinway Musical Properties did not inform the Rodgers management that any negotiations were underway. When the terms of sale were agreed to and finalized, the question then became, how should we tell the people in Oregon that they have been sold again? The late 80s was a time of a certain amount of anti-Japanese sentiment because of Japanese export success, so we were uncertain about what the reception would be. Further, as a manufacturer of cutting edge technology identified with pop and rock music, would there be a "culture clash" based on a form of product snobbishness?

During the last week in May, just a few months after negotiations had begun, a meeting of the entire workforce was held, and we were introduced as the new owners. It was literally the first news any of them had had that a sale was even being considered. The reaction was wonderful. We tried our best to explain who we were and what Roland had to offer—even demonstrating some of our newer products. The welcome we were given exceeded our rosiest expectations.

After being an independent company for about 20 years, Rodgers had been acquired by the CBS musical instrument group in 1977. Absentee senior management on the other side of the country was primarily focused on performing and recorded music, whereas Rodgers was a custom manufacturer of specialized products for a very narrow market. Ten years later, when CBS sold Rodgers to Steinway Musical Properties, ownership moved north to Boston, but was no closer to the Rodgers operation in terms of interest or enthusiasm. The Rodgers team felt isolated and ignored.

The physical plant and equipment desperately needed updating, but all pleas fell on deaf ears. Manufacturing was located in one small building; engineering and R&D were literally "housed" in a decrepit, 50-year-old farmhouse behind the factory; and the purchasing department was in a trailer located further away on the far side of the farmhouse.

I suppose the situation for the Rodgers employee group was not unlike a school-aged orphan. No longer young or cute enough to be adopted, they had come to terms with being ignored. When Roland, already an important name in electronic music, invested in Rodgers it was finally the dawn of a new day for the company.

To further signify that it was a new beginning, we changed the name of the company to Rodgers Instrument Corporation. As is true with every company in the Roland family, it is a relationship based on mutual respect, technical equality, and love of product. The joining of Rodgers and Roland has been and continues to be a solid relationship that has been in the best interest of all concerned.

And that is how we restructured our manufacturing base. Our main operations are in Hamamatsu and Matsumoto, and we have overseas operations in the United States, Taiwan, and Italy. I usually visit Oregon in connection with the Winter NAMM show in California. A month later I get a chance to go to Italy after I have attended the Frankfurt Musikmesse. After leaving the piercing cold of the Frankfurt winter, I particularly look forward to flying across the Alps and into the Italian spring.

*　*　*　*　*

In the 1990s there was another new beginning for the Roland Group. As we continued advanced research and development in the field of electronic music, we found ourselves increasingly involved in technical areas closely related to personal computers. Our research was taking us into the area of DTMP (Desk Top Media Production). This involves editing equipment for computer-music and video editing, as well as related products.

While the engineering technology of computers and advanced electronic music is similar, the market application and rates of development for the two product concepts are still seen to be radically different from each other. Although our DTMP product developments showed attractive market potential (and eventual application to the music business), it was unthinkable to attempt to conduct a business in computer related equipment in the same manner as one would engage in musical equipment merchandising.

Sophisticated video editing has already become an important part of professional concerts, where it is integrated with the presentation of the performing artists. This computer managed, combination of media will continue to spread throughout the field of performing music until it eventually is seen to be an integral part of the music field itself. However, the distribution integration of the two forms of equipment is not likely to occur in the near future. To resolve the immediate challenge of how to serve two very different markets from a single base of technology, we decided to establish an entirely separate distribution channel. Accordingly, in 1989 Edirol Corporation was created in Japan as a separate entity within the Roland group of companies. The mission of this new company was to specialize in the development and marketing of the brand of music software for computer music and the development of various image and sound data on CDs and LDs for video production. The brand name, was derived from two sources: Ed/Edition + rol/Roland. Roland Italy S.p.a. developed the original idea.

We enjoyed early success in Japan, and established a solid market share by the mid-90s. However, similar progress was not being achieved overseas. Our first focus of attention was the North American market. In 1994 we established a new company, Edirol Corporation North America, to serve the combined US and Canadian markets. In addition to being advanced in the multi-media field, the accelerating pace of economic integration between the two nations was making the combined market potential even more attractive.

To our great good fortune, Mr. Laurie Gillespie, the successor to Mr. Gene Trademan as President of Roland Canada Music, Ltd. was available. Laurie was a major contributor to the development of Edirol North America from the very early planning to the daily operation of the business. I must say that I am profoundly grateful to Laurie Gillespie for his contribution in developing not just one, but two companies of the Roland Group in North America.

To complete our distribution network for the computer markets, Edirol Europe Ltd. was founded in the UK under the leadership of Massimo Barbini, and Edirol Corporation Australia Pty. Ltd., managed by Mr. Rick Gell, was established to serve the markets of Oceania.

These four companies are positioned to offer worldwide distribution coverage for Edirol products. As sound and vision become ever more closely connected in media production, this global network will play an increasingly important role in the Roland Group.

CHAPTER FIFTEEN

VIVA ITALIA

My first visit to Italy occurred after the 1967, Frankfurt Messe (the Frankfurt spring trade fair). In addition to the general wish to pay a visit to the country, I particularly wanted to see and explore Ancona—a region of Italy that was famous throughout the world for its production of accordions. The plane from Frankfurt to Milan was a modern jet. In Milan we changed to a bi-motor propeller plane that was scheduled to make various local stops including Ancona. Of course, these stops were not guaranteed, since they could only be made during daylight hours in clear weather.

In those days there was no real airport terminal at Ancona, just a shed and a streamer pole to show the pilot which way the wind was blowing. The plane didn't actually "stop." Passengers had to get on and off the plane while the propellers were still rotating. The last step on the ramp was also the end of the airport. My traveling companion on that part of my trip was Mr. Hiroo Sakata, a personal friend and well-known novelist. It was his first visit as well, and neither of us had any fluency in Italian. To make matters even more difficult, we didn't hire an interpreter.

That was back in 1967. Today the situation at Ancona airport is vastly different. Now direct flights are offered to major European cities like Milan, Munich, and Rome. There is a full-fledged terminal building, and currently there is a substantial military presence as well. By modern jet, Ancona is only minutes away from the troubled areas of Bosnia and Kosovo. Arriving in Ancona now, one is forcefully reminded of how much time has passed since those primitive early days of a windsock flapping next to a barren field.

During my first visit to Ancona I called on several accordion manufacturers. I was actively interested in the accordion business, not with the idea of importing the instruments, but to seek components and parts that I could use for producing electronic accordions. I had a strong interest in the possible development of electronic accordions, and I believed that the product category held great commercial potential. In fact, although I didn't know it at the time, electronic accordions were already under development in Italy. They would be publicly exhibited in Frankfurt just a few years later. Although my idea for business with the product didn't work out, at least my own reasoning had been correct.

Before going to Italy I had researched the local industry as much as possible, and I selected two specific companies to visit: Paolo Soprani Menghini s.r.l., and Crucianelli. The characteristics of these two companies were substantially different, but I'm still content that they were the right selections in the context of my objectives.

I first visited Paolo Soprani. At its peak, during the accordion boom of the 1950s, the company employed about 900 workers. By the time I visited, the production staff had been reduced to about 200. The factory was located in what appeared to be a medieval mill. The workers seemed to be diligent in their tasks, but also happy and congenial. I remember that I was astonished at their work, because their products were truly the manual arts and handicrafts of skilled artisans.

I met Mr. Soprani, the president of the company. He was an extremely courteous, almost courtly, gentleman who bore a great resemblance to the first Mr. Soprani, whose portrait hung in a place of honor. The Mr. Soprani with whom I met was probably the third generation in this family-owned business. He was a rather small person, yet I was very impressed by his pleasant and gentle personality, and the cordial warmth with which he received us.

On the left is an accordian I purchased in Ancona in '67. Luigi Bruti plays a prototype MIDI accordion developed by Roland Europe.

Mr. Soprani first offered us a glass of wine. I couldn't accept his kind offer because I am allergic to alcohol. However, with my inability to explain myself in Italian, I'm afraid I did not handle the situation very well. Mr. Sakata later published a book whose title translates to *Memories of My Overseas Travels with an Inferiority Complex*, in which he gave a full account of our meeting. It was my first experience of being a character in a book.

In the afternoon of that same day we visited Crucianelli. Accordions were a diminishing part of his total business. The company was producing guitars as well as other types of electronic musical instruments. The main product lines of the company already had been shifted to guitar amplifiers and electronic keyboard instruments, and the company's range and repertoire were quite different from those of Paolo Soprani. Crucianelli later became active in the fields of organs and portable keyboards with his own brand called "Elka."

On that first flight to Ancona I happened to meet Mr. Alfred Dronge. Mr. Dronge was the president of Guild Guitars, Inc. Like me, he was making his way to Ancona on business after attending the Frankfurt Messe. Our actual business took us in different directions, but we encountered each other in the hotel lobby in the evening and had dinner together. Even though my English was very limited, we still had a very pleasant evening of conversation.

Mr. Dronge spoke at length about the U.S. market. His factory was situated in Hoboken, just across the river from New York City, and he invited me to visit the Guild factory on my next trip to America. He told me that his factory was actually next to the Statue of Liberty. If I would visit him, he would be more than glad to introduce me to her. I still remember the laughter we shared over his pleasant joke.

At the 1967 NAMM show in America, we had a chance to see each other several times. I learned that Guild Guitars, Inc. had expanded its production facilities, and Mr. Dronge actually commuted from one factory to the other in his own private plane. This American way of operating seemed to me much more efficient than the commute by train that I had to regularly make between our facilities in Hamamatsu and Osaka.

The years passed, and we couldn't seem to find a mutually agreeable schedule for me to visit his factories. Unfortunately, Mr. Dronge died in a crash while he was piloting his private plane. The crash occurred on May 3, 1972, just two weeks after I started Roland. I was never able to visit the Guild factory.

DOES TANGO HAVE AN ITALIAN ORIGIN?

After the Frankfurt Music Fair in 1994, I took the opportunity to visit our Italian factory, Roland Europe S.p.A., located about an hour's drive south of Ancona. There is a town called Castelfidardo within a short drive of Ancona. It was once the center of the accordion industry, and it is still famous for producing musical instruments. Whereas the town of Cremona has always been known for

The Japanese-made Tombo accordion displayed at the International Accordion Museum in Castelfidardo.

producing stringed instruments, Castelfidardo still produces accordions, but it is now primarily known for its production of electronic musical instruments.

Someone told me that The International Accordion Museum was located in Castelfidardo, and I could not resist the opportunity to pay it a visit. Together with Mr. Carlo Lucarelli, the president of Roland Europe, and Mr. Akira Takada, the technical director of Roland Japan, I visited the museum just before leaving Italy for home.

The museum itself was excellent—full of interesting information and a complete collection of accordions produced since the early days of the industry. One of the instruments exhibited was actually a Japanese product called "Tombo Accordion." I noticed this because the president of Tombo Musical Instrument Company, Mr. Mano, was one of my best friends. Because of the coincidence of many Japanese and Italian nouns ending in the letters "O" and "I," I assumed that "Tombo" was mistakenly believed to be an Italian brand name.

It made me proud to see a Japanese product included in the display of instruments—particularly in this prestigious location at the heart of the historic accordian industry. I told the curator how pleased I was, and I also mentioned that Mr. Mano and I were close friends.

Before we parted, the curator kindly gave me a book called *The History of Castelfidardo*, which described in detail the history and vicissitudes of the local music industry from its beginnings up to the present day. Castelfidardo is a small town. When going through the museum and experiencing the full breadth of the displays, one gets the impression that the entire town must be devoted to the production of musical instruments. The book corroborates this impression, explaining that virtually the whole population earns its livelihood from the various aspects of musical instrument production.

The accordion factories of the village ranged in size from large scale, with several hundred workers, to small, single-family shops. The village itself was made up of various specialized fields, including makers of bellows (the mechanism that channels and blows the wind), makers of reeds (the mechanism that generates the tones when wind is passed through and over them), makers of chord buttons, and also of keyboards. Finally, there were also skilled artisans who would complete the fine adjustments of the reeds to assure the instruments were in proper tune.

Among the exhibits in the museum, there was a Chinese instrument called "Sheng" and a mouth organ of the Han Chinese. The display revealed that the Sheng employed reeds, giving it something in common with the accordion. Because the tone generation of the reeds was activated by wind force (albeit, supplied by the player's lung power, rather than by a bellows), the display suggested that the Sheng could be an ancestor of the accordion. That would put the origin of the concept back to about 3,000 years ago.

Over the years, a number of traditions have been handed down about the origin of accordions in Italian history. According to the book, the one story that seemed to be the most reliable related to religious pilgrims of the 19th century. During the second half of the century, there were many pilgrimages to a shrine called Loreto, a religious sanctuary located near Castelfidardo. Pilgrims would frequently stay with families in the town. It is said that one of the pilgrims left for his hosts an intriguing small box as a token of his gratitude. The young Paolo Soprani then set about improving the device until it became the predecessor of the accordions of today. He then dedicated himself to promoting his concept of the entire town committing itself to the production of the instrument.

According to this story, the real origins of the accordion lay outside Italy, and religious pilgrims imported the idea. It is also possible that the concept originated in Italy, and then was taken back to Northern Europe by returning pilgrims. At any rate, the whole village of Castelfidardo was soon engaged in the production of accordions. Given the small size and close quarters of the village, it would have been difficult to keep secrets, so there must have been intense competition, leading to rapid innovation and product improvements.

Due to the necessity for tuning and testing each instrument, each day all of Castelfidardo would have echoed with accordion music. It was inevitable that the local culture would absorb the accordion as its own instrument of choice. The interaction of the musical tastes of the Italian people and their own festive use of the product must have promoted and accelerated further development of accordions. Musical instruments, such as accordions and harmonicas, that use reeds for making sounds can also generate a substantial range of harmonics. In addition to clean fundamental tones, rich varieties of more subtle harmonics are generated when using reeds. I suppose this is why such instruments were well accepted in outdoor music scenes such as folk dancing, back in the days when there were no microphones or amplifiers.

The Shrine of Loreto stands on a hill facing the Adriatic Sea near Castelfidardo. Since the highway was built between the sea and the cathedral, I see it from the car each time I visit the Roland Italian factory. Now it is generally a quiet and peaceful view, but a century ago the parades of pilgrims must have created needs and opportunities for vigorous commercial markets as well. Worshippers came from a wide variety of places, many with only what they could carry. In addition to the basic material needs of these travelers, there was probably an active market for religious articles. Castelfidardo is famous for producing beautiful rosaries, which would have enhanced the travelers' visit and also served as excellent souvenirs.

There are records indicating that musical instruments manufactured in Italy were introduced all over Europe by the journeying pilgrims. In addition, New York City and Buenos Aires became primary overseas destinations for shipments. New York, with its large population of Italian immigrants, and Argentina, where Italian is still the second language of the majority of the population, were both logical markets for the accordion. I'm sure that this is the reason why the bandoneon form of accordion is indispensable for performing tango music.

Although there are conflicting theories about the specifics of its origin, it is widely believed that the tango evolved in Buenos Aires during the late 19th century. The prevalent view assumes that the very substantial immigration from Europe, particularly from Italy and Spain, combined a local Argentine dance, the Milonga, with Afro-Cuban rhythms, and that the tango evolved from this stew. Early tango music was played on the guitar or the violin, but since about 1920, a bandonean—a squarely built button accordion—has become the solo instrument of choice. Its uniquely sorrowful sound makes it distinctly different from the traditional accordion and makes the bandoneon the featured instrument in most tango orchestras.

At my first NAMM in 1964, I saw a huge number of accordions. Most of the instruments were exported from Castelfidardo. On a wall in the Castelfidardo museum there was a large poster showing movie actor, James Stewart, playing the accordion. According to the museum curator, Stewart's skill with the accordion was exceptional, and that was why he was selected as a model for the poster, not merely because he was a famous actor.

YESTERDAY'S ENEMY CAN BE TODAY'S FRIEND.

The intensity of the pressure involved in creating and preserving a market position for your company tends to obscure the fact that many of your competitors are people just like you. They may speak a different language, but the best of them share the same passion for finding and developing new methods for musical expression. I think of this often when I look back over the development of electronic music.

As late as the early 1950s, a large number of accordions was exported to American music merchandisers and distributed by them throughout the U.S. market. Thanks to the marketing efforts and sales promotion of these merchandisers, an enormous accordion boom had taken place. Castelfidardo, as the chief supplier of accordions to the world, was a dominant force. Later, when sales of electronic organs began growing at the expense of accordion sales, Castelfidardo moved into the development of electronics, with the hope of distributing new products through existing sales channels. It was also about this time that Japanese manufacturers began studying electronic musical instruments, but Italian suppliers remained the most powerful, because, through their accordion sales, their distribution channels were already well established.

The largest company in Castelfidardo was Farfisa. Farfisa produced a variety of instruments, including acoustic pianos. At one time it promoted itself as the biggest manufacturer of electronic musical instruments in Europe, although Hohner of Germany disputed the claim. Farfisa also had the additional strength of a collaboration with Chicago Musical Instrument Co. (CMI) of the United States. CMI introduced the Farfisa portable keyboards to the U.S. market with tremendous success.

During those days, there was a drastic change in the popular music field, influenced by the Beatles. Portable keyboards became increasingly popular at the same time that exports of accordions dwindled. Around the world, the production of musical instruments was focusing on electronic products, especially electronic organs.

Farfisa product lines were quite powerful in the European market. Since there were no U.S. companies producing portable keyboards, Farfisa also dominated the world market for that product category. Mr. Carlo Lucarelli was the technical manager of Farfisa, while Mr. Francesco Rauchi was his assistant engineer. Both of these pioneers ultimately became part of Roland. Mr. Lucarelli is president of Roland Europe S.p.A. and Mr. Rauchi was the R&D general advisor. They both have been very active in the field of Roland keyboard production.

In the 1960s, CMI (which later changed its name to Norlin Music) was an importer and distributor of Farfisa organs. The CMI subsidiary, Lowrey Organ Company, was second only to Hammond and together they dominated the U.S. organ market. Lowrey also imported and distributed select Farfisa instruments. Mr. Alberto Kniepkamp was the Lowrey director of R&D in those days, and he naturally was involved in the design of Farfisa products. Mr. Kniepkamp is now a patent & technical consultant to Roland, and he takes an active role in Roland product development, most recently playing an important role in the development of our Atelier organ line.

In 1971, Hammond Organ Company released the world's first single keyboard instrument with a rhythm accompaniment. Since I was exporting rhythm units to Hammond at the time, I naturally became involved in the project. Mr. Jim McLinn was the project manager. The project was extremely secretive, everything operating under the code name, "MUSTANG." I made three samples and sent them to McLinn in Chicago. It wasn't until the actual product unveiling at the NAMM show in Miami that the product was introduced as the "PIPER." One of the star performers demonstrating the new PIPER was Ms. Rosemary Bailey, who is now one of the featured spokespersons for our Atelier series of Rodgers Organs.

Within a year Lowrey introduced its own new product, the "GENIE," which also featured rhythm accompaniment. The electronic organ market was reinvigorated. The development of the Lowrey

Alberto Kniepkamp, Chief Engineer of Lowrey Organ with a prototype of the MX-1.

Genie, and later the equally successful "TEENIE GENIE," was led by Mr. Alberto Kniepkamp. The competitive need to get the product into the market quickly led to the decision to ship the instrument without an owner's manual. Later, a teenage enthusiast who was still in school wrote an owner's manual for the instrument. He was Dennis Houlihan who subsequently rose to the position of marketing VP of Lowrey and is now president of Roland Corporation U.S.

When I think about the fact that we are now working with Ms. Bailey, Mr. Lucarelli, Mr. Kniepkamp and Mr. Houlihan, all leaders in the field of electronic music, as a single team, I am filled with deep emotion.

Around 1967 several Japanese companies found their way into the global market in competition with the Italian manufacturers. These included Ace Electronic (the company that I was running prior to Roland), Korg, Yamaha, and Kawai. The rivalry with the Italians was fierce.

In the mid-1970s a new product development occurred that substantially broadened the market. Keyboard instruments were introduced that were capable of producing highly realistic ensemble sounds of stringed instruments. These "string machines" drew a clear line of demarcation between themsleves and the existing portable keyboards that offered variations on more traditional organ sounds. A boom in the market then followed.

At the time Roland was exporting synthesizers to the U.S. market, and our main competitors were Moog and Arp. The Arp company placed an Italian string machine on the market with the brand name, Quartet. Thanks to brilliant product demonstrations and presentations, the product was enormously successful, and Arp became a powerful competitor. In fact, the Arp string machines were produced by Mr. Carlo Lucarelli, who had left Farfisa with two other associates and established his own company, S.I.EL. S.p.A. Of course, there was no way for us to get to know each other then, but time goes on, and now we are a team.

It can truly be said that our enemies of yesterday can become our friends of today.

Come Back to Sorrento

Since my first visit to Italy in 1967, it was my cherished dream to travel in that country without being restricted by a fixed itinerary. In 1996, at least half of my wish was finally realized. One of the Roland Group joint venture companies, Roland Europe S.p.A. ("RES"), a manufacturing factory for Roland instruments in Italy, had been established in 1988. The company had made good progress, and new government policies now made it attractive for us to take the company public.

A few years earlier, the Italian government had begun implementing a new industrial policy designed to encourage domestic companies to go public. The intention of the policy was to spur economic growth by increasing the number of publicly owned companies. Previously the industrial environment had been dominated by giant state-run enterprises. Now the government wanted to expand public participation as a way of both strengthening the stock market—the symbol of a truly free market—and of attracting additional investment capital. As an incentive, the government also offered preferential tax treatment for companies willing to go public.

It was not an easy decision to make, but I remain convinced that we chose the right course at the right time: having RES listed on the Milan Stock Exchange. It seemed to me that the negative image of the Italian industry being beset by chronic strikes was at least partly due to the presence of so many state-run companies. I cannot say to what extent this negative image was a deterrent for others, but it is a fact that very few Japanese manufacturing companies have invested in Italy.

The bureaucratic requirements for having a stock publicly listed are complex and time-consuming in any country. I had gone through the process when we listed Roland on the Osaka Stock Exchange Second Section, so I knew it could be done. Nevertheless, I was glad that this time it would be someone else's task. Carlo Lucarelli, the president of RES, had the responsibility of trekking back and forth between Ancona and Milan to see to it that the job got done.

By the end of May everything was in place. On June 22, 1996, my wife and I traveled to Milan to attend the official ceremony celebrating the listing of RES on the stock exchange. It was the first time in a long while that we had been able to travel together, so we decided to stay at the Four Seasons Hotel. Not only was it close to the stock exchange, it was also near a street called *V. Monte Napoleone*, which contained quite a few high fashion shops. Mr. Bruno Barbini, the president of Roland Italy S.p.A., made these excellent arrangements on our behalf.

We checked into the hotel on Saturday afternoon. The street was full of shoppers, and there was a sort of cordial excitement in the air. We decided to have a good rest first and then go shopping that same evening. We left the hotel shortly after five, only to find that some of the shops were already closed and that other stores were in the process of shutting down. It had not occurred to me that shops in Milan might close early on Saturday. My wife was disappointed, but I promised her we could come back tomorrow and make a day of it. We returned to the hotel, only to learn that the shops in Milan would be closed the next day as well, because it would be Sunday.

One of the wonderful things about Milan is that the city has so many places worth visiting. We decided to spend Sunday visiting the church of *Santa Maria delle Grazie* and the Leonardo da Vinci Science Museum the following day. Our intention was to see both the artistic and the scientific sides of da Vinci's achievements. By the time we arrived at the church, a substantial line had already formed to wait for the opening. Not being an expert on Renaissance architecture, I couldn't really tell the difference among the various chapels inside the church. Nevertheless, I was fascinated by them, and they were far more magnificent than the exterior of the building would suggest.

Actually, the main interest of most visitors is not so much the church itself, but the monastery building right next door. On the wall of the refectory is one of da Vinci's most famous paintings, "The Last Supper." The picture was created in 1495-96 using tempera as the medium. Over the centuries it has been subjected to a variety of abuses. It has been retouched and painted over on numerous occasions, and most recently it experienced bomb damage during World War II. When we were there it was under restoration. Although it was surrounded by scaffolding, we could still view the entire painting.

As a souvenir we decided to get a photograph of us with the painting in the background. I asked one of our fellow visitors to take the picture. When the camera flash blazed, the guard glared at us and emphatically said, "No!, No!" We realized we were in the wrong, so we left the site immediately. When we received the developed film, we saw the faces of the two offenders: my wife and me, but we had been too far away for the painting to be seen in the photo. Once the restoration work is completed, my ambition is to return to the refectory with NO camera, just to see the painting.

Carlo Lucarelli and I at the Milan stock exchange waiting to see the first price of the stock of Roland Europe.

On Monday, June 24, RES stock was officially traded on the Milan Exchange. I recalled how fascinated I had been when Roland stock was first traded in Osaka, and I expected a similar scene to unfold in Milan. In Osaka the dealers on the trading floor communicated with an amazing array of rapid hand signals, and changing stock prices were flashed on an electric signboard. When the price of Roland stock was first established, someone said "Congratulations," and a round of applause followed. Although I assumed the hand signals might be different in Milan, I looked forward to again seeing the frenetic activity of the traders and brokers.

But computerization had preceded us into the Italian stock exchange. There was no hustle and bustle on the trading floor. I felt a little letdown seeing the first price for RES stock simply show up on a computer monitor. However, the celebration and enthusiasm were real. When the first value was established (6,380,000 Lira) everyone celebrated the "birth" of a new public company with a great round of applause and firm handshakes all around.

A candid moment of happiness in front of the Milan stock exchange.

After the recognition ceremony and an official dinner in Milan, we headed for San Benedetto, where there was an office of RES. On the 26th of June there was another ceremonial party to celebrate the stock listing of RES and also to mark the 20th anniversary of the company, if you count from the establishment of the original company called S.I.EL. With all this celebrating, shopping on the *V. Monte Napoleone* had to be put off for our next visit.

* * * * *

I always enjoy traveling on the *autostrade* (highways) of Italy. On this trip we drove south from Milan through Bologna and then along the Adriatic Sea to San Benedetto. Some years earlier I had the occasion to drive from south to north, going along the Adriatic via Ravenna in order to attend a meeting of Roland's European dealers in Venice. We must have crossed the historic Rubicon River on that drive, but at the time I wasn't aware of it.

When I was in elementary school, Mr. Tago, a composition teacher, assigned us a series of readings in *Plutarch's Lives* and I still remember reading about famous heroes like Hannibal, Alexander the Great, and Julius Caesar. Among the illustrations in the book was a painting of Julius Caesar glaring at the Rubicon while sitting astride a horse. From the scale of the picture, I took it into my head that the Rubicon had to be a mighty river.

On the drive from Milan to San Benedetto, we would be crossing the Rubicon River from north to south, just as Julius Caesar had done when he made his famous crossing. I decided I could not pass up the opportunity to take a picture of the river. I asked Carlo to stop when we got there, but, although he knew about the Rubicon, he said he had no idea where it was located. Eventually we decided to get off the autostrade and take secondary roads to assure that we did not miss it. Using detailed maps, we searched the area where the river was supposed to be, but there was nothing like my Rubicon. We finally asked a local grocer for directions and learned that we had crossed the river about 100 meters back!

This was merely a small waterway rather than the impressive river of history that I had long imagined. In trying to deal with my initial disappointment, my first reaction was to assume that the landscape had been altered over the intervening 2,000 years. If I had thought more clearly, I would have realized that one cannot cross a raging river on a horse, dashing through the water and hollering "The die is cast!" When people say they are "crossing the Rubicon," they refer to a major decision. The origin of the saying was never about the size of the river, but about the symbolic courage of Caesar, who risked his life and honor to lead a civil war against the Roman senate.

Being confronted by many major decisions in life also means that you get the opportunity to make as many major choices. My visit to the Rubicon, facing the river that Caesar once faced, was a profound and moving experience. As I look back, I can see that I crossed my own Rubicon when I decided to leave Ace Electronic and its partnership with Hammond Japan. Until the moment actually arrived, I had never thought of leaving the company that I had personally started.

After I got back to Japan from the Italian trip, I checked my world atlas and found that the river branched off into three streams. I can't say for sure which stream I actually saw. But what I can say is that my image of Julius Caesar has recovered its original magnificence. I see him glaring at the river, astride the rearing stallion of my memory. The width of the river is no longer important.

After the 20th anniversary party was over, we decided to take a three-day trip without establishing any itinerary first. Carlo drove the car accompanied by his wife, Gabriella. The four of us started south. Eventually we decided to head for Sorrento, mainly because the name of the city was familiar to us through the famous song. We stayed in a hotel that offered a view of Mt. Vesuvius, and for three wonderful days we went sightseeing in such places as Pompeii, Amalfi, Positano, and Ravello.

Pompeii is a fascinating and awe-inspiring place; the world of 2,000 years ago is all around you. Thanks to the experienced guide that Carlo hired, the visit to Pompeii became the highlight of our trip. Added to that, since our hotel was located in Sorrento, we actually could "come back to Sorrento" three times.

As a souvenir of the tour, I purchased a music box of finely crafted wood mosaic. It is a special product of the Sorrento area, and we especially value it for the memories it brings back for us. We had a choice of wood finishes, but there was never any doubt that "Come Back To Sorrento" would be the melody we selected.

CHAPTER SIXTEEN

THE BIRTH OF ELECTRONIC MUSICAL INSTRUMENTS

(Note: Some of the following material has been referred to in earlier chapters. It is included here to give a clearer picture of the underlying logic and planned direction to events that may otherwise appear to have been coincidental or unrelated.)

IN JAPAN

To a certain extent, it is likely that my early curiosity about electronic music developed out of my experiences in learning about and dealing with the complexities of watch construction. The manufacture and repair of timepieces had a long history in Japan, and a body of literature existed to help me learn more about the subject. That was not the case during the mid-1950s, when I turned my attention to music. In Japan, electronic music was an unknown concept. There was neither precedent nor history, and there was no body of literature to guide me.

Of course, I wasn't alone in my wish to acquire knowledge about the emerging technology, but there was virtually no exchange among us widely scattered enthusiasts. Operating (and experimenting) independently of one another, the only "research" available to any of us was to visit the Nakanoshima Library of Commerce and Industry to look through American periodicals such as *Audio* and *Electronics*. When I learned of a relevant book having been published, I would immediately place an order, and then would have to wait as long as five months for delivery. It was only in 1962 that I was able to obtain *Electrical Musical Instruments*, which was published in the U.S. in 1958.

To say there was a technology and information "gap" between Japan and the U.S. would be a major understatement. Rather, there was a vast gulf that we had to find our way across. Although it was a slow and at times laborious process of experimental trial and error, progress was made.

In those early days the only way we could pursue our development efforts was by examining imported instruments and adapting their technology. One of the first imported instruments I had the opportunity to study was an Organo, which I had been called on to repair. Beyond occasional repair jobs, I would visit every place I could find that might have a pipe organ or an electronic organ. I learned that there were two American-made Minshall organs in Tokyo, and I had the opportunity to visit the home of the owner of one of these instruments.

When I opened the back of the instrument I could see that the design of the Minshall instrument represented an intriguing advance in technology. All electronic instruments of that era utilized the 12AX7 (twin triode) vacuum tube. However, in order to produce the same number of keyboard notes, the Minshall needed barely half as many tubes as the Organo instrument, which had pioneered the field. It was a clever design that could generate two notes an octave apart, with very few components and utilizing only a single triode tube. The Organo was still a considerably more stable instrument, but the engineering creativity inherent in the Minshall was an exciting step forward in design.

In the late 1950s *Musen to Jikken (Radio and Experimentation)* magazine primarily dealt with audio and radio technologies, but the editors were beginning to feature electronic instruments as well. In October of 1959 the magazine featured an article by Takashi Izumi titled "Making the Electolin—an Electric Violin." Subsequent articles included color photo coverage of Columbia's Elepian electric piano and a new electric instrument called the Pianette. The

November 1960 issue of *Musen to Jikken* carried an article titled, "Play It and See It." It was identified as the fifth installment of the magazine's Amateur Electronic Instrument Seminar.

The coverage that *Musen to Jikken* supplied helped to increase interest in the field and also to facilitate direct communication among the previously isolated enthusiasts. Information could now be shared directly. In 1965 I had the opportunity to write the six-part "Beginners' Seminar for Electronic Instruments" series. Mr. Izumi (real name, Haruo Noriyasu) and I became regular contributors to the magazine. We got to know each other through Mr. Kataoka, the chief editor at *Musen to Jikken*. Another organ-builder friend from those days is Ichiro Kuroda, who designed the Kuroda Tone. He had already begun commercial development of a Wurlitzer-type classical organ using reed sound sources.

As I write this book, I no longer have those back issues of the magazine. I called Mr. Izumi, only to learn that he had not retained copies either. We shared a laugh when he remarked, "In those days we were only looking forward!"

The patent system then in use in Japan was unreasonable in that importers of new products could apply for and be granted patents, even if the technology was public knowledge in other countries. The law held that their claims could not be refuted in the absence of supporting *domestic* documentation. Even if particular technology were known in other fields inside Japan, patents would be granted if the claims were limited to the field of musical instruments. Circuitry and mechanisms of American-made organs were patented "as-is," and we could do nothing to prevent the practice because such claims were legal at the time.

None of this would be allowed under the current patent system, and back then it was a source of enormous frustration for independent developers of electronic musical instruments. The amount of criticism and misunderstanding that this patent system drew from other countries also cannot be overstated.

Although it was legal to obtain domestic patents simply by importing a foreign product, such behavior was not permissible from the ethical standpoint of an engineer. However, the situation put independent engineers at a great disadvantage compared to parties who had sufficient capital to import foreign instruments. The only way to limit the damage of the situation was for amateurs and small companies in Japan to immediately publish all the information they had. By establishing the existence of domestic documentation, patent claims could be refuted.

It was in this connection that a decision was made to create a compilation of all current information available at the time. By publishing all information, we would be able to keep it "free." Takashi Izumi, Kiyoshi Hama and I worked together with many other independent developers to publish *Everything About Electronic Instruments* and *Everything About Electric Instruments* in January 1966. These two publications became the first textbooks for electronic instruments in Japan. When one looks back at the history of electronic musical instruments in Japan, the role that these two publications played was truly significant.

Of the 17 authors who collaborated on the project, I was later to work with six of them at Roland. It was a project without precedent, so we sought information from a wide variety of sources. We also interviewed six individuals who had built impressive prototypes of electronic organs. I recall being impressed that some of them presented their instruments by actually playing them themselves. One of these people was Susumu Shirashoji, who later helped us introduce semi-conductors into the Roland product line.

Since there were few people in the Osaka area who were involved in designing electronic musical instruments, I looked forward to the times that I could make it to Tokyo to gather information. There were nights that Tsutomu Katoh (then the president of Korg) and I would talk through the night about rhythm instruments. He still reminds me how he had a hard time keeping company with me because I didn't drink.

Those early days were truly special. Numerically, there were only a few of us engaged in the exploration and development of electronic music. Each of us derived strength and purpose from knowing we were not alone. In turn, that collegial rapport led to a special bond being formed. Although it has been 40 years since then, there is still a special sort of connection among us.

AMERICA: THE MOTHER COUNTRY OF ELECTRONIC INSTRUMENTS

The basis of modern music evolved over a long process of improvements to instruments created in Europe. These include virtually the entire range of modern acoustics including the piano, violins, brass, woodwinds, and the pipe organ. As the instruments developed, so did traditions about technique and proper usage. Judging from the historical fact that there were many critics of the mechanical metronome when it was invented in Beethoven's day, it's easy to imagine the conflicts and antagonisms that surrounded the new, 20th-century instruments that used vacuum tube-based oscillators as their sound source. There also must have been substantial resistance by established performers, because these new instruments not only nullified their accumulated training but also required a totally new approach to performance.

Composers, of course, tended to see electronic developments differently. These radically new instruments evoked the eager interest of the creative *avant-garde* who were not satisfied with composing strictly within the constraints of the inherited, musical status quo. However, those who were distrustful of machines and offended by the new sounds that could be generated vastly outnumbered the composers and their desire to push the envelope of musical expression.

There was also strong criticism from musical purists because it was impossible for experimental electronic musical instruments to match the tonal performance of pianos and orchestral instruments that had been perfected over the centuries. The only surviving electronic instrument of this era is the Ondes Martenot, which was equipped with a recognizable keyboard. This instrument never made it into the mainstream, since it was monophonic and technically very difficult to maintain, but it is still in limited use.

The Ondes Martenot was invented in France. The French Conservatoire ran an Ondes program and the instrument was used at major venues such as Opera National de Paris, Comedie Francaise, and Opera Comique. If I were asked to attribute a single musical instrument to the countries of Europe, my list would include Italy for the violin, Germany for the piano, Britain for bagpipes, Spain for guitars, and France for the Ondes Martenot. For me the Ondes even ranks ahead of the bandonion, whose accordion-like sounds are widely used in French popular music.

In its early centuries, America was primarily an offshoot of European culture, and thus an inheritor of European traditions. It is in America that organs expressing European musical sensitivities have been preserved. The production of pipe organs was established in colonial days, and many were installed in churches. However, in the field of entertainment, the application of electronics to create organ tones progressed in a very American way. Unlike the *avant-garde* experimentation that generated complex instruments and great controversy in Europe, the more pragmatic Americans focused on the application of electronic technology for home use. To serve that potential market, design priorities focused on stability and affordability. It was in America that the electric organ—a technology originating in watch making and pioneered by the Hammond Organ—grew into an industry.

Thomas Edison's Edison Speaking Phonograph Co. pioneered the development of sound reproduction as early as 1878. The first products achieved a form of mechanical amplification through a bell-type horn (made enduringly famous via the trade mark of the confused dog staring into the large horn that was producing "his master's voice"). By the 1920s electrical amplification using vacuum tubes and speakers had been developed.

While the Edison Company was perfecting and popularizing the electrically amplified phonograph, Radio Corporation of America (RCA), followed a parallel path and was being equally innovative in its drive to make the radio an intrinsic part of

American home life. It was probably inevitable that it would be in America, where the phonograph and the radio were being aggressively commercialized, that electronic sound production would gain widespread consumer acceptance. It is ironic that the Edison Company, although deeply immersed in the technologies needed to capture and reproduce sound electronically, never looked into the possibilities of creating original sounds.

Another element that contributed to the development of electronic instruments was the electric guitar. Acoustic guitars have a resonating body to amplify the vibration of the strings. With the advent and rapid improvement of amplifiers, solid body guitars without resonating bodies began to appear. Not only could the sound of the solid body instrument be effectively amplified so as to be heard by large audiences, the dry, non-resonating sounds opened new avenues for musical expression.

We define *electric* musical instruments as devices that electrically pick up and amplify vibrations of acoustic sound sources such as strings and reeds, and we distinguish this from *electronic* musical instruments, whose sound source derives from electrical circuits. Yet, when one considers the intermediate influence of amplification, this distinction seems dubious. Guitar amplifiers matched with speakers of limited reproduction ranges and peculiar tonal characteristics can result in aural effects that are uniquely electronic in nature.

In short, it is not the *source* of the sound that determines its final characteristics; it is the end result of the process by which the sound is conveyed to the listener. Starting with the phonograph and the radio, amplification has been the key to the acceptance of electronic sound.

When I visited my first NAMM show in 1964, electronic music was entering its growth phase. All the major components, including amplifiers and sound sources, were based on vacuum tubes. There seemed to be an almost limitless array of possibilities in this rapidly expanding field and, in truth, there was. With the development of the electronic organ and the electric guitar,

America established itself as the mother country of electronic musical instruments.

HAMMOND ORGAN

The electronic musical instrument that contributed most to this field was the Hammond Organ, developed by Laurens Hammond. It was a monumental invention that proved for the first time that organs could be brought into ordinary homes. Another important name in organs is Frederick C. Lowrey, who developed the Lowrey organ.

Technologically, there were two distinct methods of sound generation. The Lowrey organ belonged to a family of instruments that used "bright wave" sound sources. If viewed on an oscilloscope, those waves would appear as a combination of saw teeth and pulse waves. On the other hand, Hammond Organs used sine wave synthesis to generate sound. The picture of a sine wave would be a continuous sequence of smooth curves—similar to a never-ending chain of laterally connected letter S's. The sine wave is effectively a pure flute tone, whereas bright wave instruments use combined electronic sources to emulate a wide variety of sounds.

In addition to Hammond, sine wave instruments included Conn and Gulbranson, while the bright wave category included Lowrey, Wurlitzer, Baldwin, and Kimball. As the Japanese organ industry developed, most brands committed to the bright wave technology. The only major exception was the Ace Tone model GT-7. As explained below, the GT-7 was launched in 1970 as a special instrument aimed at a particular market segment.

Ironically, Hammond became particularly famous in the Japanese domestic market thanks to an unrelated design weakness, even as other organ brands were scarcely known. As the head of Ace Electronic, I had noticed a problem with the electrical contact material used in the keys of many brands of organs. I didn't know whether there was less sulfuric acid in the American atmosphere, or whether the problem was caused by humidity, but sulfurization and oxidation of key contacts was definitely a problem in the humid Japanese climate. The situation was that, in Japan, most contacts developed failures unless they were made of precious metals such as platinum, gold, or palladium.

Precious metals are extremely expensive, and virtually all American organ brands used contacts made of compounds of silver or gold plating, which performed adequately in most parts of the world. However, those contacts soon developed serious problems in the Japanese atmospheric environment. Hammond organs, because of the nature of tone wheel generation, simply had to use precious metal contacts. The fundamental Hammond problem was that the initial signal generated by the tone wheel generator was extremely weak. Therefore the instrument had to have exceptionally reliable key-contacts made of costly palladium, in order to assure that the extremely weak signal could be clearly transmitted to the amplifier.

The coincidental result was that Hammond Organs proved to be reliable in the Japanese environment, while most other brands were plagued with contact failures due to oxidation. None of this was understood by the American industry, particularly by Hammond, which took it for granted that the market simply recognized their competitive superiority. On the other hand, one of the reasons that Japanese organs were well-received around the world was because of the reliability of their contacts.

In the U.S. market of the 1960s, Hammond was the dominant brand, thanks to their pioneering of the original product concept. As the years went by, bright wave organs began to gain momentum, and eventually they surpassed Hammond in sales. In theory any sound can be created by the synthesis of sine waves, but the practical fact was that the Hammond tone wheel generation system was effectively limited to a total of ten harmonics. In contrast, the bright wave system of saw tooth and pulse waves contained a vast array of multiple harmonics. The bright wave system was far superior to sine wave organs in reproducing orchestral sounds such as strings and reeds. Bright wave organs came to be seen as desirable substitutes for pipe organs, and eventually they became the mainstream system in the home organ market.

Hammond, due to its distinctive sound, had firmly established itself as an important instrument in jazz, R&B, and gospel music. In combination with the Leslie speaker (see Appendix C), the Hammond model B-3 had become the undisputed leader in these fields. However, the Hammond management was frustrated by their inability to produce bright wave sounds. They also understood that that the inability of their products to produce sounds that decayed (such as the lingering sounds of pianos and guitars after a note has been struck) was a weakness. Accordingly, Hammond's development efforts were redirected towards making the transition from tone wheel to electronics.

By this time I had entered into the joint venture of Hammond International Japan, so I was deeply involved in the design process. An electronic alternative to the generation of the "Hammond Sound" could also resolve one of our major cost problems in marketing Hammond products in Japan. The specification of the power supply in Japan is fragmented. The eastern part of the country has 50-cycle current, while the West uses 60 cycles. This meant that we had to carry duplicate inventories of each Hammond model.

The fabled Hammond tone wheel generator was made up of a set of precision-cut, serrated metal wheels, each of which turned at a perfectly constant speed within a separate electro-magnetic field. The rate of rotation had to be perfectly constant for the tone wheel to emit a perfectly stable tone. The system worked because it utilized the synchronous motor patented by Laurens Hammond when he developed his clock business. However, since 50- and 60-cycle currents would drive that motor at differing speeds, differently serrated tone wheels had to be cut for each of the electrical currents. Thus we had to carry "East" inventories and "West" inventories. The fact that one instrument could not be used in all parts of the country also proved to be a considerable obstacle to increasing Hammond sales in Japan.

The Hammond tone-wheel system: precision engineering and perfect pitch.

Trying to resolve that problem, we set out to find a tone wheel "sound" based on electronics. We did succeed in developing an all-electronic sine-wave generator, but Hammond headquarters in Chicago did not accept our design. They had decided to build on the then cutting-edge technology of "metal oxide silicon field effect transistors" (more easily known as MOSFET-ICs), and it was this technology they built into their new model, the "Concorde."

Having been turned down by Hammond, we decided to use our sine-wave generator in the Ace Tone GT-7. The instrument became a massive hit, thanks to its low cost and portability. Meanwhile, sales of Hammond's Concorde were weak, because the instrument was plagued by IC failures. The MOSFET-ICs had an insufficient spark protection circuit, so a simple "zap" of household static electricity could disrupt the circuitry and require costly repairs. Hammond's ambitious effort to revamp their designs ended in failure. Attempts at reproducing tone wheel sounds using integrated circuits had run aground and eventual success would have to await the development of Large Scale Integration of circuits (LSI).

As things turned out, the challenges of coping with Japan's divided electrical current also contained opportunities for me and

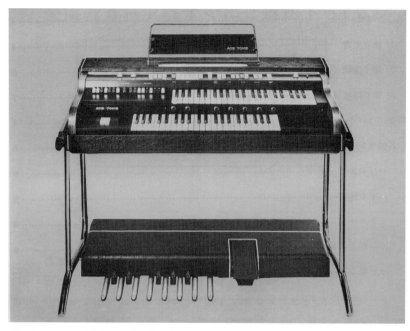

The Acetone model GT-7. The first electronic organ to produce a reliable sine-wave tone.

for Roland. Back in the mid-1950s I seized the chance to purchase nine old and severely worn Hammond organs left behind by the American occupation forces. As I had done ten years earlier when "reassembling" radios for profit, I managed to put together three operating units out of parts that I was able to salvage. These organs were all designed for 60 cycles, which was fortunate since I lived in Osaka in the western part of Japan.

In 1959, a musical group called The Three Suns—a popular band featuring a Hammond Organ, an accordion, and a guitar—toured Japan for the first time. Their tour started in eastern Japan, where renting a 50-cycle Hammond organ was no problem. However, they could not simply transport the instrument from east to west, because of the difference in cycles. They came to me, and I ended up touring with them with my organ. I was intrigued with the performance of the band's guitarist, Del Casher, who ingeniously incorporated tape echoes into his playing, to add a special sense of depth to his sound. In 1977, I asked him to come

Del Casher of The Three Suns.

to Japan to help introduce Roland's guitar synthesizer at its launching event. This relationship would not have come about if it had not been for the 50/60-cycle power problem.

LARGE MUSICAL INSTRUMENTS—ORGANS.

Historically, the organ has been an instrument ideally suited to incorporating new technologies. The process has been going on since well before the advent of electricity and electronics. Overall, there have been remarkable advances in organ development. This was particularly true in the 19th century, when the installation of organs in concert halls and theaters made it necessary to address acoustical issues in a radically different manner.

Medieval churches were the ideal location for organs because of the large amount of reverberation supplied by the vaulting stone structures. Churches generally continue to be excellent locations for organs because overall planning for the edifice includes anticipation and installation of the pipe organ. The objective is to produce a large amount of reverberation. However, these are the worst conditions in which to give sermons. When reverberation increases, the clarity of the voice drops, and it becomes very difficult to follow what is being said. Developments in sound control technology have efficiently addressed this apparent contradiction, but maintaining this balance will remain difficult. In many cases a less-than-ideal compromise has been reached by reducing the reverberation to levels that are too low. The size of new churches, and their choice of building materials, both seem to have exacerbated this tendency.

Developments in the construction of pipe organs and changes in architectural styles have continued independently of each other. However, when constructing pipe organs the building itself becomes part of the instrument. Hence, when an organ is fitted into a pre-existing building that offers only a limited amount of reverberation, there is not much room for improvement. The flexibility of electronic organs becomes apparent under these conditions. Being relatively free of structural constraints, they can demonstrate a clear superiority in terms of achieving an overall sound balance.

To improve the verbal acoustics for the minister's sermon, one can attempt to achieve better sound balance by adjusting speaker placement; this produces a more natural sound. But no matter how much we adjust an organ, whether electronic or pipe, we are still nowhere near approximating the quality of reverberation found in a cathedral built of stone. I am disappointed when I see an organ installed without due acoustical consideration. Nevertheless, one cannot judge the appeal of an organ on just a single criterion. Acoustics are very subjective, and may vary greatly depending on the venue, the organist, and the audience. Similarly, organs cannot be judged merely according to the number of pipes or the size of the church. It is the blending of multiple aspects that produces the final result.

The use of speakers instead of pipes has been a feature of electronic organs since their inception, and thus the tonal output of an electronic organ has always been subject to the state of technology in the field of amplification. Electronic organs are usually installed in buildings that are already completed, so there typically will be limitations on speaker placement, especially when compared to a pipe organ that is constructed at the same time as the building that houses it. One cannot compare the sound coverage of an electronic organ, when it is delivered through a limited number of speakers, to that of a pipe organ, which has a large number of pipes. Recent advances in amplification technology mean that speakers now may be seen as a plus rather than a handicap. The practical application of electronics technology has enabled us to get away from the acoustic and ambient limitations imposed by the church structures themselves, and has also made it possible to create entirely new sounds.

When comparing pipe and electronic organs, one aspect that has to be considered is the total cost of installation. People who judge organs by their sound tend to exclude the issue of cost from their thinking. They focus on critical evaluation of the sound that emerges, and they base their value judgment exclusively on the quality of what they hear. It would be nice if major decisions could be made without having to consider the amount of expense involved, but there are "real world" concerns that need to be addressed. I personally think it is less than prudent to compare a pipe organ with electronic organs without recognizing that the latter can produce superb sound at from one-tenth to one-thirtieth of the cost of an all-new pipe organ.

With pipe organs, much of the cost is in the quasi-architectural elements of the instrument; with electronic organs, costs are all directed to the specifics of high-quality sound. There is the cost of the console, which includes the sound generator and the bulk of the signal processing system. Then there are the costs of the sound output system, which is comprised of the amplifier, the speakers, and the system for enriching the ambient sound (components that correspond to the pipe organ's sound box). At present, by making sure we spend between ten and 15 percent of the total cost of the organ installation on speakers, we have been able to refine the acoustics to a point where it becomes virtually impossible to differentiate the sound sources.

In 1999, we conducted comparative tests in a concert hall in which a pipe organ was already in place. We installed an electronic organ, coupled with our RSS Ambient Sound System. The sound of the electronic organ proved to be fully comparable in perceived quality to that of the pipe organ, plus the electronic instrument offered the distinct advantage of making it possible to adjust the character of the reverberation to suit the preferences of the player. This was a rare chance to conduct a side-by-side comparison of an electronic organ with a pipe organ, in a concert hall that already had the pipe organ in place. The time and preparation needed in order for an organist to be able to perform this comparison was considerable. Nevertheless, I know we have been right to conduct R&D without regard for cost or considerations other than concentrating on the sound and how it moves people. Rather than a simple comparison, there is no better way to appreciate the quality of an electronic organ than by conducting a range of experiments that individually compare factors on a level playing field.

The history of the development of electronic instruments is one of reducing costs. The original Hammond tone wheel generator was a brilliant electro-mechanical device. Driven by the patented synchronous clock motor, the sine waves produced by the generator guaranteed a constant proportional relationship among the notes that made up a chord.

Until the later 1950s, the infant technology of electronics was based on vacuum tubes. It was too limited to provide a reliable, low-cost sound generator. Hammond held the lead in the organ market for 30 years, thanks to its invention of a low-cost tone wheel system. However, this method could not produce harmonic tones of a quality comparable to pipes, and there was a limit to how far one could reduce the cost of the complicated gears that were required. Eventually the company had to surrender its market lead to organ manufacturers that used less costly and more flexible electronic sound oscillators.

The constant search to improve sound generation is at the heart of the history of electronic organ development. The original Hammond organs were intended for home use, but the cost structure limited the market to only the very wealthy. Further, there were contentious issues raised by traditionalists surrounding the introduction of the electronic organ—and even the legal question of whether the new instrument could even be called an "organ." To this day there remain misconceptions resulting from comparisons of the first products with pipe organs.

In the early years the unfortunate tendency to directly compare the sound of first generation electronic instruments with cathedral quality pipe organs tended to confuse the matter. Fortunately, Hammond, Lowrey, and the managerial and technical staff from other companies, focused on lowering the cost of electronic organs, with the aim of developing and expanding the home market. Along with them, my intention has been to supply the best quality instruments to as many people as possible. I am happy to say that gradual improvements in circuit elements and components, from vacuum tubes on through to transistors, ICs and LSIs, have resulted in simpler circuits, fewer malfunctions, and a dramatic increase in design freedom.

The design freedom inherent in the development of electronic organs is a fundamental difference from issues faced by pipe organ builders, who operate within a web of tradition stretching back to the Middle Ages. The creativity of the pipe organ maker is in the customization of an organ to fit the customer's budget. This means that the cost of manufacture is not as much of a direct issue as it is with electronic organs. On the other hand, electronic organ makers continually strive to reduce their prices while achieving things that pipe organs cannot do, so that features that were previously unattainable continue to become possible.

It was in the early 70s that the promise of electronics bore important fruit. Despite its being highly regarded in terms of reliability, Hammond's tone wheel generator went out of production in 1972-73 due to fierce price competition. This happened around the time I established Roland Corporation. During 1971, my last year at Ace-Hammond, Vice President Zinder informed me that Hammond was planning to stop production of the B-3. He offered to move all production to Japan. The B-3 was highly regarded at the time, but because it was comparatively expensive and sold relatively few units, I did not feel that the plan was feasible. At that time, Japan still had lower labor costs, and so before the company ceased production there was serious consideration given to the proposal to continue production in Japan. I looked over the Hammond factory with this move in mind, and conducted a thorough analysis of both the tone generator assembly factory and the parts manufacturing machinery. My decision was to decline the offer. Sales levels for the model were dropping below what was sustainable, and we would have been unable to continue production even if we relocated to Japan. Accordingly, I had no choice but to cancel the plan. At a later date, when I was with Roland, we made the VK-9 and VK-6 combo organs featuring drawbars, and we are currently manufacturing the VK-7 and VK-77 with Virtual Tone Wheel Technology. I am sure that my experiences from that time have had some influence on the manufacture of these products.

Hammond's manufacturing facilities held a secret that I did not learn about until my final year of partnership with them. It was 1971, and Hammond was preparing to introduce their first, all-electronic console, the Concorde. The crucial turning point was the switch from a mechanical sound generator to an IC sound generator. Mr. Bob Bergslein, the head of engineering, was showing me around the factory when he pointed to a pockmarked brick wall and said, "ICs are stronger than gangs." He explained that, during the Capone era, the building had been a mafia-owned property, and they had maintained a practice shooting gallery in a secluded part of the structure. I got his meaning: tone wheels had replaced the mobsters, and now ICs had driven out tone wheels. Like Bob, I didn't feel like laughing at the situation.

It saddens me when someone tells me, "I wanted to get a pipe organ, but there was no way I could afford one, so I bought an electronic instrument instead." As an organ manufacturer, there is no polite way to reply to this. Informed people recognize that if one is using the budget that remains after building a hall, then an electronic organ is the right choice.

Recent technology makes it possible to compensate for problems with ambiance, and this means that excellent organ sound quality is possible from electronic organs. Nevertheless, however much one explains all this to fanatic pipe organ adherents, they will not show any interest. Despite having been informed, they still want to buy a pipe organ strictly on principle. The idea of spending far more than is necessary makes no sense to me. If one has beautiful organ music and a quality instrument, the physical absence of pipes doesn't seem like it should be an issue, but there seems to be no way to resolve the difference of opinion.

As far as organists are concerned, the sound has absolute priority, with no room for compromise when it comes to tone quality. In this respect, there is no difference between pipe organs and electronic organs. When creating an electronic organ, teamwork in planning, manufacturing and sales is paramount, which is how it has always been for manufacturers of large instruments.

My sole aim is to bring organ music to as many people as possible.

THE SECOND ROUND

In the early years of electronic organ production by Japanese manufacturers, we were heavily influenced by the American organ industry. We knew it would be a marathon rather than a short sprint before we could achieve technical parity with them, but we took some solace in the apparent fact that we were slowly catching up. In reality we remained a full lap behind. As we caught up to where the Americans had been, they were continuing on with their own technological advances. Ironically, when we finally did catch up with the U.S. manufacturers, global demand for home electronic organs was beginning to ebb. Synthesizers and combo organs were coming to the fore.

These trends were emerging at the same time that my situation at Ace Electronic became untenable, when I made the decision to give up my own company to start again by founding Roland Corporation. This decision was difficult for many reasons, not the least of which was my life-long interest in the development of electronic organs. It had been this interest that guided virtually all of my major business decisions. With Ace I developed rhythm units because it was technologically possible and financially accessible thanks to the relatively low capital investment required. The success of the rhythm units also funded research and development in my primary interest, electronic sound production. By the time it became necessary to separate from Ace Electronic, the Acetone organ line had achieved a solid position in the home and performing markets.

Roland was a new company with limited products and no customers. There was neither time nor money to create a new organ product line from scratch. On the other hand, I had been working on a rhythm machine almost since the time I founded Ace Electronic. That meant that Roland was able to start its existence as a leader in this field. It also meant I could stay connected to the home organ market as a supplier of rhythm technology to organ manufacturers.

In America, Hammond and Lowrey were fighting for first place in the electronic organ market, and as a result I had the opportunity of working closely with both of them. Almost from the time I made my first, tentative steps into the international organ market in the mid-60s, I developed a relationship with Hammond. By the time that relationship ended in 1972, with my departure from both Ace Electronic Industries Inc. and Hammond International Japan Co. Ltd., the relationship had grown and prospered in a variety of ways.

In 1968 Ace Electronic formed a joint venture company with Hammond. At first we were negotiating with the Hammond Organ Company. However, while the negotiations were in process, their overseas and exporting business split off from the main company to become Hammond International, Inc. (HINT). Hammond Organ Company (HOC) did the American domestic manufacturing and marketing. HINT was responsible for overseas sales and market development. This meant that organs sold in Japan were made by HOC, whereas they were imported, sold and serviced by HINT. Since the two Hammond entities vied for influence over product design and production priorities, their internal relationships were frequently less than amiable. Unfortunately, the tensions of that situation were unknown to us. We thought we were dealing with a single entity, "Hammond."

Final negotiations on the joint venture took place at the Hilton Hawaiian Village in Honolulu and lasted three days. There were four negotiators, HINT's president Don Hayes and vice president Robert Olsen, and on the Japanese side, president Kazuo Sakata and myself. During the first two days we covered organ pricing and naming for the overseas market, items that were not central to the negotiations. Details of the new structure were left until day three. That morning, however, President Sakata suddenly had to fly back to Japan on urgent business, so I was left to carry on alone. He said to me, "You'll manage all right" and left. I remember replying halfheartedly along the lines of, "If you say so...." Since I had been relying on his English language skills, it was with a heavy heart that I realized I would have to conclude the negotiations in my broken English. In order to avoid having to deal with complex negotiations, I would have to decide on our final conditions and hold to them. I approached the third day with trepidation, resolving to keep dialog to a minimum.

The first barrier to overcome was that the companies were not really comparable in size; Hammond was a much larger operation than ours was. The second problem was that there was no agreement about the percentage of interest to be held by each of the partners. On the first point I was relieved to learn that Hammond had more reasonable ideas than we had anticipated. They had no problem relative to the size of the Japanese company, and we were able to negotiate on an equal footing. It was at this point that I realized each company needed the other.

The second point had been an unresolved issue in the preliminary discussions, but an excellent solution was finally developed. We decided on a 50/50 equity stake with Sakata Shokai, Ltd. and Ace Electronic Industries Inc. sharing ownership of 50 percent of the new business, and Hammond holding the other half. At that time, there was a definite technological gap with overseas outfits, and a 50/50 equity stake between Japanese and American companies was rare. The positive impact of Hammond's readiness to accept us on the basis of equality was profound. At a later stage, Roland made it a key policy that any joint ventures it formed would be undertaken on this same *equal* basis.

As our overseas business expanded, our relationship with both Hammond companies in America became more complex. It was difficult to get the full picture when viewed from Japan, but at one point something quite extraordinary occurred.

Our popular Hammond Cadet made by Hammond International Japan (in other words, at Ace Electronic's Hamamatsu factory) was a top, international seller, and we were informed that the Hammond Organ Company had decided to sell it on the American domestic market. For us in Japan, this was very welcome news, as it meant that we could increase production, and run our factory at full capacity.

However, shortly afterwards we were amazed to hear that orders for production to be sold on the American domestic market had gone to Yamaha, Ace Electronic's largest and most aggressive competitor. This was an unbelievable decision, which resulted in much discord between the two Hammond Companies. If news of this decision spread throughout Japan, it would affect not only Hammond, but also Ace Electronic. On very short notice, we invited Mr. Hayes, the president of Hammond International, to Japan, and we convened dealers and suppliers for a party. Immediately, Yamaha invited Mr. Kutner, the president of Hammond Organ Company to Japan, and held a party that was attended by the press. As the Japanese press knew nothing about the two Hammonds in America, as far as they were concerned, one of the Hammond presidents had to be an imposter. Trying to explain things didn't help the situation, and our image suffered considerably as a result. Of course, both of the company presidents were the real thing.

In March 1972, shortly after founding Roland, I received a proposal from Hammond Organ Company to consider a merger, totally bypassing their partnership with Hammond International Japan. However, as they were offering a 60/40 ownership ratio in favor of the American company, I declined. Ownership ratios are not only related to profit ratios, but are also an indication of dominance in the relationship. From my time at Hammond International Japan, I recognized this as a rare chance, but one that I could not prudently accept.

My turning down this proposal from Hammond had the effect of deepening my relationship with Lowery Organ. I had been in touch with Lowery for a long time. Additionally, Robert Olsen, the previous vice president at Hammond International, had moved on to Lowrey, so this was a further reason for me to deepen ties with them. Dennis Houlihan, who at that time was working in management and in product promotions at Lowrey, is now the president of Roland Corporation U.S. Alberto Kniepkamp, previously the chief engineer at Lowrey, headed Roland R&D Chicago as vice president in the late 80s. These relationships have given me a belated insight into the workings of both Hammond and Lowrey, and they have helped me to better understand those earlier events that were so puzzling at the time.

And so Roland went forward. My own personal passion continued to be organs, but the market for Roland lay elsewhere. Starting with rhythm units, we developed and expanded our product lines by coming up with improved and cost efficient methods of amplification. As we moved into synthesizers, a major effort went into advancing the quality and fidelity of electronic tone generation, and advances were also achieved in the arcana of interior component design. It took twenty years, but finally we were ready. It is no secret that the fundamental elements of an electronic organ are tone generation and sound amplification, put together in a reliable and cost efficient matter. Our merging the complex technology of synthesizers with the traditional configuration of organs held the promise of creating new markets while also pleasing traditional sectors as well.

Yamaha and Kawai have long held an overwhelming share of the Japanese electronic organ market, and Technics had stepped in as a third major brand name. Roland released a home organ onto the market in 1994. Upon our announcement of the Roland Organ Atelier prototype, many people asked us, "Why are you releasing a new model onto a market that is already past its peak?" Their question had the effect of strengthening my resolve. I do not feel that the piano and organ market is in decline; rather, I see it as an important market that is going to grow. If the market eventually does decline, it will be because of a lack of effort on the part of manufacturers. They will have deprived people who love listening to and playing organ music of a valuable and unique means of expression.

I hope to be at the forefront of the second generation of electronic organs. I was happy to make the announcement of the Roland Organ Atelier, as it meant that more people around the world would be able to enjoy organ music. The number of people who enjoy playing the organ is still small when compared with those who play the piano, but the support base is growing steadily.

The Roland Atelier organ, the featured instrument at the Organ Power Concerts.

On a related note, I became aware that the NAMM Show, America's largest music show, had not had a concert sponsored by an organ manufacturer in the previous 20 years. I thought that Roland should take the initiative in putting on such an organ concert. Dennis Houlihan made this a reality on January 28, 1999, by holding the first "Organ Power Concert" during the NAMM show. Featured performers were Hector Olivera, Rosemary Bailey, Don Lewis, Seth Rye, Rob Richards and the Joey DeFrancesco Trio. It was an exciting concert, and while we were concerned at first that we might not attract much of an audience, everybody involved was very happy with how it worked out.

The members of the audience enjoyed themselves enormously, and a year later on February 4, 2000, again during the NAMM show, we held the second "Organ Power Concert." The venue was the Wilshire Ebell Theater in Los Angeles with seating for 1,100, four times that of the venue for the first concert. The help of

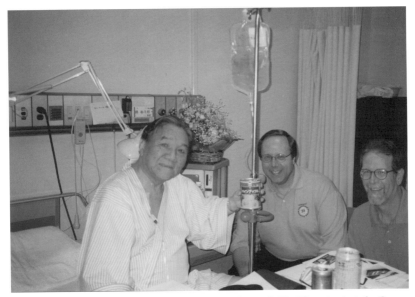

In 1998, while lying in a hospital bed, I convinced Dennis Houlihan to start the Organ Power Concerts.

local dealers insured that the concert was filled to capacity, and we ended up having to think of contingency plans in case we ran out of seating. Staff from Roland U.S. insured that the concert was a great success, and having more than a thousand people come to see an organ concert was a big confidence booster for everyone concerned.

That evening, I was very happy that we were able to invite Mr. and Mrs. Don Leslie, the former president of Hammond Organ Company, David Kutner, and his wife, and the former vice president of Hammond International and later president of Norlin Music International (Lowrey), Robert Olsen, and his wife. The performers were Hector Olivera, Rosemary Bailey, Tony Fenelon, Don Lewis, and Dan Miller, with Steve Fisher performing on V-Drums, and from Japan, Yuri Tachibana. In addition, an RSS Ambient System was used for the first time in an American concert hall. It was a stunning line-up that gave a breathtaking performance. Master of ceremonies Dennis Houlihan's presentation and management of the show enchanted everyone present. No one but Dennis, who both loves and knows organs more than anyone else, could have put on this show. After the curtain went down, it was a pleasure to hear from so many people that they were looking forward to the third Organ Power Concert.

That evening, we realized that we had begun the second round.

The following year we hosted Organ Power III at the Carpenter Center in Long Beach. More than 1,200 people were in attendance. Plans for Organ Power IV are well underway, and requests for tickets are already being received.

CHAPTER SEVENTEEN

THE DEVELOPMENT OF MIDI

REAL TIME IS FOR PERFORMERS. COMPOSERS WORK IN NON-REAL TIME.

As PCs have become widespread, more and more people are beginning to enjoy making music on computers. We can find electronic sounds in all sorts of places including karaoke and music videos. With this growing popularity, I believe that people will be able to understand the concept of how music is created with a computer by classifying musical expression into *real time* and *non-real time*.

In 1988, shortly after computer music was born, I was interviewed in London by the magazine *Making Music* about the current state and future outlook of this new form of musical expression. This was the first time I used the distinction between *real time* and *non-real time* music. Ever since then I have been drawing that distinction as often as possible. For the non-technical person, it might help to think of "non-real" time as "suspended" time. The concept of time being "suspended" might better suggest the ability to "freeze" the composition at any point so that the composer can move around among the notes that are separately suspended in time and adjust things like pitch, note length, and attack to his or her individual liking.

Acoustic instruments such as pianos and trumpets are by nature made for real time performance. In the instant the musician performs, audible music is created with these instruments for the enjoyment of the audience. In contrast to this, composers work out different melodies and harmonies on the piano, write careful notes, and save the musical notation and subsequent adjustments as they experiment until they are satisfied. Another way of understanding this is that a performer works in real time, whereas a songwriter is able to work in non-real time.

Traditionally, songwriters have made their notations on paper. Now musical specifications such as pitch, duration and accent can be entered and stored in a computer, which uses these data to reproduce the music through a synthesizer equipped with a sound source. With computer music the method of trying various ideas out on the keyboard and documenting one's thoughts has become a very different process. Songwriters can program their work directly into the computer and make adjustments while listening to it. The fundamental idea of a songwriter working on and perfecting a selection to his or her satisfaction has not changed. The important difference is that now they can enjoy much greater flexibility through the use of computers. It really isn't surprising that each day more composers are exploring the potential of this method of songwriting.

When movie music soundtracks became commercially popular, it inspired many composers. Excellent works were created for musicals, opera and other forms of performance. Although I personally regret the relative lack of new works in what we think of as the "classical" area, these days many new songs are being released as both rock and DJ-style music continue to grow in popularity. There may not be many new songs that will be remembered as classics years from now, but the number of songs being released is very large. I believe this increase has to do with the expansion in opportunities for songwriters to present their work. Compared with popular music, there are few places where new "classical music" (a contradiction in terms) can be released. But non-real time performance using computer music will surely enhance the opportunities for more classical writers. If one's work is received well in this format, the composer may very well want to record his/her next work with a live orchestra.

My statement that "real time is for performers, non-real time is for songwriters" is a generalization that contains virtually limitless possibilities. Music is an artistry of time. By controlling the time, and by infusing the writer's imagination into the music, the composer is able to choose the best overall texture, performance, tone and concept for the song. However, to achieve an optimal result when using computer technology, the non-real time method of musical composition requires a different sort of musical sensitivity. The creative feeling one gets when transferring a song from a score into the computer is vastly different from the feeling one would get from routine stenographic work of writing notes on paper, and the level of sensitivity will vary among people. Even if the same score is used, the resultant music could differ greatly depending on the intuitive feelings of the person who enters the data. The aesthetic of musical expression now includes the "music to score" mode as well as the "score to music" process of actual performance. Notation methods have become very precise in that they can now reproduce subtle nuances of actual performances, so that both aspects of expression are now influential in musical production.

Being able to give a superb performance in real time requires extreme discipline and practice. Unless the musician is able to express the concept of the song directly through his or her fingers—a feat that is usually only made possible through extensive training beginning in childhood so that the body absorbs the musical energy—the musician may be able to perform adequately but still not be able to fully express him/herself with music. The level of perfection required to realize a complete performance is extremely high, and only a handful of musicians are able to attain both the technique and the musical sensitivity needed at this level.

On the other hand, with non-real time music, theoretically one can enter the song with just one hand. This ability might give the impression that people with no prior instrumental training can create music. However, I think the catchphrase "anybody can create music" (with non-real time songwriting) is exaggerated marketing. Strictly speaking, it doesn't mean that anybody—especially if they know nothing about music—can make music. It would be more accurate to say "anybody who enjoys listening to music can create interesting music." It is important that the musician or writer has a physical sense of the music that they feel with their body, but in the realm of non-real time, the process begins with creating an image in the head and transferring the sensitivities into data that can be entered into the computer. At first, the easiest way to do this is to begin entering familiar melodies and correcting your work until you are satisfied. This is essentially the same process as practicing a performance over and over on the piano until, finally, you get it just right.

The wonder of music played live in a theater or concert hall, and played in motion pictures, provides a good example of real time and non-real time music. The former, which is a real time art, stimulates us emotionally and although there is no real conversation between the stage and the audience, the atmosphere created between the two and the common knowledge that all of this will disappear once the performance is over leaves a fresh impression on the audience. On the other hand, motion pictures, which are in non-real time, are completed after hours of work by the director, camera persons and actors on the set, in the editing room and on the story board to create images using various techniques. Movies can move back in time several centuries, or bring out different emotions by using techniques such as flashbacks. Using these various techniques, it has become a completely different art form compared to live theater.

There is little doubt that theater and cinema are both wonderful forms of art in their own right, but in its early days, cinema was not received as well as theater. Of course, this had to do partly with the material content of the early movies. Since there were no soundtracks and film duration was very limited, there was little room for creating engaging story lines.

Nevertheless, it would be a mistake to underestimate the intrinsic value of cinema as an art, simply by judging the productions made on the earliest equipment. These cinema pioneers knew that technical methods for expression would continue to improve, even though it was unlikely any people back then could specifically envision using the kind of computer graphics so impressive in the films *Gladiator* and *Titanic*.

Even in live performances, many artists use video screens at the back or on both sides of the stage. Many are also combining live performance (real time) and pre-produced (non-real time) material together. Given this aspect alone, arguments such as the one that "music must be either real time or non-real time" are becoming irrelevant. I believe the right way to proceed is to integrate real time and non-real time methods so as to create new styles of expression.

Cinema has been proving this for more than a century. We must learn from this art form and not make the mistake of condemning the future based on looking at a new technology in its earliest years. Just as cine cameras are no longer hand-cranked, new technologies may supersede traditional skills in order to improve the final product. This is simply another aspect of progress. The same explosion of opportunity is happening in computer-assisted design as well. Technologies are creating previously undreamed of avenues for expression in many different fields. It is a wonderfully rich age for artists of all sorts.

THE BEGINNING OF SYNTHESIZERS

The first wave of non-real time music composition came from the United States, when Walter Carlos released his LP *Switched-on Bach* performed on a Moog synthesizer. This first generation of synthesizers was well-suited to the musical flow of Baroque pieces, and many artists followed with similar songs

The second wave actually began in Japan. Due to the characteristics of the initial equipment, early synthesizers were not seen as compatible with the flowing themes of French impressionist music.

Four synthesizer pioneers: Dave Smith, Robert Moog, Thomas Oberheim, and me.

However, Isao Tomita's *Snowflakes are Dancing, the Newest Sound of Debussy* broke through the perceived limitations of the equipment, even though it also was performed entirely on the same Moog synthesizers. When it was released in 1974, the musical expressions in *Snowflakes* were vastly more subtle than those in *Switched-on Bach*. For someone who understood the inner circuitry of synthesizers, the artistic level of this record was astounding.

When Mr. Tomita was creating his revolutionary new recordings, the process of recording synthesizer music involved taping individual tracks on a four- or eight-track, analog recorder and then splicing the tapes together. This put a high price on the time required to produce a single completed recording.

I remember marveling at the heights of musical expression Mr. Tomita was able to achieve using the same equipment that Walter Carlos had used. The painstaking work that went into creating the kind of dynamic and deep sound in Mr. Tomita's *Snowflakes are Dancing* recording was obvious to me the moment I set the stylus on the record. I was deeply impressed by the passion for perfection that was driving him.

Mr. Tomita took his original tapes to all the Japanese record companies. Although many expressed an interest, all of them declined to issue a recording because they did not know how to deal with this completely different form of music. Eventually RCA of America released the *Snowflakes* album, and it became an instant worldwide hit. Mr. Tomita was nominated for four Grammy categories in 1974—a first for any Japanese musician. The same year the album was also named "Best Classical Record" by the National Association of Recording Merchandisers in the U.S.

In the meantime, using his original, painstaking technique, Tomita released versions of Mussorgsky's *Pictures at an Exhibition* and Stravinsky's *Firebird* in 1975, both of which became best-sellers.

From the beginning our goal at Roland was to create synthesizers that were easy to operate and whose pitch was stable despite considerations of time and temperature. The original System 700 achieved these objectives, but the price tag of 2,400,000 (JPY) for the entire system was prohibitive. To create an instrument in a more accessible price class, we subsequently developed a lower cost module called System 100.

A major advance in music production was ushered in by the development of the sequencer. A sequencer is a machine that repeats the identical musical information that a performer plays on the keyboard: which key is played, how firmly it is struck, how long the note is held. Sequencers—along with the synthesizers used with them—have always been an important area for us. The Micro Composer MC-8 that we developed in 1977 was a computerized sequencer that had eight analog outputs. When connected to an analog synthesizer, the MC-8 could simultaneously generate up to eight different notes, provided that eight oscillators were used.

One of our important objectives was to increase the market penetration of analog synthesizers that students could afford, such as the Roland SH-1, SH-2 and also the SH-3, which was slightly larger. There was also a large market for unique orchestra solo voices that electronic organs could not produce. This even-

Winter NAMM 2001: members of Roland's international family.

Introducing the newest VariPhrase technology at Winter NAMM 2001.

At the Nethercutt Collection, producing a public interest video "Fascinating Organs" about the history of organ development. With me are Mr. Dan (the new CEO of Roland), Tony Fenelon of Australia, and Hector Olivera from Argentina.

Organ Power II: some of the performers (Rosemary Bailey and Hector Olivera are off camera).

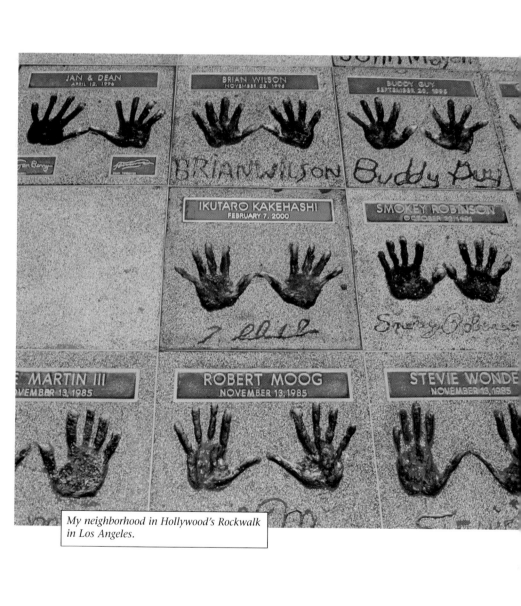

My neighborhood in Hollywood's Rockwalk in Los Angeles.

Don Lewis and I visit with Alan Kay (L.) in front of the baroque pipe organ in his music room.

Discussing design issues with Albert Kniepkamp.

Members of the Joey DeFrancesco Trio.

International joint venture partners, June 2001.
The cooperation of these fine people is the heart of the Roland Group.

Receiving an honorary Doctor of Music degree from Lee Berk,
President of the Berklee College of Music in Boston.

While visiting Spain in 2001, I was fortunate to be given a tour of the Ramirez guitar factory by Amalia Ramirez, the 4th generation head of this prestige manufacturer.

Godin Guitar Company and Roland are allies in promoting innovations in the electronic guitar. Here Robert Godin, President, and Brian McConnell, National Sales Manager of Godin, join Paul Youngblood of Roland U.S. and me at the 2002 NAMM show.

*Ray Charles was a special visitor to our stand at NAMM 2002.
Here he is along with Dan Giffen of West Los Angeles Music
and John Eganhouse of Roland U.S.*

*Working in my office with Seiko Yoshimura and
Anita and Bob Olsen during the editing of this book.*

tually led to the development of Jupiter-4, which was capable of generating four notes at once. When the Jupiter-8 was developed, it was accepted by an even larger market segment. The Jupiter-8, considered to be a classic among polyphonic synthesizers, could generate rich sounds that were very unusual for synthesizers of those days, and it sold well despite its 980,000 (JPY) price tag. This price was obviously not for everybody, but it was received very well by musicians and contributed to spreading the Roland name around the world.

Around 1980, the American synthesizer manufacturers began to focus on large machines. We realized that it would be extremely difficult for Roland to compete in that product class against companies that had already formed ties with various universities and research institutions. Instead of following their lead, I decided that Roland should focus on the development of synthesizers for rock groups, the general population and, possibly, for solo voices incorporated into organs, instead of large-scale synthesizers.

We discontinued all large-scale, analog product lines including the System 700. The decision to discontinue our original product line was a big one, and it was not easily made. It was a struggle between my ego and the task of managing the company. One can never be sure about "what might have been," but I don't think Roland would exist today if we had not chosen to change directions then. Almost certainly we would have experienced the same fate as most manufacturers who took the large-scale route. Eventually they disappeared from the market.

THE START OF THE DIGITAL ERA

A breakthrough in the digitalization of synthesizers came with the introduction of the hybrid concept that uses both digital and analog circuitry. This enabled us to dramatically lower the price of our six- and eight-note polyphonic synthesizers. In fact, the synthesizers started to sell well as soon as they became more

John Chowning and me trying to play the Theremin at the Museum of Making Music located at NAMM headquarters in Carlsbad, California.

affordable and easier to transport. Roland was not the only company that released products based on the analog-digital hybrid concept. Several competitors released synthesizers based on the same idea and the market became filled with such products. Large-scale analog systems remained in use exclusively in institutions and laboratories.

Next, in 1983, Yamaha Corporation released a digital synthesizer based on FM oscillation (Frequency Modulation synthesis). This FM system, developed by Dr. John M. Chowning of Stanford University, was an innovative system that allowed the generation of new sounds with great flexibility. I had known about this system and Dr. Chowning's research, so I visited him at Stanford before Yamaha's FM synthesizer was released. Unfortunately, he had already signed a contract with Yamaha six months prior to my visit and could not enter into a license contract with another company. From the viewpoint of commercializing the FM system, it was natural for Dr. Chowning to partner with Yamaha as they had the capability of developing Large Scale Integrated circuits (LSI) in-house. Although we were not able to license his FM technology, Dr. Chowning was kind enough to give us a tour of his other topics of research. I got the sense we were witnessing the arrival of an entirely new wave. For me, this visit to Stanford was the turning point for my becoming convinced that we were entering the digital age.

Roland had already been producing first generation digital products, but the technology of our most advanced research efforts was much further ahead than what we had on the market. The questions of how far and how fast we should proceed became crucial. Historically, the market has never flocked to a new system or sound, no matter how innovative. FM synthesis had a great impact from a technological standpoint, but my greatest interest then was "How much longer will analog synthesizers continue to sell? When will they be overtaken by digital synthesizers?"

Although these questions were extremely important in terms of determining our product strategy, nobody had the answers and it was useless to ask others for advice out of anxiety. To compete against FM synthesis, we had to develop a new full-digital system unique to Roland. "What other methods do we have at our disposal for achieving this?" was another important question. By then, several schemes for changing the entire synthesizer to fully digital had been suggested, but the availability and the cost of semiconductors with the necessary capacity were also pressing issues.

As things turned out, our analog-digital hybrid synthesizers sold for longer than we expected. However, in a market that was awash with digital products and at a time when people were excited about these new digital synthesizers, I must admit that it was difficult to lead the company with confidence when our flagship product was an analog-digital hybrid. It was particularly difficult to prevent the morale in our sales force from deteriorating. In the end, the number of Roland analog-digital hybrid synthesizers sold during the years of competition did not differ greatly from the number of fully digital Yamaha DX-7s that were sold. Nevertheless, we had to wait until the release of our D-50 in 1987—a fully digital synthesizer based on our proprietary Linear Arithmetic synthesis system—to recover our position as the top manufacturer in the synthesizer market.

THE BIRTH OF MIDI

By 1980, many manufacturers were marketing electronic instruments, but musicians were not able to operate a unit made by one manufacturer that would be compatible with an instrument made by a different manufacturer. Although microprocessors made it possible to digitally control the instruments, each machine had a proprietary interface that only allowed connection to machines of its own brand.

Given this state of affairs, a movement began to create a universal method of transmitting musical information between different synthesizers. Various research efforts were launched in the early 80s, and heated debates went on with respect to a digital standard for connecting multiple electronic instruments. Unfortunately, most of these exchanges consisted of unstructured conversations among developers from different companies when they happened to meet at various international trade shows. It took quite a while until a formal meeting was called to establish a universal standard.

One of basic issues that needed to be resolved was which interface to adopt—either serial or parallel—for connecting the instruments. The majority of American makers who concentrated primarily on large-scale system synthesizers supported the parallel interface for its transmission rate. The only supporters of the serial interface were those whose primary focus was on portable synthesizers, such as myself and Dave Smith of Sequential Circuits. With regard to standardization, there was no doubt that a single standard would be most desirable, but both schemes had their advantages and it was difficult to decide on either one of them at that point.

I came up with the idea that the supporters of the serial interface should design one standard, and supporters of the parallel interface should come up with their own. Roland and Sequential Circuits decided to co-develop a digital interface for electronic instruments. This collaboration was the first step toward connecting electronic instruments together regardless of manufacturer.

Roland had already developed its own serial interface for electronic instruments called the "DCB Bus" (Digital Communication Bus"—with the word bus generally signifying the format in which electronic information is transferred between circuits) in 1981. In 1982, we released the Jupiter-8 and Juno-60 synthesizers along with the JSQ-60 sequencer, all of them fitted with a DCB bus using a 14-pin connector. We proposed to Sequential Circuits that we proceed with joint development based on the DCB bus. In the meantime, Mr. Smith had completed a serial interface using regular two-wire phone cables, announcing this at the AES Convention held in November 1981.

At Roland we had known through experiments that the phone cable scheme would work for connecting one synthesizer to another, but it was prone to problems such as ground hums caused by phase differences in power supply. A phone cable system would not be practical in situations where, for example, two synthesizers with analog outputs needed to be connected, or when making complex connections between synthesizers and sequencers. As a solution Roland developed a system of electrically isolating the ground lines of the two units using photo-couplers, so that only the digital signals were transferred.

Initially, we had been using 14-pin connectors, which would offer better support for future expansion. We soon realized, however, that this configuration would be too expensive for the entire industry to adopt as a standard. Therefore, we decided to propose the use of five-pin DIN connectors, which were cheaper than the 14-pin connectors and would also support the photo-coupler-based ground hum cancellation scheme. We also believed that this would be advantageous for a new standard, because DIN was a European standard and was not widely used in either the

U.S. or Japan at the time (and particularly not in the field of electronic instruments).

By disclosing Roland's ideas and protocols, including data transferring know-how and information on suppliers of parts such as the DIN connectors to Sequential Circuits, we were able to speed up the development of our new interface considerably. Soon, other companies began to show support for the standardization process initiated by our two companies. In mid-1982, the new standard was officially named MIDI (Musical Instrument Digital Interface). In October 1982, we released the detailed "MIDI 1.0 Specification." This was the birth of MIDI—a worldwide standard.

Sequential Circuits and Roland immediately designed new synthesizers supporting the MIDI standard. At the 1983 NAMM Show, we connected Sequential Circuit's MIDI synthesizer Prophet 600 and either the Roland JP-6 or JX-3P for the first public experiment of digital transmission between MIDI instruments. (My own recollection is that the Roland synthesizer connected with the Prophet 600 was actually JX-3P, but that differs from the memory of others, and I can find no written record.) When a key on one synthesizer was played, the information was instantly transmitted to the other synthesizer and a sound was produced. The historic experiment was a success, although as I remember it, we had not even invited representatives of the press to this auspicious moment. There were no more than 20 people from both companies gathered around these two synthesizers, applauding the fact that the synthesizers worked as they were designed. Looking back, I now realize this was a significant turning point in the history of electronic instruments: for the first time, instruments were able to communicate with one another.

The story behind the birth of MIDI is also covered in depth in Mr. Joel Chadabe's book *Electric Sound: The Past and Promise of Electronic Music*.

After the MIDI 1.0 Specification was released in October 1982, MIDI became a universal standard and it is not an overstatement to say that there are no instruments today that have not been affected by MIDI in one way or another. For the first time, electronic instruments acquired the ability to communicate directly with other instruments and computers. MIDI brought many benefits, including the improvement of sound and functionality through digital control, but I personally feel this capability of an instrument to communicate with something other than itself is the largest benefit to electronic instruments. This function enabled instruments to transcend the traditional boundaries of music. MIDI enables people to fuse images and music at will. Of course, I believe various other interfaces other than MIDI will be developed in the future, but I also believe that the current functions of MIDI will be incorporated into these, and that they will continue to be used.

One musical area vastly improved by MIDI is karaoke. In the early 1980s, most karaoke music was recorded on eight-track tapes, and this was followed by Laser Disc karaoke in the late 1980s. When karaoke using data transmission was introduced in 1992, it rapidly replaced the previous systems in most karaoke bars in Japan. This system used MIDI as a way of handling musical data digitally, so suppliers were able to offer a much wider repertoire and deliver the songs much more quickly. Users could also control the tempo and pitch to their preference—something that was unthinkable in the days of recordings or tapes. It's not unusual now for mobile phones to play a tune when they receive a call. This is also done using MIDI information to generate a melody on the phone's sound chip. Thanks to MIDI, users can download the latest tunes and begin using them immediately.

Since MIDI uses musical information in digitized form, musicians are able to control pitch, tone and timing as digital data. This functionality revolutionized the process of recording and subsequently the recording equipment itself. For example, during the days when tape was the primary medium for recordings, if one wished to overdub several parts, engineers had to synchronize the previously recorded track with the new track, regardless of whether or not the first track was good—a painstaking job. With MIDI, the song's tempo can be changed on the fly, retakes are easy to perform and, if one wishes, the same performance can be repeated over and over again. In addition, if the MIDI information is pre-programmed, it can transmit various types of control information to other electronic instruments and recording machines at the desired point in time. In short, MIDI has had the effect of expanding the musical instrument industry into the realm of recording devices.

Traditionally, musical instruments and recording equipment—although both are deeply related to music—were made by completely different industries. Musicians performed music on the instruments, and the recording process was completely separate from this. Therefore, instrument makers made only instruments and most of the companies that made recorders and mixers tended to be audio equipment companies. However, as more and more musicians and singer-songwriters began to appear, instrument makers began developing recording equipment. By the 1960s, microphones, which had been a product of the electrical equipment industry, were being manufactured by musical instrument companies. By the mid-1990s, digital became the norm in recording and digital recording equipment made by instrument manufacturers became the standard. In recent years, many types of software-based recording systems using computers have been released by companies formerly thought of as being limited to the production of musical instruments.

As digital technology evolved, this digital recording equipment and computer software became easy enough for musicians themselves to use and prices have come down to levels that are affordable for the ordinary consumer. Ten years ago, it would have been a dream to create your own CD at home, but now, anyone can create CDs at a relatively nominal cost.

It has been 20 years since the establishment of MIDI, but in the long history of musical instruments, we have only scratched

The Roland VS-880 Workstation. It was the first fully digital hard disk recorder. It included MIDI, and it was fully portable.

the surface. The advancement of digital technology will expand the potential of MIDI and we have yet to see products that utilize the full potential of this standard.

CHAPTER EIGHTEEN

THE FUTURE OF ELECTRONIC MUSICAL INSTRUMENTS

PREDICTIONS AND OUTCOMES

The decade of the 90s was a time of upheavals in social systems, fluctuating exchange rates, and explosive technological growth. In the midst of this climate of instability, all manner of predictions were made—particularly regarding economics and telecommunications, where the information revolution was developing into a major force. Looking back we can see that the large majority of these "forecasts" were substantially off the mark.

In Japan, as in most of the industrial world, the "science" of futurology became a vogue during the 1980s. Futurologists—both academics and self-appointed prognosticators became the economic gurus—confidently offered definitive insights into what lay ahead. As a group, much of their credibility disappeared (along with a good many of their predictions), with the collapse of the bubble economy. Nevertheless, I have great respect for those who approached the forecasting of future developments with seriousness and courage and announced predictions according to their own personal views at the time. Obviously it isn't a realistic expectation for any set of projections to be 100 percent accurate. I believe it is more important to evaluate predictions based on the extent to which they have matched general trends, rather than to calculate the exact percentage of detailed accuracy.

Even if a given prediction turns out to be inaccurate or mistaken, the attitude shown by those who state their opinions clearly is of value. Such people are more courageous than ordinary economists who merely issue vaguely worded conjecture based solely on past data. Harry Truman, when he was president of the United States, publicly complained about predictions he would receive. He explained that whenever he asked for an economic forecast, his advisors would boldly answer his question one way, but then they would say, "On the other hand," and proceed to contradict their own forecast. He found them to be no help at all, and said that he would prefer to work with one-armed economists, so that they couldn't offer him their other hand.

Forecasting based only on past information can lead to some remarkably inaccurate conclusions. In the early Victorian era of the 19th century the steam locomotive was put into practical use. Accounts relate that the world's first passenger trains ran at the speed of eight miles per hour, and that even faster speeds would soon be possible. No one knew what sort of impact high-speed travel might have on the environment or on the human body. Scientists predicted that speeds in excess of 50 mph would cause gigantic tornadoes to form, or that the 50-mph barrier could not be broken due to air resistance. The most extreme view was from one scientist who maintained that traveling faster than 100 mph would suck all the air out of the train and suffocate the passengers. Today, passengers on Japan's Shinkansen (bullet trains) or the TGV in France can comfortably enjoy having a drink, engaging in conversation, or dining as they ride at speeds in excess of 150 mph.

Every year, on the day before the NAMM show opens, there is a new product preview meeting to which major U.S. dealers of Roland products are invited. For the 1999 meeting, invitations to the dealers were accompanied by a cleverly conceived gift. The following "Words Of Wisdom?" were printed on the six sides of the box that contained the present.

1) "The telephone has too many shortcomings to be seriously considered as a means of communication."— *Western Union internal memo, 1876*

2) "Everything that can be invented has been invented."— *Charles H. Duell, Commissioner, U. S. Patent Office, 1899*

3) "Stocks have reached a permanently high plateau."— *Irving Fisher, Professor of Economics Yale University, 1929*

4) "I think there is a world market for maybe five computers."—*Thomas Watson, Chairman of IBM, 1943*

5) "We don't like their sound, and guitar music is on the way out."—*Decca Recording Company, after rejecting the Beatles, 1962*

6) "There is no reason anyone would want a computer in their home."—*Chairman of Digital Equipment Corp, 1977*

All of the above were predictions confidently offered by presumed experts. By pointing out historically hilarious errors made by people who ought to have known better, Roland U.S. was reminding the dealers that they should never underestimate the potential that lies in the future.

It's hard enough to understand the past—predicting the future is vastly more difficult. Had I been alive at that time of those various predictions and asked about the same topics, then (except for the music of the Beatles, about which I had strong, positive feelings) I seriously doubt that I would have been able to produce comments any better than those given.

As a businessman, I am constantly challenged to anticipate the future. It would be nice to be able to read tomorrow's newspaper today, but that's not going to happen. No matter what our business is, we can't read, scan, or download tomorrow's news until tomorrow. The only way to affect tomorrow's news is to make tomorrow's news ourselves. The implications of that responsibility are quite heavy. In any line of work, today's business (and today's crises) must be managed effectively, while at the same time it is vital to never lose one's sense of direction regarding mid- and long-term objectives.

It is truly difficult to make day-to-day decisions without losing sight of a longer-term sense of direction. In my own way I have consistently tried to maintain a clear sense of focus on what the future will be. That does not mean that I have locked my company into an irreversible course based on my intuition. It is necessary to try to predict a business environment ten years hence, but, instead of locking in on plans and investments, I think it's better to frame your plans in terms of goals in which you have invested your own will and pride, and then keep these goals clearly in front of your whole organization. Only by making daily efforts toward realizing these goals can one hope to achieve the future one seeks. This means you must follow through, backing up your own words with action. Of course, difficulties will be encountered, and changes will have to be made, but your "predictions" will never be off by much. In fact, in my experience, some of these goals became reality sooner than predicted.

During an interview for a Japanese trade magazine in 1976, I was asked to predict the future of electronic pianos. When I mentioned that electronic pianos would account for as much as 50 percent of the total piano production, both my interviewer and I burst into laughter. In those days Roland was the only company offering electronic pianos for the home market, and my prediction about electronic pianos making up 50 percent of the total market certainly seemed to be an extravagantly optimistic forecast. Even I myself thought that my comment was a little bit exaggerated. In all truth, I wasn't so sure myself—but it was a goal I believed in.

By 1985, the production of electronic pianos had already reached significant quantities. In an interview that year, my earlier prediction was mentioned, and it no longer seemed so far-fetched. Instead of laughter at the thought of electric pianos achieving a 50 percent market share, this time the interview merely ended with a little grin. In 1989, 13 years after I first made my 50 percent prediction, we indeed reached that figure. In fact, the production of electronic pianos has now surpassed that of acoustic pianos in terms of units produced, and recently in terms of earnings as well.

Roland wasn't the only company moving towards this achievement. The fact that my prediction came true is also due to other companies entering the field of electronic pianos, or perhaps I should say that the competing manufacturers unintentionally cooperated with me to make my prediction come true. In any event, one thing I do know for sure: There is no sustainable prosperity where there is no competition. Roland was the first company to undertake manufacturing electronic pianos for home use. Once we demonstrated that the market potential was there and that the technology could be harnessed, other companies entered the field and contributed to the market expansion.

At times it can be a real struggle to maintain belief in one's own predictions, but I think it is much more difficult to sit and listen meekly as others point out one's mistakes, than it is to try and predict future opportunities and then set goals that will influence the outcome.

EVOLUTION OF ELECTRONIC MUSICAL INSTRUMENTS

In the 1920s and on through the 1930, there was a major flowering of invention in the area of electronic music, and the first generation of electronic instruments was born. A look at the circuitry used in the instruments back then makes it immediately obvious that the vacuum tube, the newest component of the time, was the primer. Although the new instruments were monophonic, they were the very first musical instruments whose means for producing sound were not mechanical. I have previously mentioned the Theremin (1920) and the Ondes Martenot (1928) as successful examples of this early experimentation. Another interesting instrument was the Trautonium (1930). All three of these devices were created in Europe.

In addition, we cannot overlook the enthusiastic efforts of composers and the existence of electronic music studios that were behind these inventions. The Italian composer Ferruccio Busoni (1866-1924) was enthusiastic about experimentation with new sources of sound. It was his position that, "The development of music can be hindered by the limitations of musical instruments." Research also flourished after World War II, especially in Germany, which boasted five electronic music studios. Japanese composers also traveled to Germany to learn about the electronic music studios at Technical University of Berlin and the West Germany Broadcasting's Electronic Music Studios (in Cologne). Toshiro Mayuzumi, who in 1954 composed "Ectoplasme," a work for the Ondes Martenot, once told me about the studio he visited in Cologne. He mentioned that the studio was what spurred the Japan Broadcasting Corporation to build its own electronic music studios.

In the 1950s with Ace Electronic, I was struggling to create prototypes of new musical instruments and I was still having difficulty trying to create an instrument that would work reliably. When I learned that a patent for the Ondes Martenot had already been granted back in 1928, and that numerous musicians were currently using the instrument in composing music, I was again amazed at how pioneering musicians are. But progress was being made. The November 1953 issue of the Japanese magazine *Rajio Gijutsu* (Radio Technology) carried an article in which I wrote on a prototype sweep generator, a test instrument for television. The April 1956 issue of that same magazine carried two important pieces: "Lullabies for the 20th Century?! Special Feature: Let's find out what Electronic Music is?" and composer Makoto Muroi's report and opinions about his visit to the Cologne Broadcasting Station. Even today I am still amazed at how pioneering composers had managed to advance their research to such heights, while I was still building televisions and struggling with prototypes of electronic instruments. I was living in Osaka then and knew virtually nothing about the studio advances taking place in other parts of the world.

In the 1950s the usual method for recording contemporary music featuring electronic instruments involved using tape recorders. When I think about methods using modern equipment, these old processes must have been incredibly tedious. Even tape recorders were not available in the 1920s and 1930s, so that the only way to hear a performance using electronic instruments was to attend one. That was a time when the mere amplification of sound was thought to be a major advance.

There is one exception. Analog records were already fairly popular, and the sound of the original Theremin has been preserved. There are film images as well. Performances by the violinist Clara Rockmore created quite a sensation. I myself have a recording of her performance. For me, the sound is very similar to that of a musical saw. In terms of musical expression, however, hers was a major step forward.

The Theremin, both because of its intriguing sound generation principle and its place in history, has continued to fascinate design engineers. An LP recorded in July 1975 had a wiring diagram of the Theramin printed on the record jacket. Robert Moog was listed as the recording engineer. I tried making a Theremin for myself, but even though it did produce sound, I was completely unable to play it. Although it is comparatively simple to put one together, it is remarkably difficult to perform on it, and I couldn't use it for anything other than sound effects. My own experience made it very clear to me just how marvelous Clara Rockmore's playing technique was. The fact that no concert-level Theremin players have appeared since Ms. Rockmore is also indicative of the difficulty factor.

The August 27, 1953, issue of the periodical *Soviet Culture* carried a report about the closure of the electronic music production department, which had been an approved organization of the Soviet government. The reason given was that "performances of electronic music are antithetical to Socialist realism." The official position appeared to be that the ability of the electronic instruments to do things freely, which could not be done with conventional instruments, was not acceptable to the authorities.

In reality, this coincided with the Soviet Union's focus on nuclear development and rocketry. By comparison, the government may have considered the project of developing electronic instruments as having no urgency and little importance. Seeing also how this came about during the political turmoil associated with the end of the Stalin regime, it is most likely that the unfortunate cessation in the development of electronic instruments in the former Soviet Union, where the Theremin originated, was due to shifting winds in politics and ideology.

It wasn't just the Soviets who had their doubts about electronic music. The Second International Catholic Music Conference, held in Vienna in October 1954, resolved that it was "opposed to pipeless electric organs." This is perhaps not so surprising, because there were some churches in the Middle Ages that even opposed the introduction of pipe organs. In the Gothic era, the objection to installing them in churches was that the "pipe organ is much too acrobatic an instrument."

Despite various types of institutional opposition to change, the thinking of musicians at the beginning of the contemporary music era embodied a search for something new. Again quoting the composer Ferruccio Busoni, writing in the early 1920s: "Contemporary musicians clearly were tired of antiquated instruments, for example ones made of wood, horsehair, copper wire or plate brass, and their opposition to such conventional instruments was quite obvious. The *avant-garde* bared their defiance for playing their music with such traditional instruments. Their reason was that such old acoustic instruments were imbued with an immutably fixed character that inevitably elicited cultural, historical, and emotional associations to listeners."

"Conventional instruments," a contemporary of Busoni said, "are burdened with something that cannot be measured, and are replete with 'character-imparting' memories. They are flutes, horns or oboes, namely instruments of the past; and are relics of tradition both literally and formatively. They cannot easily be liberated therefrom."

These were statements by leaders in the early days of modern musical instruments who had begun to glimpse the potential of new sound-source materials. When I compare their statements with my own work today, I realize that the process of development is a never-ending one. We have reached the point where we can envision the possibility of presenting forms of expression that might even include three-dimensional sonic images, and it is impossible to envision an end to the potential for future developments.

Regarding the development of electronic musical instruments, extensive research also took off in the United States—the country where they tackle everything enthusiastically. In 1976, Herbert A. Deutsch published his book titled *Synthesis*. With the author's permission I translated and published a Japanese edition of that book in 1979. It also was a wonderful opportunity for me to expand my knowledge of past developments. I learned a great deal about the history of electronic music from the text. I still remember the excitement of discovering so many fascinating facts. Among other things, it became clear to me that, in the early days of electronic musical instruments, it was definitely the composers and performers—those in charge of the actual music (so to say "software")—rather than the manufacturers (in other words "hardware" people), who were the ideological vanguard.

Jögensen Electronic of Düsseldorf started sales of the Clavioline in the mid-1950s. This portable and affordable melodic instrument, a monophonic three-octave piano attachment, used a single vacuum tube (with a pair of triodes). I was greatly influenced by the Clavioline when I designed the Canary, the Acetone melodic instrument that I hand-carried to my first NAMM show in 1964.

Monophonic electronic musical instruments eventually reached a satisfactory level in the context of musical expression. The next stage was inevitable. People came to look for a keyboard instrument capable of producing chords. For me the next concrete goal became developing an organ to produced polyphonic sounds—that is to say, an electronic organ.

ADVANCES IN TECHNOLOGY

I believe it is easier to understand the progress of technology used in electronic musical instruments by looking at the subject in terms of changes in sound generation. The original development of electronic organs started with efforts to design electronic replacements of various pipe organ functions. Over time, a series of major improvements have been made in the ability of an electronic instrument to perform with acoustic precision.

Adjustment of Sound (Producing and Stopping Sounds, and adding Different Groups of Tones)

The first important step occurred in the early 1930s with the creation of experimental instruments using keyboards. On a pipe organ, the pipes produce pitches that correspond to the keys that are pressed. When different tones are desired, the air path is switched so that a differently shaped pipe of the same pitch is played. In simple terms, the pipe organ's pipes are replaced by the electronic organ's electronic sound generator (initially vacuum tubes, then transistors and now the CPU). A major difference is that whereas the pipe organ's sounds come from its pipes, the electronic organ's tones come out of speakers.

Although each key on an organ is responsible for starting and stopping notes, it was not capable of adding anything further in the way of musical expression.

Adjusting Harmonics (Selecting the Harmonics)

In 1935, Hammond Organ Company launched sales of its first mass-produced electronic (electric) organs. These organs featured sliding drawbars, which enabled performers to freely choose combinations of harmonic structures. Hammond's was the first organ that allowed performers to choose combinations of harmonics freely and promptly—in my own terminology, I would call it "the real time manner."

Because this by itself did not produce any undulations in the sound, an improved electronic organ was subsequently produced that featured an "attack" function making it possible to add accents.

Adjusting the Sound Envelope (Changing the Form of Sounds)

Just as the piano plays sounds that decay and the organ plays sustained notes, the way sounds begin and fade is different for each instrument. The next goal of electronic musical instruments was to reproduce the varying wave forms of the sounds of different instruments.

To control the progress of a sound, such as the process the sound starts when a key is first pressed and the way the sound fades after the key is released, parameters called Attack (A), Decay (D), Sustain (S), and Release (R) were devised. These A, D, S, and R parameters were designed to be adjusted freely which made it possible to create various sounds—even sounds that do not exist in nature. The development process was begun in the late 1940s and fully realized about 1965, with the appearance of analog synthesizers. It took another ten years and the application of integrated circuits in order to reach the point where the sound envelope could be controlled for every key on the keyboard.

Time-based Adjustment of Harmonics (Continuous Change of Harmonic Structure)

By enabling the tone to change with time, greater expressiveness can be added to musical sounds. With the acoustic piano, for example, the sound that occurs when a string is first struck includes numerous harmonics, resulting in an extremely complex waveform. On the other hand, when the piano key is held down, the sound is gradually attenuated. The tone becomes progressively softer, and it develops a sine-like waveform as it naturally fades out.

This process expresses changes in the harmonic structure over time, and a major effort was undertaken by the industry to achieve these characteristics electronically. The technology that was created in the process of synthesizer development was extremely useful in perfecting this new technology.

Today's electronic organs, electronic pianos, guitar synthesizers, and other electronic musical instruments were developed by implementing not only the functioning of adjusting harmonics and adjusting the sound envelope, but also plenty of the functioning of the time-based adjustment of harmonics as well.

Sampling Technology (Storing Waveforms)

By the early 80s, technology for creating electronic music had achieved a high level of complex sophistication. If the sound of a conventional instrument were required, the instrument's sound was recorded directly, then converted to wave data and stored in memory. After that, it became a simple matter to produce the sounds by pressing keys on the keyboard. Lower costs for computers and memory led to the successful practical application of this concept.

However, there are drawbacks to this approach as well. Although the sounds are realistic, they, like still pictures, lack animation. The human voice in particular presents many limitations and is difficult to work with. Despite these limitations, the sampling process itself is extremely convenient, and it is used extensively in the various venues where music is created.

VariPhrase Technology (Thinking in Phrase Units)

The Greater implementation of digital technology has been accompanied by advances in technology for sound and waveform synthesis, resulting in numerous commercial products that have combined several of these approaches in various ways. Although many musicians ceaselessly look for new possibilities in sound creation, in many cases the grounds for their dissatisfaction are vague and difficult to articulate. Hence it is very difficult to precisely satisfy their needs. Various companies are now pursuing independent research in the development of electronic musical instruments, working toward solutions through methods that blend elements of the adjustments mentioned earlier, or experiment with waveform synthesis, physical modeling, or a variety of combinations of the preceding.

It seems to me that sound-generator formats used in electronic musical instruments basically resemble the languages initially used in writing computer programs, such as machine languages and assembler languages. I do not mean to state that today's technology is immature. Rather, I think that the means that existing technology provides are still not perfectly suitable for musicians who on the whole tend to use an intuitive approach in getting "that sound," that is, the unique sound that comes from within their mind.

I believe the ability to think of music in terms of phrases, rather than just individual notes, would open up a completely new area for creating music.

The next target is ambience. Ever since their advent, electronic musical instruments have been destined to use speakers as the output ports for their sounds. In the case of an instrument such as a pipe organ, which is constructed as an integral part of the building in which it is installed, a hall with good conditions produces superb sound. Conversely, if the conditions in a building are not good, or if there are problems in the way the pipes are arranged, there is no more room for improvement. In this regard, because an electronic musical instrument projects its sound from speakers, the instrument itself can be moved as desired, and the volume can be adjusted to whatever level is necessary.

Electronic musical instruments continue to be handicapped relative to the ambience created by an excellent concert hall. Especially with organs, comparisons of extremely expensive pipe organs with electronic organs costing one-tenth or even many tens of times less has gone on for decades. In spite of the handicaps we see today's computer technology promising to provide an answer to this issue of controlling the ambience.

In 1939, not long after sales of the Hammond organ began, speakers equipped with coil springs to produce reverberation appeared on the market. A successive array of improvements and modifications have been devised and incorporated in the circuitry of electronic organs, including circuits for varying delay times to produce chorus effects. Some even feature a combination of two types of sound generators, which are the most expensive component parts. I do not think the success of the Hammond organ would have been possible without the existence of Leslie loudspeakers. Hammond always strove to find its own solutions to the challenges it faced and tried every means to counter Leslie loudspeakers, but musicians never lost their faith in Leslie and would not stop using Leslie products. The ambience created by Don Leslie and his speakers has been beneficial to electronic musical instruments. Their contributions have been immeasurable.

I believe there is tremendous potential for even greater developments in ambience technology. Twenty years ago, we couldn't even imagine that speakers, which heretofore had been seen as a limitation of electronic musical instruments, would be transformed into a powerful tool to improve performance.

Volume and richness of sound have completely different meanings. The sound of pipe organs is very rich even when heard on a compact portable radio; the magnificence of the sound is immediately apparent. Conversely, music that you don't much care for seems noisy even when the volume is not very high. Music can sound completely different depending on where it is performed. When we listen to an orchestra in a hall that does not provide enough reverberation, the separate parts do not blend, resulting in a dry, flat sound, the bane of any orchestra. The right amount of reverberation in a space acts as a natural mixer, and hall selection is one of a concert promoter's major considerations.

In some other cases, even when everything sounds fine during rehearsals, characteristics of the reverberation often change in surprising ways once the seats are filled with people. The amount of such difference varies widely depending on types of hall and sometimes differences of as much as 0.3 to 0.6 seconds may appear for reverberation time alone. If you take a look at the seating in Milan's La Scala Theatre, with its arrangement of four floors of box seats lining the walls, you will find that the 1,437 seats are wrapped around the stage in a slight curve, and that the hall design has been carefully considered in view of influences that may be felt with a full house.

I have not yet been lucky enough to attend even a single opera at La Scala. However, I was able to inspect an exhibition room in the building. I had a chance to view the stage from a third-floor box seat, and I believe I could understand the reason that people can enjoy opera performances without microphones.

After having the Roland Sound Space (RSS) system installed in my house, I am confident that we are now capable of creating an environment that is as good as listening to music in the box seat of a concert hall. Owing to the advancement of recording technology, which can be summarized by the transition of recording media including SPs, LPs and CDs, it is now possible to install high quality audio systems even in homes. Tremendous advancements have been made in playback devices along the way, but reproduction of ambience has only just begun. When all is said and done, the absolutely critical factor is acoustic ambiance. No matter how fine the technology, the only test of acoustic quality is the final product itself.

THE DOOR IS NOW OPEN

The guitar has ancient roots. It is hard to determine what served as the original model of today's acoustic guitar, but it is clear that the guitar is one of the most highly perfected musical instruments of all. It has been called a "little orchestra" because it is possible to play melody, accompaniment, and even rhythm all on this single instrument. The guitar ranks with keyboard instruments as among the most popular instruments, and it is enjoyed by a great many people.

The resonator in the guitar's body adds rich, swelling reverberation to the sound produced by its six strings. Compared with other instruments, though, the guitar does leave something to be desired in terms of volume, and microphones are often used to provide a boost. Solid-bodied types that have no resonator and instead amplify the sound electrically to enhance the volume are generically called "electric guitars." Strings used in the electric guitars are made of steel. Vibrations from the strings are converted into electric signals by pickups, and all the sounds are output from speakers. As a result, this provides sufficient volume, and once electronic circuitry was adapted to create a variety of new sounds, a whole new field of music evolved.

The scale of guitar concert performances has also grown, and guitarists often perform on center stage. For a time, electric guitars were more popular than acoustic guitars, but folk, rock, and country music fans never wavered in their loyalty to the more traditional instrument. The broadening of musical genres has led to a revival of acoustic guitars and an increase in the number of players. The electric guitar made significant contributions to producing volume and new sounds, but because the string vibrations were relayed for amplification by a single pickup, the resonance produced was unlike that of an acoustic guitar.

Providing the guitar with six separate pickups, and adjusting the volume and acoustic qualities for each string individually, enables a reproduction of guitar sound in stereo and makes it possible to give each string a different tone. The possibilities arising from being able to electrically control each of the six strings independently have offered musicians new vistas that transcend the limitations of the world of stringed instruments up to that time. I refer to the guitar synthesizer. The world of guitars expanded from the traditional acoustic guitar to include the electric guitar, and then the electronic guitar. I believe that each type of guitar has its own musical realm, with each complementing the others.

Twenty-three years have passed since Roland introduced the world's first guitar synthesizer, the GR-500, in May 1977. This may seem to be a short time in the history of musical instruments, but when one considers how brief the entire history of electronic

Del Casher (and Godiego) demonstrating the Roland Guitar Synthesizer model GR-500.

musical instruments is, it is clear that we have spent a considerable proportion of time on guitar synthesizers. The announcement of the GR-500 took place at the Hotel Grand Palace in Tokyo, at an event attended by many members of the media and dealers. The new product was demonstrated by Del Casher, who was invited from the United States specifically for the performance. We enjoyed a propitious beginning, with the GR-500 even being covered by the Japan Broadcasting Corporation's (NHK) morning news. But one month later ARP Instruments announced their own guitar synthesizer at the June NAMM Show.

Five or six other companies entered the guitar synthesizer market thereafter. Although this new entry in the field of electronic musical instruments did attract a lot of attention, it could not achieve widespread use in the market. The early guitar synthesizers were not yet perfected as musical instruments, and they had performance limitations.

With the release of Roland's VG-8 guitar synthesizer in 1994, independent guitar manufacturers began producing guitars designed for guitar synthesizers, earning acceptance for the "electronic guitars" in the music world. During the development process, we came to realize that aspects of sound usually thought

Bill Schultz, CEO of Fender Musical Instruments and me marking the alliance of our companies to expand the market for guitar synthesizers.

of as problematic in music, such as various types of distortion and noise, had actually come to be viewed as essential ingredients of musical expression. Traditionally, these elements had been considered to be "contaminators" of desired sounds, and they were likely to be eliminated. Now they are confidently used with the aid of electronic technology. This constitutes a major advance in terms of expanding the breadth of musical expression.

If we talk about typical types of "distortion" alone, there are as many as five major types. The fuzz box, an effects device producing distortion for guitars, was introduced in the 1960s. This, in combination with high-volume amplifiers, produced sounds which have become essential factors in rock music.

Deviating from the topic for a moment, I'd like to say a little about the *shamisen*, a Japanese three-string plucked lute, and its

The traditional Japanese shamisen.

unique "fuzz" sound. There are many different theories in the world regarding the roots of three-stringed instruments, and none of them is definitive, but it is certain that an early prototype entered Japan by way of Okinawa from somewhere on the Asian mainland. It is also clear that although the *shamisen* was influenced by instruments originating on the Asian continent, the *shamisen* itself was developed in Japan.

The *shamisen*'s second and third strings cross over the upper bridge at the top of the neck, but the first string, which is the thickest of all three, is completely separated from the bridge. This causes that first string to produce a sound with a distinctive resonance: the fuzz sound we have been discussing. This structure is called *sawari* in Japanese, and it dates back several centuries. This means that the fuzz sound had already been sought out using only the ears, without any electronic circuits, and so I suppose that the fuzz sound can be deemed a Japanese invention.

The impact of electronics on traditional music has been as rapid as it has been beneficial. Enormous strides continue to be made in applying sophisticated new technologies to the task of creating music. In order to produce sounds, electronic pianos do not require costly and sometimes fragile mechanical actions in order to cause cloth-covered hammers to strike metal strings. Nor do they need massive soundboards. With electronic pianos the sounds are produced by solid state circuitry and articulated via digital speakers. In the area of traditional organs, costly and unwieldy pipe organs are being replaced by hybrid technology that combines the beauty of pipes with the genius of digital electronics.

Drums and drum sets, once dependent on the uncertain consistency of animal hides for drum heads, and plagued by size incompatibility among the brands, are now built to standard sizes using laboratory developed synthetic material for the drum heads, thus assuring performance consistency (see Appendix B). At the beginning of the last century there were only acoustic guitars. In the 1930s Leo Fender and Les Paul led the way in developing electric guitars and basses. In the 1990s electronic guitars opened an entirely new avenue of expression for guitar players.

The first synthesizers looked like old-fashioned telephone switchboards, but rapidly adopted the standard keyboard. Subsequently the concept and techniques of synthesis have been adapted to other families of instruments, so that "synthesizing" cannot be confined to a single instrument or concept.

New musical needs have given rise to new sounds, and I think the future will see more of such solutions that address needs that are sure to arise. The creation of original sounds with electronic musical instruments began with the analog synthesizer built by Dr. Robert Moog, and since the advent of the digital age we have continued to think up new ways of fashioning new sounds. Thus far we have only been able to apply a limited range of processes and techniques to human voices, so the opportunities for advances in that area are particularly attractive.

Roland succeeded in announcing its new VariPhrase technology at the NAMM Show in February 2000, making it possible to create entirely new sounds by analyzing, processing, and re-synthesizing the three elements of sound, namely pitch, time, and formant. I consider this a tremendous accomplishment for Roland's development team, headed by Mr. Tadao Kikumoto, senior managing director and head of Roland's R&D Center. I look forward to seeing how many new sounds musicians will create with this VariPhrase technology.

Tadao Kikumoto with the TR-808.

While continuing to expand our product lineup, from automatic rhythm machines to synthesizers, microcomposers, echo machines, guitar synthesizers, digital pianos, electronic organs, DJ devices, and digital recorders, we at Roland have also developed a number of fundamental technologies, specifically:

MIDI	(Musical Instrument Digital Interface)
S. A. System	(Structured Adaptive Synthesis)
L. A. System	(Linear Arithmetic Synthesis)
COSM	(Composite Object Sound Modeling)
R-DAC	(Roland Digital Audio Compression)
R.S.S.	(Roland Sound Space)
F.F.P.	(Feed Forward Processing)

There is an accelerating trend towards specialization in technology relating to electronic musical instruments, and Roland has responded by continuing to create new subsidiaries. It is fewer than 70 years since the electronic music market was established, and I believe it is still a young and growing field.

Roland VariPhrase processor VP-9000.

Roland V-Arranger Keyboard VA-7.

Turning imagination into sounds, images, and even shapes, then combining them to produce new solutions—this is the great challenge that Roland is looking at. We are determined to continue creating in the twin fields of sound and dynamic visuals. Roland's message, "we design the future" is not merely symbolic. The opportunities inherent in the new technologies have erased the line between present and future.

CHAPTER NINETEEN

KEYBOARD INSTRUMENTS, THE MONARCHS OF MUSIC

The earliest origins of organs as musical instruments are lost in the mists of time, but precursors of the instrument can be traced to well before the advent of the Christian era. On the other hand, the modern piano evolved from the harpsichord into its present form in about 250 years. Even though the organ had a 2,000-year headstart, there are many more pianos in the world today. When one considers the physical nature of the two instruments, the reasons for this numerical imbalance can be readily understood.

Apart from the earliest, historic versions, a standard pipe organ is actually a part of the building in which it is housed. The pipes themselves are immovable, and they usually form an important element of the building's décor. The process of sound generation in an organ is dependent upon a keyboard that operates valve mechanisms for selectively admitting wind into individual pipes. This requires that construction of the organ include a provision for a large device needed to generate wind. On the contrary, pianos are completely self-contained, and are deliberately designed so that they can be moved.

In the two instruments the method of sound generation is also fundamentally different. The piano's mechanism allows the loudness and softness of notes to vary in accordance with the force with which the keys are struck. Therefore the "touch" of a piano keyboard is vastly different from that of an organ.

Considered from the point of view of sound source, the piano can be called a stringed instrument, because the vibration of the strings is communicated to the soundboard. Pipe organs are nothing but wind instruments. Of course, when both are manufactured as electronic instruments, sounds are transferred through speakers. For all practical purposes, there is no visibly discernable sound source. The engineering complexities of electronic sound-generating devices are virtually incomprehensible to the layman, and I suspect the arcane nature of the field is a contributing factor to misunderstandings about the "legitimacy" of electronic musical instruments.

In the 1970s, with its significant breakthroughs in the design and manufacture of electronic sound-generation devices, the production of electronic organs increased dramatically. By the early 1980's sales of electronic organs were on a par with piano sales, and the specialization of electronic instruments was beginning to be accepted. The initial marketing appeal of the electronic organ had been that it was an instrument that could be used to play all types of music from jazz to classics. In fact, as the industry became more sophisticated, it was recognized that tones and touches required for each field differed from each other, and not all discrete features for all types of music could be contained in one single type of instrument. Three different types of instruments evolved:

- Classic type: for musical scores written for church and traditional concerts
- Jazz type: for jazz, rock, and contemporary pop music
- Home type: for general applications

Prior to the breakthroughs in electronic design, virtually all organs were variations within the general category of the classic type. The type of architectural structure and the purpose for which the instrument was being installed largely influenced this process of design variation. In addition to churches and chapels, organs came to be installed in secular venues for the purpose of giving concerts, and the necessary acoustical conditions varied according to the type of concert. During concerts in which only an organ is played, acoustics as great as in cathedrals are anticipated. But when the instrument is played in combination with other musical instruments it becomes more difficult. Then the organ still must sound like an organ, but the reverberation of the instrument has to be controlled or the total effect will be less than satisfactory. Highly complex skills are necessary for adjusting organs so that they suit every situation.

A major application of classic-type instruments outside of churches and concert halls was in the area of theater organs. Starting in the late 1880s, classic organs were adapted for use in playing accompaniments for silent films. With its capability to produce various special effects and imitated sounds, the theater organ made remarkable advances and was well accepted by the general public. Particularly in the United States, Great Britain, and Australia, there is still active support for the remaining theater locations. Groups of theater organ fans will organize to restore and preserve instruments, because of the great nostalgia that is felt for them.

"The world's largest," is a standard of comparison used throughout the world for virtually all categories of things, and no exception was made for organs. At an exposition held in St. Louis in 1904, a huge organ with a five-rank console, 232 stop controls and 18,000 pipes was demonstrated under the rubric of being "the world's finest organ." In 1917 the organ was transferred to Wannamaker's Department Store in Philadelphia, and the size of the instrument was doubled. The race for bigger instruments continued. In 1932, the virtual nadir of the global financial depression, a mammoth organ was installed in Atlantic City. It had a seven-manual console, 1,233 stop controls, and 32,882 pipes.

At almost the exact same time that the race to build ever-larger instruments was going on, Laurens Hammond was developing his Hammond Organ for commercial production. It could produce the sounds that were already familiar to people who were used to organs in churches and theater organs. The Hammond Organ was introduced to the market in 1935 and was an immediate success with the general public.

Those first electric (electronic) organs were focused on emulating the sounds of pipe organs. Mr. Hammond's invention was a brilliant success. When it was introduced in 1935, some of the early purchasers included Leopold Stokowski, Sir Thomas Beecham, George Gershwin, and even Henry Ford. Ford, always fascinated by inventive genius, placed an order for one as soon as he had a chance to see the design drawings, more than a year before actual production. I was only five years old at the time, so my yen for organ music was not at the level where I also could place an order.

Hammond applied for the patent in January of 1934. Normally, patent applications take many months or years to issue. But patent number 1,956,350 was granted to him in April of 1934, less than 90 days later.

By looking at the drawings attached to the patent application document, one can tell the perfection of the product design. I am particularly delighted by one aspect of the contents of the drawings. Hammond had earlier developed a highly reliable synchronous motor, and on this invention he based his tone-generating system. The system consisted of a set of serrated wheels revolving at an absolutely even rate of speed within a magnetic field. Once the driving motor was up to speed, it could be played with a 60-cycle power source available in every standard home. The original drawings included a manually operated crank-handle as a starter for the synchronous motor! It is understandable that Henry Ford should be interested in the new musical instrument. Like one of his early cars, it needed a crank to get started.

The first Hammond organ was priced at $1,250. In 1935 that was an enormous amount of money, but it was a fraction of the price of a pipe organ. In 1937, two years after the introduction, the Federal Trade Commission (FTC) entered a complaint against Hammond using the word "organ." A comparison test was arranged. Thirty people (15 students and 15 professional musi-

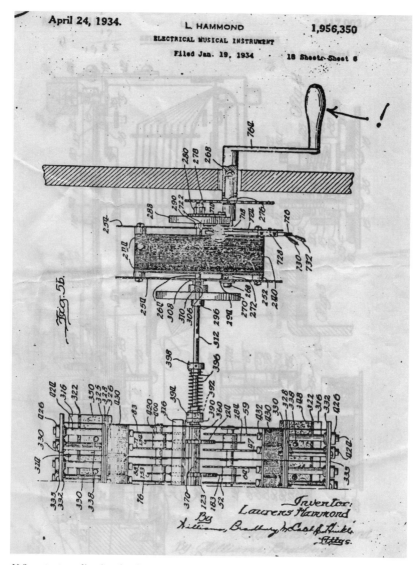

U.S. patent application for the Hammond tone generator. (It has a crank!)

cians) were assembled for a blind test. Behind a curtain two instruments were played, and the jury tried to decide which was a Hammond and which was a pipe organ. The results were inconclusive; the jury could not consistently agree on which instrument was a "real" organ.

At the time of the test, the price for a pipe organ was around $75,000, while the largest Hammond organ sold for about $2,600. There was no basis for price comparison. But the tonal comparison was another matter. A year later the FTC finally conceded that the Hammond products could legitimately be called "organs." The patent application had taken only 90 days, but it took more than a year for the FTC to accept aural reality.

When did the original FTC complaint arise? It is fair to assume that entrenched academics were very much against the idea of letting Hammond products be called "organs." They liked things the way they always were. Thanks to the result of the test and the subsequent FTC ruling, Hammond products were recognized as musical instruments, rather than as merely machines. This breakthrough, I believe, was an enormous encouragement to creative people who wanted to create new forms of electronic musical expression.

Roland was also the target of a complaint. Competitors argued that we should not be allowed to use the name "piano" for our electronic pianos. The basis of the complaint was that the use of the term "piano" was misleading. People might become confused between electronic pianos and acoustic pianos. They objected to the name: "Roland Piano." Even though the sound sources were different, tones and playing techniques were completely the same for both electronic and acoustic pianos. I was mystified; if it looks, sounds, and plays like a piano, what should we call it?

Then I recalled the stubborn opposition that Hammond had to confront. We simply proposed to add one word: digital. The Roland digital pianos now have been on the market successfully for more than ten years, with no serious complaints about the legitimacy of calling the instrument a piano.

Earlier in this chapter I explained that, compared to the long evolution of the organ, the history of pianos is quite short. The invention of the first example of what would become the modern piano took place only 250 years ago. It represented a major technological shift away from its own immediate forerunner, the

Piano of the type actually used by Mozart. At the keyboard, Patrick Rucker, Project Director and Co-Curator of the Smithsonian's "Piano 300" exhibit.

harpsichord, which had achieved widespread acceptance from the 15th through the 17th centuries.

The revolutionary implication of the piano is that it is capable of playing notes at degrees of loudness, in response to changes in the force with which the keys are struck. On the other hand, strings of the harpsichord are plucked rather than struck, and that system is not capable of producing significant changes in loudness. The importance of this advancement is evident in the very name, *piano*. It is, in fact, a shortening of the earlier term, "pianoforte," i.e., "soft-loud," which is how the new instrument was differentiated from the harpsichord.

Naturally, different playing techniques are required for playing the two instruments, even though the physical layout of the piano is almost the same as the harpsichord, namely seven scale keys and 12 notes in an octave. It can be assumed that the invention of the piano with its full range of tonal dynamics gave enormous advantages to contemporary composers and players. One can imagine the intense experimentation and development that must have gone on to perfect the design of dynamic piano actions, so that new music could be composed and performed successfully. The final design of piano actions was far from being an overnight creation. All told, it took about 50 years. But each improvement must have spurred further effort, with composers and artists enthusiastically encouraging and welcoming developments.

Of course, this process was taking place within the context of a solidly established musical culture, and there must have been considerable resistance from traditionalists who felt that each note must be played exactly as written by the original composer. The invention of the piano introduced the need for an entirely new playing technique that included the dynamic of loudness and softness in tones. The composer could only hint at this subtlety of expression, so the player now had to add his own interpretation. The rapid speed of experimentation and development must have brought out strong opposition within the artistic community. Not only were there conservatives who were opposed to change on philosophical grounds, new instrument concepts were not always well thought out, so that players would be reluctant to accept all changes until enough time had passed that the worth of a new change had been clearly established.

During the period of tumultuous change in the evolving concept of the piano, the design of the harpsichord remained generally stable with only minor modifications. Two hundred years later, the harpsichord still has not significantly changed. This is probably because there is no strong demand for changes to the instrument. Music for the harpsichord was written centuries ago, and musicians playing pieces from that time understandably would wish to perform on the instrument for which the music was composed. In addition, original harpsichord music was composed in a variety of tonal temperaments. There are significant differences among the temperaments used then and the uniformly adopted "equal" temperament currently used on contemporary keyboard products.

The subject of temperaments introduces an interesting contradiction. In olden days string instruments contained only three octaves or so. Except for the harpsichord, instruments could be tuned at various pauses in a concert. This was important, because the instrument itself could go out of tune, and because songs to be performed would have been composed in a variety of temperaments. The harpsichord player could surmount this problem by having two instruments, each tuned to a different temperament for the performance of different pieces. The invention of the piano introduced solid stability of pitch. That gave the player greater confidence, but it limited his ability to perform music which had been composed in alternative temperaments. Nevertheless, the introduction of the equal temperament was a great help to the evolution of pianos and organs.

Harpsichords have been a major beneficiary of digitalization. They do not benefit from the ability to adjust volume, because their traditional performance criteria did not include volume dynamics. But with digital electronics, harpsichords now have instant access to a variety of temperaments with the added benefit of stability of tuning. Modern technology now makes it possible to enjoy the rich, full sounds created by plucking two strings simultaneously, while a coupler function allows the simultaneous playing of the tune in a different voice and octave.

There was an attempt, about three hundred years ago, to create an instrument that combined the performance characteristics of a harpsichord and an organ. I suspect it was developed in response to stated wishes of contemporary players. The resulting instrument was too large to be commercially feasible, so only stories about it remain. But the idea was and still is interesting. Digital harpsichords produced by Roland include aspects of compact size organs, and the feature is well accepted. I can well understand why such an experimental instrument was created more than 300 years ago.

Keyboard instruments are capable of playing melodies, accompaniments or rhythms of their own. At the same time, they

The Grave of Laurens Hammond in Connecticut.

are capable of playing accompaniments for other solo instruments such as flutes, clarinets, oboes, or human voices to give depth and breadth to the entire harmony. With that sort of flexibility and vast potential, the evolution of keyboard instruments must have stimulated the development of increasingly sophisticated composers.

If it were not for the history and present existence of keyboard instruments, it is impossible to speculate on how music might have evolved. Titles given to the instruments, namely, "the organ is the King of instruments and the piano is the Queen" are well deserved. The harpsichord may be a royal uncle, or perhaps grandfather, but as a family, keyboard instruments are definitely the monarchs of music.

CHAPTER TWENTY

SHORTCUT TO A MUSIC PARADISE

When you are pursuing an endeavor that interests you, you don't become easily bored. Conversely, with an activity that is easy to master, one tends to lose interest in a relatively short period of time. It is more interesting to learn when there is a challenge involved. This is particularly true in the field of music.

Although many people enjoy listening to music, only a comparative few will extend their interest to learning how to play. From within this group there is an even smaller number who are willing to try their hand at composition. Enthusiasm among young people may be great, but looking among my friends and colleagues, it is apparent that not very many of them have sustained their passion for musical composition as a hobby—probably because composition requires highly developed skills, even at the entry level.

People who started their music-related experiences from infancy are the fortunate ones. By growing up with music an integral part of their experience, they become comfortably accustomed to the presence of music in their lives. Even if, at some point, they discontinue their childhood lessons and pursue non-musical careers, their lives will always be enriched because music will always be with them. Once learned, the lessons remain. Most people will choose to keep music as a part of their lives. As adults, those who drifted away from their early training may choose to resume musical activity or learn new instruments, and their progress will be swift.

The Japanese system of music education that started 120 years ago in the Meiji Era has gone through many modifications, but the results, both in the domestic population and by international comparison, continue to be outstanding. Of course, there are many drop-outs in the field of musical education, but that is to be expected. The path is challenging in its own right, and excessive parental expectations at times can be counter-productive. The fact remains that a large segment of the total population actively enjoys music in all aspects of life. Those attuned to music constitute a growing proportion of the population, and this must be attributed to the continuing emphasis on music education in the elementary schools of the country.

The popularization of personal computers has now opened whole new possibilities for musical entertainment. Johann Sebastian Bach was once asked how he could play so skillfully. He replied to the effect that he merely pressed the right keys at the right moment, as called for on the sheet music. That may have been easy for him to say. It can be considerably more difficult for the average person than it was for Johann Sebastian Bach. The tangible act of playing an instrument is performed in real time; both accomplishments and mistakes are heard by all at the precise moment they occur. However, if the average person could handle the timing and the musical scales as digital data and input them to their personal computers, they might be able to design their own music in a "non-real time" manner.

Granted that computer music does not necessarily require diligent finger training needed for real time play, but other complex efforts and talents are required to create impressive and unique music. Creating any music requires the same quality of sensitivity that is needed for playing music on traditional musical instruments.

Before the birth of electronics, there was only one narrow way to achieve entry into the "music paradise" where you could entertain yourself and others by playing an instrument well. Today the paths to music satisfaction are increasing and more options are available. In my boyhood, the dislocations of World War II precluded even traditional music training. My access to music was via those radio broadcasts that absorbed my attention in the early postwar years. When I finally arrived at my own version of the music paradise, I discovered a world of interesting people there, and I felt truly lucky to have been able to join them.

Most of the time I was too busy to dwell on the awareness that I was actually progressing on a path toward an objective. There are no shortcuts to any kind of worthwhile endeavor. However, I never felt tired during the journey, because I was always moving toward the goals that I treasured. Someone said, "work is what you are doing when you would rather be doing something else." Applying that definition, my life has involved a lot of effort, but it wasn't "work," because it was what I wanted to do.

I truly believe I live in that "music paradise."

CHAPTER TWENTY-ONE

GRACE NOTES

Because it is fundamentally based on aesthetics, the world of music is a very special place. The sole reason for music to exist is as a means of human expression and satisfaction. Perhaps that is why the musical world is populated with such a high percentage of good and thoughtful people.

Devoting my career to music has given me wonderful opportunities to achieve a full and happy life. I have had the chance to meet and become friends with wonderful people. By succeeding with Roland, I also achieved the satisfaction of knowing that there are many people who have been able to earn their livings and follow their own dreams because of their association with our product lines. Whether producing, marketing or playing electronic musical products (for fun or for profit), there are substantial numbers of people who are part of the Roland global family.

But friendships and good feelings are not the only gifts I have received from my chosen profession. Thanks to the world of music, I have been able to begin to see and be thankful for the unity of human values that exists among virtually all peoples, despite cultural differences. Following are some thoughts on a few of the abstract issues of life that I have learned about during a lifetime in music.

Beginner's Luck

When I arrived in Vancouver, Canada on a business trip some years ago, my Canadian business partners, Mr. Trademan and Mr. Gillespie, invited me to go salmon fishing. I was intrigued by the idea, so we flew to a region about 100 kilometers north of the city. At dawn the next day we headed for the fishing grounds, each of us going out in a separate fishing boat.

It was my first experience at fishing with no friend to advise me, so I decided to put my trust in the young captain and follow his instructions in everything I did. The captain's name was Steve. Rather than being a professional fisherman, he actually was a full-time college student working on a temporary basis during the fishing season. Nevertheless, Steve definitely knew his way around those waters. My trust in his ability was not misplaced.

Everything that happened during that expedition was a new experience for me. In my entire life, my only experience with fishing had been my boyhood excursions to the Yodo River in Osaka. What I caught in the Yodo were small fish. What amazed me on the salmon expedition was that fish used as bait were bigger than any of the fish I had ever caught.

The fishing in Canada was genuine sport fishing. We used fishhooks without barbs, so a delicate sense of timing was required to reel in the fish, or it would escape. I faithfully followed every instruction that was called out by Captain Steve regarding every aspect of playing the fish. As much as I could, I followed his orders as to when to reel in and when to let run. The results were most gratifying. I easily caught my legal limit of four large fish.

When the expedition was over, I paused to consider the experience. In light of my quick-tempered personality, I should not have been able to endure the boredom of fishing. Fishing requires quiet patience, and that has never been my strong point. Much to my surprise, the five hours on the water had passed quickly.

I asked one question of 22-year-old Captain Steve. "I assume that you have been serving many types of fishing customers. Do

Beginner's luck. Fishing with Eugene Trademan.

you believe in beginner's luck?" For me there really was no question. It had to be luck; I didn't know what I was doing, and yet I had enjoyed outstanding success. The Captain did not hesitate to say that he definitely agreed.

On my way home, I was content with his answer. After I arrived back in Japan and boasted of my successful fishing trip, I posed the same question to one of my friends. Even more quickly than Captain Steve, he responded with an emphatic, "Yes." But then he continued his opinion. "It is because beginners are very obedient, and they are willing to follow instructions given to them by experts. Since they do not insist on their own way, they simply believe that fortune smiles on them naturally."

The photograph of me along with my catch is now put in a frame, more as proof of my beginner's luck than to commemorate my fishing expertise.

ART AND TECHNOLOGY

In the early postwar years in Japan, virtually anything could sell regardless of quality. The undersupplied market offered few if any choices to a public that desperately needed a wide range of items. Gradually market pressure for higher quality and lower cost accelerated the development of mass-production. A byproduct of the process was that the products of small shops and individual craftsmen came to be seen as obsolete.

As supply lines finally filled, indiscriminate consumer demand for production volume began to ebb, and more attention was paid to considerations of fashion. By then the public believed that "high quality" was something it had a right to expect. What then evolved was today's market of diversified segments, each expecting differing levels of quality, style, and price. Looking back, one can see that the period in which mass-production was uncritically worshipped actually was rather brief.

It is inarguable that the technology developed for mass-production will continue to be extremely important. But, as is true in the rest of the industrialized world, today there is a growing segment of consumers who look for products that combine the artistic skill of traditional craftsmanship with the benefits of mass-production. It is only a slight exaggeration to say that Japan's experience in the 40 years after World War II was a condensed reproduction of the 150 years of changes in the West since the Industrial Revolution commenced.

Semiconductor products are the classic representatives of today's high technology. Even though most of the processes for manufacturing semiconductors are fully automated, the end results of the finished products are stunning in their ordered complexity and remind us of the zenith of artisans' spirits.

If you look at a magnified view of a microprocessor, you will see complicated circuits placed in orderly rows on an almost microscopically thin layer of silicone. Tens of thousands of these elements are aligned with artistic precision. It is utterly impossible to create such complicated yet precise designs by hand. The entire process of design work has to be computer operated. However, even though most of the manufacturing processes of semiconductor products are mechanically performed in "clean" rooms without the need for human assistance, the final product is entirely the fruit of human imagination.

As for software programs used to operate computers, well-designed programs reflect a level of craftsmanship fully equivalent to the artisans of earlier times. There is no contradiction in thinking of the artisan spirit while looking at state-of-the-art technology. While some people may believe that "art" and "technology" are mutually exclusive terms, I am confident that I am not alone in seeing them as parallel expressions of a single creative concept.

The people of ancient Greece did not even have different words for "art" and "technology." They used only one word, *ART* to express both meanings. Both artists and technicians were regarded as expressing the same set of aesthetic skills. In Renaissance Italy, a man like Leonardo da Vinci was respected as an ideal person because he represented both forms of creativity.

Now the time has arrived that one might safely refer to as an era of "New Artisans." These are creative and productive geniuses in a field without precedent. They have mastered novel and complex technologies in order to exceed the mechanical limits of mere machinery. They truly create a new horizon of possibilities.

Memory: Human and Otherwise

In an amazingly short period of time, computers have become an integral part of our daily lives. Within the computer itself, the memory function has the central role, and semiconductor memory chips are the focal point of the continuous development of memory technology. For data processing purposes, both erasable and permanent information can be stored on the thin silicone membranes of memory chips.

While the chip capacity to store information keeps increasing, the price for high-density memory chips has steadily declined. It has reached the point that, in addition to the keyboard-operated computers with which we are familiar, these chips are also used in low-cost, hand-held electronic devices that can combine the functions of a calculator, data recorder, and even such uses as language translation. Nevertheless, the fact is that the memorizing capabilities offered by these high-tech marvels still falls far short of the flexibility of the human memory.

If only a slight portion of the information stored in the computer memory is altered, the computer will not operate correctly. Compared to that sensitivity, the system of human memory is vastly more adaptable. There are even wiser ways of learning for human beings, for example, to let your body learn things through physical repetition. Practice doesn't necessarily make "perfect," but for learning skills as diverse as piano technique or a golf swing, physical practice is the only way for the body to learn and the mind to remember.

Human memory is inherently ambiguous; we often forget important matters while recalling trivial things. Sometimes mixed up memories can confuse us so that we are unable to determine the sequence or specific relevance of remembered information. Other times we may bring to mind general situations while specific facts elude us. In those cases we are certain that we know a name or a fact, but at that moment we are unable to think of it. Hours later, or in the middle of the night, we suddenly blurt out the fact that had been hiding from our conscious mind. Remembering things "vaguely" is not the sort of thing of which a memory chip is capable.

There are even some people whose memories appear to randomly shut down regarding specifics. An individual may be totally unable to recall an incident or an event, even though it is clearly stored in his or her memory. What amazes me even more is the fact that people equipped with that sort of haphazard and wooly memory are nonetheless capable of achieving significant accomplishments.

It is an interesting phenomenon that recently such ambiguity of human memory, in other words, "fuzziness," has become one of the important subjects of study in the field of computers.

We tend to think of all memory in human terms. A typical human gesture for jogging a vague memory is to symbolically rap one's forehead as if to "loosen" a fact that is "stuck"; another gesture is to lightly pinch oneself on the arm to "stimulate" clearer thinking. These are the same people who slap computer monitors or fiddle with the electric plug when the operation of their computer also appears to be stuck.

One of the most interesting yet mysterious capabilities of human memory is that, as time goes by, the recollection of events involving hardships or sadness sometimes can transform themselves into pleasant reminiscences.

Whenever I pause to consider the complex excellence of human memories, I am awestruck by the God who designed such great devices.

SISTER CITIES

It seems clear to me that climate and geography play important roles in shaping personality characteristics. Probably the easiest example of this effect is the accuracy of general stereotyping relative to regional and even national characteristics. For example, no one argues with the general truth when someone says, "Swiss are meticulous," or "Americans are enthusiastic," or

"Japanese are orderly." What I find interesting is why these generalizations tend to be true.

In Japan we have a structure of regional governmental units called prefectures, which are similar to the Australian or American concept of "states." In all three nations, it is frequently said that people of each separate unit have distinctive personality traits—presumably influenced by the physical environment of their home regions.

I live in Shizuoka Prefecture. The prefecture extends along the shore of the Pacific Ocean, and features a fertile, coastal plain between the sea and the lofty mountains to the north. Within the boundaries of this prefecture there are three geographically different areas. Although the mountains and the sea define the entire "state," each of those areas has its own distinct characteristics in terms of geography and industry. Within Shizuoka Prefecture itself, the separate areas are frequently contrasted. It is thought provoking to observe peoples characteristics that are unique to each area. However, when the prefectural trait of Shizuoka people as a whole is compared with those of neighboring prefectures, it is immediately apparent that the people of Shizuoka Prefecture share common features as a single group.

In 1988, when Roland Corporation decided to purchase the Rodgers Organ Company of Hillsboro, Oregon, it was necessary for me to make multiple visits there. The closest airport was in Portland, only a few miles away from Hillsboro. After flying for hours over the Pacific, the view coming into Portland was dominated by a combination of a huge volcanic mountain covered in timeless snow, Mount Hood, and the broad swath of the Columbia River watering the plains at the foot of the mountains.

I experienced a strong sense of recognition. Except for the fact that we were landing west to east, this might have been coming home to Shizuoka, with the snow-capped peak being Mt. Fuji rather than Mt. Hood.

At the time of my first visit, I was prepared to be treated as "foreign," but that isn't what happened. I immediately discovered that the people of western Oregon are as warm at heart and as open as the people of Shizuoka. Taxi drivers were as helpful as those in Hamamatsu. In my Portland hotel I received a wonderfully cordial welcome.

There is a global organization, "Sister Cities International," which helps cities establish relationships among foreign locations with which they have much in common. About 20 minutes outside of Portland is a town called Camas. It is a "sister" city to the Japanese city of Hosoe, where I live and where the main Roland factory is located. The town of Camas is only a 40-minute ride from Hillsboro, my regular destination. I was fascinated to learn that Hillsboro also has a sister city in Shizuoka prefecture, Fukuroi. Not only is Fukoroi in Shizuoka, it also is about the same distance from Hosoe as Hillsboro is from Camas.

If further evidence of the similarity in cultural geography were needed, one need look no further than the Oregon city of Eugene. It, too, has a sister city—Kakegawa, which, not surprisingly, is located in Shizuoka. In geographic terms, the respective location of the three Oregon cities is virtually identical to that of the three Shizuoka cities.

I was intrigued by the geographic comparability of the two sets of locations, so I made inquiries into how the individual relationships came to be established. I learned that each of the sister city engagements was made independently and coincidentally. Nevertheless, the facts that western Oregon and Shizuoka share geographic conditions as well as the distinctively warm humanity of their people must have been major contributors to establishing each of the sister city relationships. It is no surprise to me that more than 20 Japanese firms already have established their presence in Oregon.

In the year I was making my frequent trips to Oregon, economic conflicts between the governments of the United States and Japan were intense. Using a law known as "Super 301," the U.S. administration had imposed a ruinous tariff on the import of Japanese-made semi-conductors, effectively closing the U.S.

market to Japanese laptop computers. The situation was extremely angry and tense. However, thanks to the warmth and consideration of my own treatment during my multiple visits to Oregon, I was encouraged to realize that friendship among the people of our two nations could continue to develop, despite policy conflicts at inter-governmental levels.

The prologue to this book was written almost two years ago. I spoke of looking back from "the autumn of my years." That was my point of view then. However, now that I have revisited (and to a certain extent re-lived) all of the events and experiences related in the preceding pages, I do not feel that "autumn" was a completely appropriate metaphor. An individual's lifetime may have its seasons, but a lifetime in music is a song without end. I am proud of the global Roland family. The satisfaction I derive from it is because it is a vibrant part of the vast and timeless "world of music."

ORGAN JOURNEYS

All my adult life I have been fascinated by the science of sound, and my personal focus has never wavered from the organ as the most complete musical instrument. My career has been devoted to electronics, but I have never passed up the opportunity to learn from and admire famous installations of pipe organs as well. Here are some of the more memorable locations I have had a chance to visit.

ST. THOMAS CHURCH, LEIPZIG

Trade fairs dating back to Medieval times still are hosted throughout Europe. The Frankfurt Musikmesse, which virtually the entire music industry attends every year, is one of these traditional fairs. In Germany, the city of Leipzig also hosts an annual fair that can trace its history to the Hansiatic League. In 1967, I attended the Leipzig Fair for the first time.

In those days, Germany was still divided into two bodies, East and West, and visiting Leipzig in East Germany was massively inconvenient. Unless you could prepare and submit necessary documents for attending the trade fair, it was even difficult to obtain an airline ticket. Having learned about the difficulty of going there, I wanted even more to visit the country. On my way home after the Frankfurt Musikmesse, I somehow managed to obtain an entry permit and could attend the fair called *Die Leipziger Messe* (The Leipzig Trade Fair).

At the Frankfurt Musikmesse, I had seen various types of musical instruments exhibited in a large exhibition booth of "Demusa," the state-operated manufacturer of musical instruments of East Germany. Although there was not a single electronic instrument in their booth, almost all types of traditional instruments were exhibited, and the quality of their instruments was fairly good. Thus I felt I needed to learn more about East Germany.

The flight to Leipzig from Frankfurt was very short, but in sensory terms Leipzig seemed far away. I had to check the map to confirm that the two cities were indeed geographically close. The Leipzig airport facilities were substantially less sophisticated than those in Frankfurt, and I was unnerved to see a line of soldiers with automatic rifles lining the ramp to the terminal. Immediately I felt tense, unsure of how dreadful the place might be. I actually started to worry about whether I would be able to go back home. After going through the strict entry procedures, I was finally "inside" the German Democratic Republic. I left the airport immediately. I had no reservations at any hotel nor had I any other plan in mind. I am still intrigued as to why I behaved in such a reckless manner; perhaps it was a form of panic brought on by the line of soldiers with the Kalishnakov weapons.

Following instructions that were posted at the airport, I went directly to the city hall after clearing immigration procedures. There I stood in a queue before a counter that dispensed assignments for lodging.

Every decent hotel in the city was full, and I was instructed to take my lodgings at a private tourist home. By that time I would have been happy just to find a place to sleep. They gave me a note indicating the address of the tourist home, but I had no idea how to get to the place. There was no such thing as a professional taxi in the entire city. You had to pick up one of the unlicensed taxis temporarily recruited during the fair period, in order get to a house of a private citizen. Without knowing what I should tell the driver in the German language, I showed him the note, and off we went.

Luckily, the room assigned to me was very comfortable; in fact, it was part of a private apartment house. Good hot water was in plentiful supply, thanks to a boiler with a faucet that was equipped with a lever to provide both hot and cold water. In Japan in those days, only a very few houses came equipped with facilities for hot-water supply. For me, who had only learned that the Communist countries had low standards of living, it was a great surprise to see the actual living conditions for families in East Germany. Compared to all other experiences that I had to confront by then, including the airport soldiers, the queue formed in the city hall for lodging assignments, and the negative factors of public transportation typified by unlicensed taxis, the condition of the private tourist home was unexpectedly good. To a certain extent it eased my tension. Still, I could not overcome the feeling that I had come to an awful place.

I went to the exhibition early in next morning. The exhibition site was larger than I expected. In fact, it was surprising to me that such a large-scale trade fair could be held in a place like Leipzig, a part of the Communist bloc in which cultural exchange and communications were heavily restricted.

Inside the fair, various kinds of items from large-sized construction machines to musical instruments were exhibited. However, the booth for musical instruments was a small one. Only pianos, harpsichords and accordions were on display. There was not much to learn from the presentation. I was frustrated, but I wasn't ready to give up, because I had gone to a lot of trouble to get to Leipzig. Accordingly, I negotiated with a person in charge of the display and told him that I wanted to visit their factories. I was taken aback when he immediately gave me his approval for a tour of their accordion factory. I had to decline when I learned that it would take more than five hours to go and return from the factory. That might have been okay, but I was then told that there was no available transportation to return to the tourist home from their factory.

On the other hand, when I referred to electronic musical instruments, they clearly became enthusiastic. They told me that, although they were not manufacturing such items yet, they were working on experimental samples, and they would be happy to show me their work. They even suggested that they would consider a technical tie-up with our company. I immediately forgot about the accordion factory and focused on visiting their laboratory of electronic musical instruments. It was only a two-hour round trip to the lab, and furthermore they offered me a ride back to the tourist home.

The lab was just a two-room apartment, and what I saw there was a makeshift instrument made of pieces and components taken out of Italian and Japanese instruments. It was by no means a marketable item. Although I felt disappointed, I was reassured to learn that at least there were people working on the project of electronic musical instruments, even in this Communist bloc. What I really saw there was an image of my Kakehashi Musen Radio Shop experiments more than ten years earlier.

Having promised the engineers that I would send locally available parts after I got home, I left the lab. During that two-hour visit, I had to cope with a storm of questions that they rained down on me. When I left, I was exhausted. Now it is one of my good memories; we could understand and communicate with one another through circuit diagrams and English technical terms. Afterward I became depressed when I thought about the future of those earnest and eager engineers. The visit to their lab left me with a strong impression that electronic musical instruments would not thrive in the Communist bloc. Then I recollected the first worries I had when I first stepped off the plane at Leipzig airport, and I decided that the trip had been worthwhile thanks to the enthusiasm of those engineers. Nevertheless, I still knew that I would not come back for a while. In fact, it was 20 years before I visited Leipzig again.

On the next day I decided to forget about the trade fair. Instead I visited St. Thomas Church, which had been the other objective of my Leipzig trip. I headed for the church in the morning. The building itself was not very large, but was cunningly built, so that it projected a sense of "welcome" and nestled into the surrounding cityscape. It was less inspiring that I had anticipated, but I was truly satisfied that I was at the very place that Johann Sebastian Bach had played the organ.

St. Thomas Church, Leipzig.

Visibility inside the church was limited. The only available illumination came from filtered light provided by the stained glass windows. I discovered, embedded in the floor, a brass plate with a variety of German writing and a prominent display of the name of Johann Sebastian Bach. There was a small bouquet placed on the plate. For some reason or other, my attention was so totally focused on the metal plate and the stained glass, that I forgot to observe the organ. I remember having seen the pipes, but I did not look at the console. At any rate I was truly satisfied for having seen the epitaph of Bach.

My second visit to Leipzig was twenty years later, after the Berlin Wall had fallen. Again, the main purpose of my business trip was to attend Frankfurt Musikmesse and the Leipzig Trade Fair. In the entire city, time seemed to have been at a complete standstill. The Leipzig fair had not improved from its conditions of twenty years earlier; there still was not very much to see. Aside from the fair, I

photo by Haruaki Matsushita

Bach's memorial plate in St. Thomas Church.

visited the places that had originally impressed me, namely St. Thomas Church and a semi-basement restaurant where I had enjoyed delicious soup. These two were the only purposes of the trip to Leipzig other than the trade show, and both of them were accomplished.

I remember that I was again deeply impressed by St. Thomas Church, just as I was the first time. This time I was determined not to miss seeing the organ. The organ console seemed relatively new compared with those in the era of Bach, but there was no attendant I could ask about it. There was no brochure either, and I never did learn the facts about the date of the console.

At the time I first visited the church I was with Ace Electronic, manufacturing electric organs. The second time I visited St. Thomas Church I was trying to figure out when I could really set about developing organs, now that the work at Roland was taking favorable turns for both synthesizers and electronic pianos. My mind has always been filled with ideas for organ developments, which made the second visit even more memorable and emotional. I knew that there was no practical answer to be found at St. Thomas. Rather, I was seeking something to stimulate my thinking on the subject. It turned out to be an empty quest, but I do not regret the visit. I was in a searching mood during that second visit.

While in Leipzig, I also questioned people from Demusa regarding the laboratory of electronic musical instruments, but they seemed to know nothing about the lab. Tradionalists may refer to Germany as the "mecca" of organs. But even the manufacturing of organs can disappear because of the social structure. Looking at the streets that had not changed at all for 20 years intensified my sense of isolation, as I considered how helpless I was to find out what had become of those bright-eyed engineers, with whom I spent such an intense two hours, 20 years earlier.

Wondering how they might be getting along, I realized how very lucky I was to be able to devote myself to the creation of musical instruments in Japan. This thought helped me to recover my natural sense of optimism, and I focused again on the future. I decided that things would probably work out for the best as long as I continued my own efforts.

In the pictorial book called *Journey of Mind—Churches and Pipe Organs of Europe*, the church of St. Thomas is introduced on the first page. Looking at the picture, I found a bronze statue of Bach standing in front of the church. I missed that one on both of my visits, and its discovery gave me cause for elation: it's good to have a reason to visit St. Thomas one more time.

ST. PETER'S BASILICA, VATICAN

In the late spring of 1995, my wife and I had a chance to spend a full day in Rome as tourists. It was her first visit to the city, and I would say it was truly a "Roman Holiday" for both of us. We started out bright and early to see the city. There were a few places I had already seen that I wanted to share with my wife. We decided to visit as many famous spots as possible, using taxis to get from one place to the next.

I hoped we might be able to listen to the organ being played at St. Peter's Basilica during the morning service. Accordingly we reached it at around 10 A.M. The Piazza, a perfect ellipse of open space in front of the Basilica, was already filled with people, and we had to work our way through the crowd to get to the entrance.

Organ Console of St. Peter's Basilica.

Unfortunately, Swiss Guards were there to prevent us from entering. I was surprised and very much embarrassed; the last time I was there I got in with no hindrance at all.

We finally understood that there was going to be a service celebrated by the Pope himself! It was a ceremonial occasion, and admission was restricted to invited guests who were formally attired for the event. Sightseers and tourists were not invited. We had just about decided to leave the place, when some of the tourists told us to try another entrance at the back of the shrine.

The back entrance was a narrow door, but people were going in and out freely. There was no guard, either. Entering into the chapel, we found ourselves in a place about 30 to 40 meters from the worship altar that was so huge that it loomed over the multitude. Soon we saw a line of monks approaching from the right, each bearing a swaying censer that emitted clouds of perfumed smoke. The Pope was within the line. Since we were not far away from the aisle, we could see the Pope's face very well. I started to feel a little nervous thinking that perhaps we should not be there with the Pope, particularly in an area where there was no guard. Rather than call attention to ourselves, we quietly participated in the ceremony along with the people around us.

The Pope was now at the altar, showing his back. Suddenly the organ started to sound. The organist in a white gown was playing it leisurely. The four-manual organ console was fairly large and magnificent, and its cabinet including sleeve boards seemed as wide as three meters or greater. The organist started to play the organ very naturally without seeming to be unnerved by the solemnity of the ceremony. I had no idea how he could determine the precise timing of the ceremony, but he clearly seemed to know each interval. He played and stopped and then started to play again. The entire ceremony took about an hour.

Since the church was quiet, with no commotion in spite of the multitude inside, I could not move around to see the organ console or look at the pipes. Still, I was very pleased that I was able to listen to the organ in the same chapel with the Pope. Later in 1999, I saw an on-the-spot telecast of a Christmas Mass at St. Peter's, and it was explained that as many as 7,300 people attended the service inside the basilica, while a crowd of more than 50 thousand people gathered in the Piazza. Looking at the chapel on the TV monitor, the altar in the center looked even larger than what I remembered from my earlier visit. I must admit I was disappointed by the TV coverage. I hoped to see a close-up of the organ console. The TV camera visited virtually every nook and cranny of the entire basilica, except the organ.

TRINITY CHURCH, BOSTON

In 1997 I had the opportunity to visit Boston's famous Trinity Church, considered to be a masterpiece of American religious architecture. According to the brochure supplied by the church, it was originally established in 1773 and subsequently moved to its present location a hundred years later. In addition to its architecture, the church is also famous for possessing one of the few remaining Aeolian-Skinner Organs. The organ has a three-manual console and 6,898 pipes, including 32-foot pipes. I had long looked forward to the chance to attend a service and hear the instrument being played.

The church's choirs are famous as well. The front of the chapel is hollowed out in a circular shape and the choirs stood in that space, facing the congregation. The chorus sung in that hall was echoed throughout the entire chapel, producing splendid effects.

At the conclusion of the service, I asked to see the organ console. In 1988, when Roland purchased Rodgers Organ Company from Steinway Musical Properties, Inc., we learned that Rodgers owned a complete set of drawings of an Aeolian-Skinner Organ. In those days the main target of every electronic organ manufacturer of church organs was how to compete with pipe organs, and accordingly the design drawings were considered highly important as reference information. However, I have no intention of producing or competing with pipe organs as such; I am absolutely committed to the creation of electronic organs. Accordingly, we are going to present the detailed drawings to a qualified custodial institution, in order to assure that the plans are carefully protected and preserved for future study. I mention this because of the coincidence involved. I never imagined that one day I would encounter the actual organ that was the basis for the drawings we had accidentally acquired.

Aolien-Skinner organ of Trinity Church.

Trinity Church is famous as a sightseeing spot and is included in every tour guidebook of Boston. The church stands in a thriving business district lined with modern buildings and it offers a magnificent view. If you take an interest in organs, then the church is even more worth visiting. Recently I had another chance to go to Boston and I returned to Trinity Church. This time, being guided by Mr. Paul E. Murphy, Jr. of M. Steinert & Sons in Boston, I noticed that, on the other side of the church's square, there was another church building featuring a Gothic tower. I asked someone about this building, and they told me it is called the Old South Church. I was surprised that two large churches of different denominations were located so close to each other.

The Old South Church also had a very impressive Skinner organ with wooden pipes lined up perfectly on both sides of a stained glass window. The internal design of the chapel was splendid, and the placement of the organ console was different from any arrangement I had ever seen. The console was placed in

Paul Murphy Jr. in front of Trinity Church.

a low area in the front of the chapel. I had never seen an organ console placed in such a way that the congregation looked down upon it. I was not able to hear the instrument played, but I was amazed and enthralled by the fact that two different Aeolian-Skinner organs were installed within a few hundred yards of each other. I was profoundly impressed by the depth of American organ culture.

Rodgers Organ at Second Baptist Church.

SECOND BAPTIST CHURCH, HOUSTON

Shortly after the purchase of Rodgers Organ Company by Roland, the Second Baptist Church in Houston, Texas, finished preparations for the dedication concert of a new organ. A five-manual console built by Rodgers was placed in the middle of the Worship Center, along with 10,761 pipes. The Worship Center was enormous, and the entire view was magnificent. It was June of 1988. The installation of the instrument was complete; the building was beautiful, all seats were filled.

The organist was Ms. Diane Bish. She was unhappy. Due to the fact that final adjustments to the organ had not been completed until the day before, she felt she had not been given enough time to set up her registrations. While it was good that the installation and adjustments had been completed in time for the opening, it was disturbing to have the recital start with a comment by the player that she had not been provided with enough time for practice. Indeed, I must admit that at least one whole day is absolutely required to master the registration of a five-manual console.

This was my first introduction to a new Rodgers custom installation, and her complaint made me feel a certain amount of nervousness. As matters turned out, her playing was excellent, and the concert was completed without a hitch. Not surprisingly for an inaugural performance, there were a few technical problems related to specific components. However, the congregation was clearly delighted with the performance and the installation of their custom-designed organ.

What started out as a very tension-filled affair turned out to be a happy occasion. The initial technical problems have long since been addressed, and the organ in the Second Baptist Church of Houston is one that I really want to hear again.

BAMBOO ORGAN, MANILA

As a musical instrument and as an element of church architecture, organs have always been associated with the process of instilling and encouraging faith. In turn, it is frequently thanks to people's faith that historic instruments can be saved from destruction.

The country of the Philippines was a colony of Spain until the end of the 19th century. During the period of Spanish rule, Augustinian monks came in as missionaries. In the process, they built churches and installed organs. They did not attempt to bring pipes from Europe, preferring instead to use bamboo which was abundant in the islands. That was the birth of bamboo organs.

It was in 1969 that I first visited Philippines, and during my trip I went by taxi to a village called Las Pinas on the outskirts of

The Bamboo Organ at Las Pinas.

Manila. I had been told that that village had one of the few remaining bamboo organs. Eventually I did indeed find a small church that contained a pipe organ made of bamboo. Unfortunately, the keyboards were in terrible condition. It was clear that the instrument had not received any maintenance for a very long time. Such sound as could be generated by the organ could hardly be called music. Soon a half-naked boy was brought in by a nun. He sat on the bench and abruptly started to play the organ. I had no idea what song it was. Since he had to skip broken keys, whatever he was playing could not be called beautiful music.

The result of my visit to the church was limited to just hearing the sounds played by the boy, but I was really impressed by the passion and energy of the original monks who took up the task of making organs out of bamboo almost 400 years ago.

Later in 1994, 25 years after the first visit, I again went to Manila. I asked Mr. Philip Yupangco, the president of our Filipino distributor, G.A. Yupangco & Co., Inc. to visit the same church

Mr. Yupangco, Roland Distributor in the Philippines and my guide to the Bamboo Organ.

with me to see the bamboo organ again. The organ must have received good repairs; it generated sounds much better than the last time. However, the construction materials were quite old, and the condition of the instrument was not still good enough to be genuinely musical.

There was an organist who kindly explained to us the special aspects of the organ structure, and he even played a few pieces. Among other things, he told us that freshly cut bamboo pipes had to be aged in mud for a long period of time, in order to obtain stable pitches. I told him that I had visited the church about 20 years earlier, and I asked him if he knew anything about the boy who played the organ for me. I was delighted to learn that he had been that little boy. When the demonstration was over, he brought us to another room where an excellent modern pipe organ was installed. He explained that the newer instrument was for giving organ lessons.

When I first visited in 1969, I had only a small amount of money with me, due to the governmental restriction on the amount of foreign currency allowed to be taken out of Japan. I donated a modest amount for the sake of the organ reconstruction saving the balance of my funds for the taxi ride back to the city. From the progress that had been made, it was obvious that more and more supporters contributed to assist in the renovation of the bamboo organ, as well as the propagation of organ education. I was greatly impressed having seen that the bamboo organ was so well-renovated by the faith of such people.

Later I learned that two sets of pipe organs were brought into Japan in 1579, and also some sets of bamboo organs were made in Japan around 1600. Again, I am amazed at the passion of Christian missionaries in those days and the broadness of the area in which they were active.

Bel Air Presbyterian Church, Los Angeles

On January 17, 1994, I was staying at the Torrance Marriott Hotel, in order to attend the NAMM show in Los Angeles. As the sun rose that morning I felt a very strong shaking, and the room swayed slightly. In the costal areas of Japan, seismic activity is not unusual, and I recognized the event as an earthquake. Since I was on the 14th floor, and the intensity of the quake did not seem very serious, I decided to stay in the bed, rather than running down all those stairs in my pajamas. Soon the shaking ended, and I went back to sleep.

Perhaps because the hotel location was far away from the epicenter, it never occurred to me that the earthquake might be a large one. Instead of worrying about damages that might have been caused by the earthquake, I was concerned that attendance for the NAMM might be reduced due to news about the quake. (In fact, some people planning to attend the show from Japan did cancel their trips.) The truth was that the quake (later to be known as the "Northridge Earthquake") had done extreme damage in some specific areas, including ruptured freeways and building collapses, along with various other disorders and confusions peculiar to the auto-centered society of the United States. The entire west coast of California is known to be a seismic zone, but no one seriously expects their location to experience a major quake.

Exactly one year after the earthquake, I was again staying at the same hotel in order to attend the NAMM show, and I received word of the catastrophic, Kobe earthquake. The earthquake devastated the city and caused casualties of nearly 6,500 people. It was in the afternoon of January 16, 1995, that I learned from TV news that the damage was enormously serious, almost equal to the great Tokyo earthquake of 1923. Still, the entire picture was not available to me. I tried to call from Los Angeles to Japan, but the line seemed to be permanently busy. When my call finally went through, all that I could learn was more vague than what I heard on U.S. TV, and I felt even more confused. In Japan, various precautions had been taken for possible earthquakes in the Tokai area (Central Japan on the Pacific rim *including the Hamamatsu area*!), but scarcely anyone had imagined that Kobe would be struck by so massive an upheaval.

In 1997, three years after the Northridge quake, I visited a Los Angeles showroom of Robert Tall & Associates, Inc. The visit had been a promise for a long time. Dr. Robert C. Tall is an owner of the company which is one of the most excellent dealers of Rodgers organs in the United States, and he has a profound knowledge of organs. Our first, indirect contact had occurred back in 1976. Roland Corporation had introduced a sound system called REVO-30. It was a unit that could be easily attached to an electronic organ, and it would produce rotary effects and chorus sounds in order to improve the original sound of the instrument. The product was primarily targeted at the home and amateur musician market. I later heard that there was a retailer actually selling that product for the classic organ. That person was Dr. Tall. Although we did not meet until much later, Dr. Tall and I had been doing business together for more than 20 years through our products.

That day in 1997 turned out to be the Organ Day for me,

Bel Air Presbyterian Church.

because he arranged to show me Rodgers organs (three-manual and four-manual) placed in three different churches. Furthermore, we were supposed to visit Mr. and Mrs. Don Leslie at their house on the way back. It was such a special day with special schedules, and everything we did was related to electronic organs and Leslie speakers.

The highlight of the tour was the organ at the Bel Air

Presbyterian Church, in which I had maintained a strong interest. Luckily, we were in company with an organist named Hector Olivera, and I was very pleased that I could confirm the true sound of the organ with my ears. During our visit, people of the church including the resident organist and various church officials were very kind and guided us. I still remember that I was very pleased with the view of Los Angeles that could be seen from the church window and felt that I was truly happy

In 1991, a new Casavant pipe organ had been constructed in the Bel Air Presbyterian Church. When it was damaged by the Northridge earthquake in 1994, nearly 65 percent of the pipes fell, and the console was severely damaged as well. The church had to face a great problem concerning the rebuilding of the organ, in view of time and cost. As possible solutions, the entire body could be replaced with digital technology, or they could attempt to overhaul it. Not all the pipes were broken, and in fact one-third of them were still usable. Since people had a strong admiration and affection for acoustic pipes, the decision had to be made carefully. They finally decided to interface the original organ with a four-manual Rodgers console, while utilizing the remaining undamaged 60-rank of pipes as they were. In addition, 151 digitally sampled pipe voices were selected from the Rodgers' custom library to be controlled using 118 stops. Having replaced the essential part with the digital technology, the Bel Air Church organ was renovated as the largest pipe/digital combination instrument in the world.

I assume there were spirited discussions and debates before the final decision to proceed with a hybrid approach was agreed upon. In order to cope with the unusual situation caused by the earthquake, people had to carry out more investigations and studies than when they installed the original new organ. I can imagine how complex it must have been to pull together a list of technological issues and then find and agree upon a resolution for each item.

Considering just the technical side, you can immediately list difficult issues that would have to be resolved: how to seamlessly integrate analog pipe sound and digitally processed sound; how to achieve and determine conformity of the composite tone; and the issue of interfacing remaining pipes and the new console. And that's only the beginning of the list. They had to deal with the question of how to maintain the appearance of pipes and remaining parts perfectly; where to install the speakers to balance the output within the complex architecture of the church building, or even how and when to determine that the work was in fact complete. When I looked inside the pipe room and saw the position of speakers, I could understand the efforts and difficulties that confronted them.

Comparisons between pipe organs and electronic organs have been a contentious issue in the industry since the beginning of electronic musical instruments. Advancement in the adaptation of electronic technology to musical applications has been remarkable, especially in the last decade, but it takes considerable time to let every organist fully understand the present state of technological achievement. It is also extremely difficult to create an opportunity for organists to simultaneously compare both types of instruments in tests of playability. It is inevitable that the stops on electronic organs and on pipe organs are completely different from each other, which makes it even more difficult to achieve a direct comparison.

In the Bel Air Church organ, both electronic sounds (CPU sourced) and acoustic sounds (pipes) are generated using a single console, and if one form were superior to the other, the result would not make sense as a musical instrument. Since it is hardly possible to modify pipe sounds, there is no other way than to match the electronic sound to the acoustic standard. Thanks to the flexibility of electronic technology, this difficulty was resolved. In the case of Bel Air, the most important concern was how satisfactory the sounds can be in a musical sense, so that there is no indication at all whether pipe or electronic sounds are better. If you could hear it play, you would understand that the combination of both has yielded excellent results.

Down through the centuries, there has been a continuous

process of modification and improvement to pipe organs, both in physical structure and in functional aspects. I believe that it is now time for pipe organ traditionalists to accept the revolutionary change to utilize sound generators. This integration brings changes not only in the sound generator itself, but also in the relationships between organs and the scales of chapels. With wind-operated pipe organs, in order to obtain desired sound you have to determine the location of the console and the exact pipe arrangements at the time the building is being designed. In addition to being acoustically legitimate, the electronic system is the key to overcoming the architectural difficulty as well. The Bel Air Church organ is a sign post relative to the benefits that the combination of the pipe and the digital will yield. I truly admire the church people who made the decision and Dr. Robert Tall who accepted the project of the organ reconstruction.

In order to introduce the fascinations of organs to as many people as possible, we arranged an interview regarding the Bel Air organ and made a movie of their services performed on January 30, 2000, using a HDTV system. The final movie describes circumstances of the organ from its experiencing the earthquake in 1994, till the renovation was completed. Thanks to the cordial consideration of Dr. Michael H. Wenning, the pastor and the organ committee, we were able to attend two worship services held that morning. The organist was Mr. Hector Olivera, who played "Joyful, Joyful" (Beethoven's "Ode to Joy"), brilliantly enhancing the gracefulness of the services. The organ, in which traditional pipe organ technology and digital sound generation were harmonized perfectly, produced magnificent sounds.

As a commemoration of the event, I received a hymnal personally autographed by the officials of the church. Considering the devastation that had been caused by the earthquake, and the six years of devoted effort that went into creating one of the world's first custom organs combining digital and traditional technology, it was a day of true happiness for all concerned.

INTERVIEW WITH REMO BELLI

In discussing music, it is customary to think in terms of three families of instruments: Wind (including brass and woodwinds), Strings, and Percussion. In whatever culture and whatever time period, the shape and nature of instruments may differ, but percussion is always important.

The application of electronics to drums contained special challenges. In the early 80s the Simmon's Company of England introduced the first generation of electronic drums. The public seemed to be ready for the concept, and Roland also entered the market. There was an early surge of consumer interest, but then sales went into irreversible decline. To play drums proficiently, the player needs a tactile response from the drumhead. The first generation of electronic drums could not offer that characteristic.

We spent years seeking a solution, and Roland engineering finally developed mesh drumheads. I then turned to Remo Belli to learn if the material could be produced in quantity. In collaboration with our engineering department, Remo succeeded, and we finally had the drumhead we needed for the Roland V-drums product line.

Although most famous for their drumheads, Remo produces a wide range of percussion instruments. The founder, Remo Belli, brought a special expertise to the business because he actually started as a professional drummer. However, he does not limit his creative interests. A few years ago he began experimenting to see

Chatting with Remo Belli.

if he could create a cost effective version of the classic "Taiko" drums of Japan, using wood fiber as the primary material.

It seemed like an unusual effort, so I asked the reason for his interest in what was essentially a "folk" instrument of a foreign culture. Mr. Belli saw it differently. Because Taiko was so tradition-bound, to the average Japanese it simply was unthinkable to consider changing material. Remo said that Taiko is a wonderful instrument, but the price is too high. He believed that a quality product at an affordable price would substantially widen interest. When I finally had the opportunity to hear the Remo Taiko, I was amazed at the quality of the acoustics. It is no surprise to me that the Remo Taiko is very well received in Japan.

Remo's latest contribution to percussion is in traditional Japanese instrumentation, but his lifetime of contributions covers almost 50 years. He is the first manufacturer of musical instruments to be inducted into Hollywood's Rockwalk.

In 1999 Mr. Belli visited the Roland factories and consented to the following interview.

Kakehashi: Thank you for coming to Hamamatsu to visit Roland. As I explained, we have an internal magazine for our workers, and we try to share information with them. Your visit is an excellent opportunity for us to interview you. Everybody would like to know how you got started in the drum business and what your views are.

Remo Belli: OK. First of all, I am a drummer. It's a good reason: the number one reason. I have been a drummer since the age of 12, and I became a professional drummer at the age sixteen. I had a very good life as a drummer in the United States. Then I started a drum store in Hollywood. I had a very nice, successful, specialized drum store in Hollywood. And I had the pleasure of knowing the great drummers of the world, when they came to visit California.

While I had the drum shop I experimented with various materials to make a display—not to make a drum, merely a display. I became familiar with a particular kind of material made by the Dupont Company in the United States. In trying to make the display, I made a drumhead with it and I was surprised at what I heard: the possibilities were intriguing. So I found a chemist and we worked together, perhaps every night for three or four months until we developed the method of how to use the material. And that's how the drumhead was formed. It was the first time in the history of man that there was such a possibility, and it changed completely and forever the whole relationship of the drum business.

K: I agree. I think that we could not even achieve the characteristics of today's beat, without the plastic and new materials that have been developed. With animal skins the sound is a little dark.

B: That's correct. And besides, there were not enough animals— not enough animals to make animal-skin drumheads of good quality. At that time also, there was no control over drumhead size in the world of music. So we established the standard for the whole world. I went everywhere, and I said, "Hey, look. When the drummer travels from New York to Tokyo, and he needs a drumhead, they use the drumhead the same size, the same thing!" Everybody thought that's a pretty good idea.

And I used to come to your country many years ago. At that time there were 23 drum manufactures in Japan.

K: In Japan? Really?

B: Most of them in Nagoya. Everybody was making drums. And you used to export to the United States twenty-four thousand drum sets a month.

K: A month? Twenty-four thousand?

B: Yes! Can you imagine? It could not happen with animal-skin heads. It changed completely the drum business. I was very surprised that I was part of it. Because I did not do it on purpose.

K: As a result you saved a lot of animals and also contributed to the environment.

B: Oh, yes. But I guess the most important thing that I've always appreciated, is that it made a very major contribution to the possibilities in drums and music. That's what I like about it.

K: The key is the fact that your background is in drums.

B: You know we make drums. We also have developed a whole new idea that we call "World Percussion." And as you know, I worked with music product industry association NAMM, and I'm on the board of directors of NAMM, and I work with your Dennis Houlihan. I enjoy working. Now we do a lot of research in music and uses of music, and I have worked for ten years now in music therapy. I'm also on the advisory counsel of the United States for music education. We are learning how to understand music, and how playing other instruments makes the quality of life better. So I think the message for you and for all the employees of Roland is that the music industry is really a very safe place to be. Because it will grow very much.

Steve Fisher of Roland. One of the key contributors to the development of the V-drums.

We have an expression in the United States that "you do well by doing good." OK? If you think about that expression later, that's where I believe that our industry will be going. Because our industry now does not have to look only for musicians. It's no longer true. Because, now everybody that is alive is the customer. No questions about it in my mind. We make products starting for six months old. We have a system now within my company. We deal with six months old to the time you are dying. OK? So my plans are just exactly that people will realize that there is very strong connection between music and life. As you know, my wife is a doctor and we do a lot of research. We go to many research conventions and I speak at doctors meeting. The nice part about it is that everybody agrees. We are lucky. Nobody disagrees with what we are doing.

K: Now we need action.

B: I know for what we're growing, and how we're growing, that the concept in the mind of people is already beginning to change. The concept that says music is good for you is becoming important. We

Tommy Snyder. Another of the key R&D contributors to the V-drums project.

in the industry made a mistake, because we always sold music at something that was culture, something that was refinement. And that's OK. We don't have to change that. We don't have to change anything. We just have to give the added value that we now have. So, that's what's going to happen with us.

K: Thank you. Now the next question. We are now enjoying the product we call the V-drums. Without your help we could never have achieved the present level of success. I am deeply grateful for your assistance. It is my philosophy that Roland must cover all of the musical instrument groups, including percussion. Similar to what we have done with guitars, I wanted to combine electronic technology with basic areas like drums. That's why we started the V-drums. What do you think of combining electronics with drums? What are your thoughts about an electronic type instrument?

B: Yes, I can comment from two different points of view. One point of view is that when somebody within Roland discovered the mesh material and then asked us if we would try to use our system to make a drumhead with the material—it was very fundamental to the success you are having. Let me explain. In the early days of the electronic drums, there was a psychological problem and there was a physical problem. The drummer who normally played on a membrane was used to an entirely different feel, and physical reaction. The drummer could not ever feel the same way with the different surfaces of the early electronic drumheads, and so you had very big problems. You had physical problems and you had psychological problems. It's honestly true. OK? Since your staff was able to solve the material problem, we were able to cooperate with you to produce what we do for you. That's basically why you are having success with that instrument; technically you have done a good job of developing it. It simply has to have and we will have a very good market share, because it plays an important part in everybody's need. I believe that the Roland contribution to the development of the drum, although it's electronic, is no problem. No problem.

K: Thank you for that. Without our working relationship, it never could have happened. I'm very, very happy.

B: Me too. I'm very happy with it. For all of your employees, I just encourage you to keep making, keep developing. I hope we can be proud of everything.

K: Thank you. I very much appreciate your time and your giving us your opinions and comments.

B: My pleasure.

INTERVIEW WITH DON LESLIE

Whether strings, winds, or percussion, all electronic musical instruments share a common need: they depend on amplification to be heard. In the field of electronic organs, Mr. Don Leslie has been a pioneer in the development of truly innovative speakers. He also has given a great part of his life to thinking about the nature of sound and the best ways to reproduce it.

It is fair to say that commercial acceptance of electronic music got its start with the introduction of the Hammond Organ. Even in the depths of the Great Depression, the product was an immediate success. Don Leslie was a young man who loved pipe organ music, and he was frustrated that the original Hammond organ sound could not be more faithful to that of a majestic theater organ. Accordingly, he set to work to study the problem. What resulted from his experiments would revolutionize the home organ industry and thus help to accelerate acceptance of all forms of electronic music.

However, the Hammond Organ Company was less than enthusiastic to have such a major improvement created outside of its own organization. Instead of welcoming the invention, it spent years trying to prevent its success. Don had to go it alone in bringing his invention to the world. As I mentioned in the prologue to this book, his reminiscences in *The Don Leslie Story* tell a fascinating story of courage and creativity.

Ultimately, the Hammond management had to change its mind and recognize the improvement in sound that Leslie speakers

My first meeting with Bob Campbell of Electro Music, Pasadena, CA.

brought to the Hammond organ. This change in Hammond policy occurred in the mid-60s. Accordingly, when I agreed to become the importing agent for Hammond Organs in 1967, I could also get the agency agreement with the Electro-Music Co. I immediately went to Pasadena, California to meet with Bob Campbell, the president of Electro-Music, in order to establish the agency agreement. By this time Don Leslie had retired from active management of the company, but arrangements were made for me to personally meet him. Unfortunately, my travel schedule required my return to Japan on the day of the appointment, so our first meeting could not take place for several more years.

In 1971 we decided to build small-size Leslie speakers into our organs for export. As we had very limited knowledge regarding aspects of the rotor technology, Mr. Harada and I decided to go to the States to learn from Mr. Leslie himself. He met us at the airport and gave us a ride in his Mazda RX-2 sedan. In those days the RX series was a world-wide sensation as the car with the rotary engine. Possibly because of his invention of the rotary speaker, Mr. Leslie

Don Leslie inside the "Leslie Wall of Sound" in his house.

continues to be enthusiastic about rotary engines in cars. On later visits with him, I learned that he continued to drive Mazda models such as the RX-4 and the RX-7. I look back on that first visit with special fondness. Considering my limited facility with English, Mr. Leslie was wonderfully good-natured during our technical meetings. He worked with us with unstinting patience until it was clear that we completely understood.

In 1997 I visited Mr. Leslie at his home and he demonstrated his own, custom made "Leslie Organ." Starting with a console of a Rodgers organ, he had turned it into his own unique design by re-engineering it with a wide array of modifications and internal alterations. The biggest mystery for me was how such impressive sound could be created without any visible speakers. Don solved the mystery by guiding me into a room beside the organ console. The entire wall was lined with sophisticated amplification and sound modification equipment, including a 50-channel amplifier, speakers (both traditional and Leslie), processors, and percussion instruments that worked with solenoids. The entire wall of his spacious living room had been turned into a "Leslie Wall of Sound."

We invited Mr. and Mrs. Leslie to the second annual "Organ Power" concert, which Roland U.S. presented at the Winter

Masako and our daughter Junko visiting Mr. and Mrs. Leslie.

NAMM show held in the year 2000. I had the opportunity to sit down with Don and interview him regarding the history of the Leslie speaker and some of his views on the field of electronic music. In addition to being a successful inventor and entrepreneur, I think of Don as a philosopher of acoustics, and I'm sure you'll find his comments interesting.

Kakehashi: Where did the idea for rotary speakers come from?

Leslie: It was one of many things I tried. It grew out of my experiments in trying to make the Hammond Organ sound better. I tried many things, and the first thing that really sounded better was when I put a speaker at each end of the room and then gradually changed over the volume from one end of the room to the other at a tremolo speed. That had at least some substance to it, and it improved the sound a lot. From that experience I learned that location and change of location had something to do with substantially improving the sound.

Another thing that I had observed, and I was just tumbling to at the time, was that when you play a pipe organ the sound jumps around among the various pipes. That virtually continuous movement of the source of the sound tells you it's coming from a big instrument, even though it might be playing quite softly. The sound source doesn't have to be loud to be a truly "big" sound.

K: I see. It's not necessarily the volume.

L: That's right; the sound can be "big" simply because it's moving around. Also, I noticed that when an automobile or train went by, it would rise in pitch and then lower in pitch and I wondered what the fact of movement had to do with it. So I decided, I'm going to get some speakers and rotate—move—the speakers and see what happens. So I bought 14 little speakers, and mounted them on a cylinder and rotated them.

K: Rotated physically?

L: Yes. I mounted them all the way around a large drum (they were only four-inch speakers), and with bearings and a motor I rotated the whole big drum of speakers. Going slower didn't seem to do anything, so I kept speeding it up and speeding it up, and the results were a terrible racket, with each speaker emitting a pulse as it went by, until the whole thing was simply clacking.

I was disappointed of course, but I got to thinking about it and I decided I should try a different approach. I tried phasing the 14 speakers: half of them plus, and the other half minus. When I then increased the speed up to tremolo, the effect was beautiful. That was much better. Next I started disconnecting speakers, one at a time. Much to my surprise, I discovered that I actually only had to have one speaker to achieve the improvement in sound.

K: From the beginning had you been experimenting based on your understanding of the Doppler effect?

L: No, I can't say that I was. Of course I was aware that there was a frequency change going on, but I didn't realize the importance of it at that point. The sound was wonderful, but I didn't really know why it sounded so good. My next step was to go from the lab experiment with a four-inch speaker to a practical unit offering commercial range and power. That was a long and complicated process. In particular, I could not find a way to maintain a power connection to the rotating speaker without an unacceptable level of noise. I was stumped until I realized that the speaker itself didn't have to rotate.

It could remain stationary within a rotating drum that projected the sound via a bent horn. That was the big breakthrough.

K: But would such an arrangement create a problem of balance?

L: No, not really. You see, when the horn is coming towards you, the pitch and the volume both rise. Then, as the drum continues to turn, the pitch and the volume both lower. That sounds simple, but it's only a part of the story. Because the sound that is coming at you, is also going by you and bouncing off the wall to come back at you. This is happening from every direction in the room, so there is a virtual infinity of sound movement occurring simultaneously. People tend to marvel at the "width" of the sound.

It is an effect that is almost impossible to duplicate, and all it takes is rotating the source of the sound in order to accomplish it. Since it is a physical effect on the ears, apparently it takes a physical process to achieve it. I couldn't figure out how to do it electronically, no matter how vast an array of components I had.

K: Another question: When it came to negotiating with the individual organ manufacturers about the use of your product, what was the most constructive instance, and what was the most unsatisfactory?

L: Well, I can't say I ever had a truly "unsatisfactory" case, because I sold a whole lot of speakers to everybody. But in order to do that, I did have to go through some unpleasant experiences. I was sort of a necessary evil. In order to sell their organ, they had to have my speaker, but they didn't want it. And of course the first one that didn't want it was Hammond.

K: That's a famous story that deserves to be told by you.

L: Well, I had the idea for a revolutionary new speaker, but I didn't have a business. I needed to find out how this product was going to be accepted by the manufacturers. Laurens Hammond had invented the entire industry, and the Hammond Organ absolutely dominated the market, but they were a tough outfit to deal with. To present the product in public, I put together a unit designed to commercial specifications. It delivered first class sound, and it was designed for mass production techniques.

In those days, Hammond owned its own retail store in Los Angeles. It was called Hammond Organ Studio. There was a cocktail lounge across the street from the Hammond store where the Hammond salesmen would stop for drinks. I arranged for a friend to use my speaker when he played the Hammond Organ there. The Hammond salesmen were enthusiastic about the sound, but they knew nothing about the source of the marvelous new speaker.

A few days later I called the Hammond Studio and offered to give them a demonstration of my invention, and they invited me to come as soon as possible. The day came, and they had brought in close to 50 people to hear the demonstration. There were professional organists, and a wide range of other "experts." They even had a phone hook-up back to Chicago so that Laurens Hammond himself could listen in.

It was a triumph! With my speaker, the sounds were vastly better than anything they had ever heard. All afternoon the demonstration went on and on. While all this was happening, I personally heard the Hammond manager tell one of his subordinates, "Don't let him know it's any good." That was a pretty good clue that it wasn't going to be smooth sailing. It was a darn shame, really: I had designed this speaker specifically to work with the Hammond organ, and I strongly believed that Hammond should have it. However, I knew I couldn't wait forever. When I left the store with my speaker, I told the Hammond manager that I would wait 30 days. If I hadn't heard from Hammond by the end of that period, I would start making and selling my speakers directly to the retail trade.

It's just as well I didn't wait by the phone, *seventeen years* later the President of Hammond called me and wanted to buy my company. In the meantime we had become hugely successful, but it was accomplished with a lot of unnecessary anguish, particularly since Hammond did everything they could to try to stop me.

K: It seems so strange to hear that. It seems impossible to think of listening to a Hammond without a Leslie. Together they are a perfect package.

L: You're right. (*laughing*) The sum of it is, they fought me, and I won. They ended up putting my speakers in all of their organs and my name on their instruments as well. Aside from Hammond, the other manufacturers did well with Leslie speakers from the early days onward. Of course, there was some hard negotiating along the way, but I can't say I had serious problems with them.

K: New question. I think every organ player knows your name and knows the Leslie Speaker. However, you are an inventor, and I am sure your creativity was not limited to just speakers. Tell us about some of your inventions in non-music fields.

L: I'm flattered that you think that, but that's not really the case. Being an inventor I do think of things, and I do have about 50 patents, but they're mostly in organ designs. There are two other fields I hold a few patents in: one is in model train control, and the other is in technical aspects of swimming pools. My ideas were good enough to be patentable, but there was not sufficient market potential to aggressively pursue development.

K: In the field of electronic music, the sound produced by musical instruments must go through a speaker to be heard. In terms of the entire spectrum of electronic music, what do you think are the most important considerations relative to speakers?

L: What do I think of producing music through speakers?

K: Yes, but from the point of view of creating electronic music, speakers are not optional, they are an integral part of the process. What do you think are the most important consideration for the future development and application of speakers in the system of electronic music?

L: Well, unfortunately, speakers sound like speakers. Even if you had the world's best speaker, let's call it a perfect speaker, you would still have the problem that you cannot squeeze all that music through and shoot it out of one spot. It doesn't sound right; it isn't anymore the thing that it started out to be. I would say 20 poor speakers are better than one perfect one. In my opinion there isn't any such thing as a "perfect" speaker that will sound exactly like the real thing, because it could not encompass enough of the physical acoustics that are necessarily beyond the scope of any single speaker.

So in designing speakers, while it's important, I don't think we should strive to get a "perfect" speaker, because I don't think we're going to know the difference. For example, in the organ I put together in my home, I use about 50 speakers. For the horn voices, I use horn speakers, and so forth. That's the way I think about speakers; they have a duty in a small area, they can't be everything all at once.

K: That's very good advice. Now here is a final question. Looking to the future, what advice do you have for the organ designers and engineers of tomorrow, with respect to sound?

L: As a general statement, I have a good feeling about the future for organs, because technology is advancing so fast in so many directions. I believe that, in order to make electronic instruments of any kind—pianos, organs, or anything else—sound more like the real thing, we need to present the sound to the ear, just as though it were coming from the real thing. New technology should bring us closer to that objective.

You know that I personally prefer "natural" instruments because of the physical reality of the acoustics. But that doesn't mean that we cannot continue to come closer and closer to the real sounds. Technicians must pay attention to what the real thing is doing in all respects. This is a complex challenge, because harmonics are coming from different places at different times. But technical innovation is expanding all the time. Not too long ago, two channels of sound was considered sophisticated; now we can begin to talk in terms of 150 channels! If tomorrow's technicians will keep in mind that we hear with two ears, and that sounds come to those ears from all directions, the new technologies can be applied in creative ways that will offer vast advances.

As I said, I have a good feeling about the future.

K: Thank you very much.

INTERVIEW
WITH ISAO TOMITA

Music can truly be a universal language, and for that reason it is particularly pleasing to see that more and more Japanese artists and composers are becoming internationally active. In the 130 years since Western music was introduced to Japan, it has taken strenuous effort and great sacrifice to overcome the difficulties of cultural and linguistic barriers, but wonderful progress has been made.

One of the major events in the acceptance of Japanese artists on the world stage occurred 30 years ago, when Mr. Isao Tomita made his worldwide debut as "Tomita—the world artist." He emerged as a star at a time when the development of electronic music in Japan was just getting underway, and Tomita's triumph was a matter of great pride for those of us who were engaged in producing this new category of musical instruments. His enormous achievement was truly an epoch-making event. In addition to increasing the prestige of Japanese performers, Tomita's success also significantly enhanced the worldwide appreciation of musical instruments manufactured in Japan.

I had the opportunity to visit Mr. Tomita at his home and interview him on November 30, 1999—just as the new millennium was about to dawn.

Kakehashi: Although you achieved world renown in 1974, with your Grammy nominated synthesizer album *Snowflakes Are*

Isao Tomita, Hector Olivera, and me.

Dancing, you actually had more than 20 years experience as a composer and musician before your "overnight" success with *Snowflakes.* Please tell me about your career before starting on synthesizers.

Tomita: My first work was in 1952. I was to create music for one of the minor TV programs of NHK (the call sign of Japan Broadcasting Corporation). In those days there was nothing like synthesizers, and we were using real orchestras and real-time musical instruments—in other words, acoustic musical instruments. Although Hammond Organs were electric, when I started my career as a musician, acoustic instruments were regarded as the only legitimate instruments in the world. The only limited exception might have been vibraphones, in which motors were electrically driven.

In those days I was particularly interested in a radio program called *Rittai Ongaku-do* (Stereophonic Music Hall) to which I devoted most of my time. It was an experimental program using two radio receivers. The "1st Station" and the "2nd Station" of NHK Radio broadcasted simultaneously, so that one served as a left channel and the other the right channel. This resulted in the combined broadcasts being heard as stereophonic.

K: I think I remember the program. Didn't it start with an announcer asking, "can you hear from the right?" and then, "can you hear from the left?"

T: Yes. That's correct. The program always started with an announcement asking audiences to adjust the balance of volumes. The announcement continued on for as long as three minutes, and then the actual program started. I was in my 20s and a novice in the industry. And I was entirely absorbed in working for the program, because I was allowed to use a large-scale orchestra consisting of approximately 80 players. At that time the compensation policy of NHK for musical arrangements or compositions was set on an hourly basis, so that there was barely any difference in remuneration whether your work was written for a small group of four or five players or for a large-scale orchestra with 80 players. Frankly speaking, experienced arrangers did not wish to work under such conditions. On the contrary, young novices were willing to take the job, and I was one of them.

K: I see. That created an opening for young composers to get serious work and important experience.

T: As you know, back in those days audio systems were equipped with only one speaker in the center, which we called the "one-eyed goblin." It was a dream-like experience for me to work in a program that used an audio system with speakers installed on both sides, effectively putting the listener with his two ears in the center of a world of sound. In fact I developed a special sense of almost every sound while I was working for that program. For instance, I realized that sounds such as the oboe and the flute could never be merged as one. Even if both were played in unison, they would always be heard simply as a mixture of two different sounds. And in case of duets, I came to understand which instrument, oboe or flute, should take the higher section in order to create more effective harmonies. I also learned effective ways of using stringed instruments. To tell you the truth, most of my fundamental techniques for playing the synthesizer were acquired through that job.

K: You went on to achieve a certain amount of local fame through writing the theme music for the TV program *Shin Nihon Kiko* (New Travels in Japan—a popular show exploring unique Japanese locales from unusual perspectives). When was that program on the air?

T: That was probably between 1955 and 1965. The opening theme played under film footage of a steam locomotive chugging along a single track. For many years now the rail system has been virtually all diesel engines running on double tracks, so it had to be at least 40 years ago. That was long before synthesizers too. We had to collect players to put together an orchestra in order to play the theme music.

Speaking of orchestration, I was an ardent admirer of Rimsky-Korsakov, the celebrated Russian composer of *Sheherazade*, and also of Ravel and Debussy, both of whom were associated with the French Impressionist movement. I was also enthusiastic about works of Stravinsky and Respighi. They also were influenced by French Impressionism. On the contrary, orchestral music composed by Mozart or Beethoven, for me, seemed somehow monochromatic. I was particularly interested in reasons why there were such big differences in tones even though they were played using the same types of musical instruments.

K: For those of us who were working on the development of synthesizers, a record called *Switched-on Bach*, created by Walter Carlos, was very impressive—as was his subsequent work as Wendy Carlos. In the midst of the excitement about the creative work of both Walter and Wendy Carlos, your record called *Snowflakes Are Dancing—The Newest Sound of Debussy* was released.

Your record consisted of absolutely astounding pieces. Listening to your music, we were stunned by the contrast with what we previously believed was possible. We felt as if we were looking at a fascinating painting, delicately woven using impossible curves and previously unimaginable colors immediately after having seen a monochromatic picture containing only straight lines. To us, who were especially aware of the difficulties of creating such sounds, it seemed like yours was a type of music that we would not even dare to create or would think that we could create. It was really a tremendous shock for us.

I assume that your challenge for synthesizers must have been based on the background that you just mentioned, in other words finding interests in Debussy or in Stravinsky. I am sure that the challenge was really difficult for you.

T: In those days in Japan, we had almost no information about what a synthesizer was. Although we had heard that some sort of product called "synthesizer" had been created, we knew nothing about it or what we could do with it. It was not until 1969, a year before the Osaka EXPO, that I clearly understood about synthesizers. While I was looking around shops of imported records in Osaka, I came across the *Switched-on Bach*. Listening to the record, I came to realize that it might be possible for a single person like me to produce orchestra sounds. That was the very first clue for me.

However, I could not find a synthesizer at all, although I searched everywhere that I could think of. I even sent inquiries to Hong Kong because they had access to imported products such as Gibson guitars before those products became available in Japan, but still there was barely any information at all. I also contacted Yamaha, because they were acting as an agent of various foreign manufacturers, but they even said they knew nothing about it.

Eventually I learned from a local trading company that there was a company manufacturing what was called Moog Synthesizer in Buffalo, New York. Although I did not have any exact information about the company nor any reason to be particularly confident, I decided to import the synthesizer through the trading company; it was the only source that I could count on. In the meantime I met Dr. Robert A. Moog who told me that there was an excellent engineer of musical instruments in Japan named Kakehashi. You had already met him before I did, is that right?

K: My first meeting with Dr. Moog was in Frankfurt. We eventually got acquainted with each other, for instance I visited his house and so on.

T: I remember having wondered who Mr. Kakehashi was, as I was not aware of your name in those days. The *Switched-on Bach* surely consisted of great music, but as you mentioned, the individual numbers were sort of a "line-drawing" type. I think most music composed using synthesizers in those days was created without giving much consideration to tones. Rather the tendency was to use several straight sounds mixed together. On the other hand, I aimed at another direction. My focus had been mainly in orchestration, seeking to create "colorful" type of sounds. I noticed, while experimenting with different filters of my synthesizer, that various types and complexities of sounds could be produced using the synthesizer. It occurred to me that I might be able to be competitive with the *Switched-on Bach* which was rather "line-drawing" Baroque type, if I, as an Oriental, would create pieces based on tunes of Debussy, especially the "not colored yet" type of his piano tones. You know that the French musical Impressionism was in fact generated under the influence of Oriental music affected by Japanese Gagaku (Japanese court music) players who visited Paris EXPO back in the 19th century.

That was how I set about creating with the synthesizer, and it was truly a hard work. To begin with, I had a great deal of trouble in importing. The custom officer yelled at me "Are you trying to fool me? This is not a musical instrument. Show me the proof." What could I do for him, because it definitely was a musical instrument? I had no other choice than to send a telex to Dr. Moog asking him to send me a document, but his answer did not arrive quickly. I was really disturbed because the customs clearance was suspended until I could satisfy them. I even showed a record jacket of *Switched-on Bach* on which a Moog synthesizer was displayed. They instantly denied accepting that, since the guy on the jacket looked so eccentric. They even said that the player wasn't really playing the instrument in that picture. Finally I showed another photo in which Keith Emerson was playing the synthesizer in a concert, and at last they granted me permission. It was quite a lot of trouble.

In the meantime, the synthesizer was stored in a commercial warehouse, because they said the government warehouse in Tokyo Airport was full. It took more than a month for me to obtain customs clearance, and then they charged me a storage fee. I was mad at them, because I did explain from the very beginning that it was a musical instrument. On the contrary they persisted that the fault was mine, because I was not able to clearly prove that it was a musical instrument and therefore I had the obligation of settling the storage charge. If I kept fighting with them, I would not be able to get the instrument, so I decided to pay the charge. There was no other choice. That was only the first part of the trouble. Even bigger trouble was to come.

K: In spite of all those troubles, you finally completed the record *Snowflakes Are Dancing—The Newest Song of Debussy,* and then introduced it to Japanese record companies. What was their reaction?

T: I personally contacted each company and visited them with cassette tapes of the record. Some of the younger generation directors showed positive interest, and a few asked me to show them the synthesizer, because they could not clearly grasp the concept based solely on the sound. When they came to my studio and realized that such a strange-looking machine was capable of creating such interesting sounds, they actually became excited. Watching their reactions, I thought that things would work well. However, after they consulted with the company's sales divisions, the situation became awkward. They couldn't decide in which part of a record shop my record should be displayed. They thought *Snowflakes* could not be included in any of existing categories, such as popular music, classics, film music or anything else. I checked where the *Switched-on Bach* was displayed in a shop and found out that it was placed next to a record called "Good old steam locomotives" among records in the sound-effects section. Because it defied traditional classification, heads of record companies decided that my record was really peculiar and would not sell, so they ended up denying my proposal.

I already had spent nearly a year producing the record, and during that time I had purchased not only the synthesizer but also various equipment including an echo machine from AKG Acoustics, a Compu-Mix and even a 16-channel recorder from Ampex. One of the Japanese record companies offered me a contract at a very small price, but I couldn't accept such a cheap offer, and that was why I decided to go to the United States to show my records there.

I learned that the director who produced the *Switched-on Bach*, Mr. Peter Manves, had moved to RCA from CBS Columbia. Since he clearly understood the potential of synthesized music, I contacted Mr. Manves directly. I was confident that my pieces showed completely unique characteristics written with a concept of "colorful" styles, and that there was no other music of the same sort. I hoped that he might be looking to repeat his earlier success, and I was right. He asked me "why don't you publish it in Japan?" I said, "I guess Japanese record companies are wondering in which section of a retail store my record should be placed," And then he said, "Go to a local record shop, and you will see my *Switched-on Bach* everywhere, I mean in the classic corner, the popular corner, the electronic music corner, and of course in the sound effects corner. It is in everywhere, so check it out. If I were you, I would go ahead and not worry about what shelf it ends up on." And I tried what he recommended, and it worked. He even organized press conferences. Eventually, I received quite a few phone calls from various Japanese companies offering to sell the records through their companies, because they somehow knew that my records were selling in New York.

K: After that success, you enlarged the scope of your music theme aggressively, for instance, taking an interest in the universe. I am still very proud of having supported you with the data coding for *The Bermuda Triangle*. I keep telling people that I once co-starred with Mr. Tomita.

T: Yes, I am deeply grateful for your help of that time. In those days the "gaaa" noise of computer was quite unique as itself, and I asked you to make the noise as an established sound.

K: To tell you the truth, I was greatly surprised that you stayed with noise sounds like "piii's" and "gaaa's."

T: I believed that such sounds were just right for that situation as effective sounds to simulate signals dispatched from a UFO carrying celestial aliens.

K: It was really remarkable. I was so impressed by your using such a noise as one of musical notes. Later on you became interested in sound-images, and what was the trigger for that? For instance, in the album *The Bermuda Triangle*, I noticed the launching sounds of rockets. Could you please tell me the story of how you became especially conscious of such three-dimensional sound-images?

T: In Japan around 1970, four-channel stereos were very popular. I was fond of the RCA type in which the JVC system was adopted. In that system everything was designed discretely, and I was especially interested in its capability of generating sounds from various directions.

In general classical music concerts, sounds usually come from a stage on which players are aligned, meaning that sound is over there and can be heard by the audience in a three-dimensional way. I believe that so-called stereo systems are based on this mechanism. On the contrary, however, in case of my synthesizer music, sounds are recorded in multi-track system, so that there is no fixed sound formation since there is actually no player. Therefore it is all up to me how I align each sound, move it around or whatever. In case of acoustic instruments, such performance would sound rather unnatural, but in case of synthesizer sounds, it is by no means unacceptable. Just like fantasy animations, there is no original state from the beginning. Therefore I decided to use the four-channel stereo and involved myself in it, thinking that multi-track recording was the best choice for my synthesizer music. I actually created several works, but unfortunately the four-channel stereo system didn't last as long as I had hoped. Nowadays I can use DVD audio systems and perform controls of six-channels, so once again I am trying to pursue my dream.

The relationship between audience and players in concerts, namely the audience on one side and the players on a stage on the other side, is just a custom through the history of music. I believe that sound fields can exist anywhere, for instance on the spot that you are standing right now. In our daily lives, you can hear various sounds from every direction whether you are walking in a downtown or playing on a beach, meaning that you are living in a certain universe of sounds. I couldn't help but feel that I could create such a universe in the world of music, and that is why I decided to set about my experiments in the three-dimensional sound fields. For me, that kind of approach is the best way to satisfy my listeners. Unfortunately audio players of CD or records mainly use two or three channels, though....

K: That's right. There are still limitations in conditions or circumstances in which the audience can listen to such music at home.

T: Yes, and I can't help feeling sad because I have a sense that listeners are, at this moment, listening to reduced versions of my music. I hope that I will be able to create works that will include the sound fields that I really have in mind.

K: Recently when you did a concert of your new piece, *The Tale of Genji*, you used our RSS (Roland Sound System) in various ways, and I appreciated your experiments. Luckily our RSS system was completed at the very moment to which Mr. Yamato (an engineer at Roland) had committed himself. We were all pleased that we could meet your requirements in that very challenging time frame. Speaking of the RSS, for us it is rather easier to implement sound effects that you call "moving" and "running," but implementing effects like "floating" or "stopping-right-there" is quite difficult technically. What was the base of your conceptions of having an evil-spirited ghost drift within your music?

T: As I was conducting the orchestra on the stage, I could not actually hear the effects with my own ears. But, according to the response from the audience, I knew that my scheme was achieved as I had intended. As you know, if you simply move sounds between right and left speakers, one sound gets smaller while the other gets louder. But using the RSS, it was highly successful in creating live effects in which the jealous spirit of the Rokujo lady appeared suddenly on one spot and then faded away. In the process, you could almost feel a sensation that her cold hand would touch your face sooner or later. I believe it was a real success. Westerners are even more fond of ghosts than we Japanese, (laughter), so it was really effective.

K: As a manufacturer of musical instruments, we have been associating with you through technical collaborations as well as experiments with equipment. Our first collaboration was over the MC-8 (micro composer), which was one of the products that brought me into the world of computers, and the latest collaboration is with the RSS that you have just mentioned.

I believe that the finest musical instrument among all existing instruments is the human voice. However, until recently, it has been considered impossible to "play" human voices. Human voices are in fact excellent instruments in which pitches are organized in a total manner, and furthermore they are capable of presenting "meanings."

Using the technology that we are currently developing, we see more and more likely possibilities of playing "human voices" in the context of the MIDI system. First of all we focused in the technology of manipulating the human voices, but as we went along, we understood more and more that the possibilities are not limited to that area alone. Now, as we proceed with the project, we are receiving enthusiastic responses from creators of sound-sources for computer-aided music. It is clear that the prospect of a technology in which the human voices can be used as material is tremendously exciting to them. A while ago we introduced the same technology to you, Mr. Tomita, and by now it has come to be even more usable. I am confident that you will be able to develop new and fresh applications as we continue to refine the system.

T: That sounds great.

K: The relationship that exists between hardware and software, in other words between the producer of musical instruments and artists, has remained unchanged from the days of Beethoven. Only very recently have materials such as semiconductors or silicon come to be accessible to us. Both you and I have lived through the times of vacuum tubes, transistors, and IC's, and now we have come to the period in which we are freed from worries about costs of CPU's and memories. Can you describe for me your dreams of the new fields of music that are to come in the near future?

T: People in general tend to make a distinction between acoustic instruments and the others. Talking about myself, I entered the world of music starting from orchestras and then met synthesizers. There is no such artificial distinction in my thinking.

Electricity has existed from the beginning of the earth as a form of lightening and thunder. People in the prehistoric ages heard the roar of thunder exactly as we do today. Not just human beings but other animals as well, while living in a world of acoustic sound, have kept the balance of their lives by harnessing the electrical mechanisms within their bodies. In a similar sense, for me, there is no difference at all between acoustic instruments and instruments that use electricity. In other words, flutes or pipe organs were created taking the advantage of natural resources, while electricity is just one of the same natural resources.

You know that mechanisms used in pipe organs are tremendous. The invention of pipe organs took place in an era when only primitive musical instruments were played, and its significance was great, because it enabled us to perform sounds greater than orchestration even as a single player. Eventually excellent pipe organs were invented. Initially, electricity was not adopted in the instruments. Thanks to the wisdom of human beings, the mechanism to control natural air flows was created—first human beings treading on a great bellows and now, sophisticated electrical generators. Do you have any idea how many years ago the pipe organs were actually invented?

K: The other day I saw a TV news program featuring a Hydraulis organ that had been excavated in Greece. I understood that it was more than two thousand years old. Amazingly the Hydraulis was properly equipped with pipes and keyboards.

T: Did they use white and black keys in the Hydraulis?

K: No, there was no black key, and to tell you the truth they used a reversed musical scale in that instrument, meaning that intervals become lower as you go rightward. As a power source, a water pump was used.

T: That it is one of the mechanisms I have been talking about. Whether you are using water power or electricity, both of them are natural energy originally, so that it is never necessary to distinguish one from the other. What we must pay more attentions to is the diversity of musical instruments. Thanks to that diversity, guitar players who could only play guitars can now use their instruments to control synthesizers. The birth of electronic musical instruments has broadened the scope of expression.

Musicians now have access to an expanded array of available resources, so that they are now capable of expressing sounds that previously could only exist in their minds and imaginations. In addition, people whose musical expression was artificially limited because of the physical properties of traditional musical instruments can now increase their creativity thanks to the arrival of the synthesizers. I see more and more people finding their way like that. As for myself, I am thankful to synthesizers, because they have given me access to forms of expression that simply are not possible with traditional orchestras alone. That does not mean that I don't love orchestras. But I believe that we will see more composers who feel the same as I. I expect a brilliant future. Not just for musicians but also for listeners who will have wider selections of what to hear.

K: I really enjoyed talking with you, and thank you very much for your interesting stories.

T: Thank you.

Bibliography

1   Alan Douglas : *The Electronic Musical Instrument Manual*, 1976
2   Peter Williams : *A New History Of The Organ*, 1980
3   William H. Barnes : *The Contemporary American Organ*, 1930
4   Walter & Thomas Lewis : *Modern Organ Building*, 1986
5   George Ashdown Audsley : *The Art Of Organ-Building*, 1965
6   David L. Junchen : *Encyclopedia Of The American Theatre Organ Vol. I*, 1985
7   Q. David Bowers : *Encyclopedia Of Automatic Musical Instruments*, 1997（再版）
8   Frank T. Hubbard : *Three Centuries Of Harpsichord Making*, 1972
9   Herbert A. Deutsch : *Synthesis*, 1976
10   David M. Rubin : *The Audible Macintosh*, 1992
11   Jerome Markowitz : *Triumphs & Trials Of An Organ Builder*
12   Andre Millard 著／橋本毅彦訳：エジソン発明会社の没落 （朝日新聞社, 1993）
13   *The Story Of Hammond Organ Company ; When Electrons Sing* Hammond Organ Company
14   *Fifty Years Of Musical Excellence 50th Anniversary 1394-1984*   Hammond Organ Company
15   Mark Vail : *Vintage Synthesizers*, 1994
16   Mark Vail : *The Hammond Organ ; Beauty In The B*, 1997
17   Don Leslie : *The Don Leslie Story*（個人の執筆物で未刊行）
18   Richard H. Dorf : *Electronic Musical Instruments*, 1958
19   Alan Douglas : *The Electrical Production Of Music*, 1957
20   James A. Koel : *The Lowrey Story*
21   Laurens Hammond : *U. S. Patent 1,956,350*, 1934. 01. 19
22   Laurens Hammond : *U. S. Patent Reverbration Apparatus,* 1939. 10. 07
23   Laurens Hammond : *U. S. Patent Musical Instrument*, 1940. 07. 30
24   Desmond Briscoe & Roy Curtis Bramwell : *The BBC Radiophonic Work Shop*, 1983
25   Stevens Irwin : *Dictionary Of Hammond Organ Stops*, 1939
26   Stevens Irwin : *Dictionary Of Electronic Organ Stops*, 1968
27   Jack C. Goode : *Pipe Organ Registration*, 1964
28   Joel Chadabe : *Electric Sound*, 1996

The following titles are available only in Japanese language editions:

29   團伊玖磨：私の日本音楽史 （日本放送出版協会, 1999）
30   大崎滋生：楽譜の文化史 （音楽之友社, 1993）
31   檜山陸郎：洋琴ピアノものがたり （芸術現代社, 1986）
32   檜山陸郎：楽器業界 （教育社新書, 1977）
33   藤枝守：響きの考古学 （音楽之友社, 1998）
34   A. T. サリヴァン著／岡田作彦訳：ピアノと平均率の謎 （白楊社, 1989）
35   長嶋洋一、橋本周司、平賀譲、平田圭二編：コンピュータと音楽の世界 （共立出版, 1998）
36   吉田実、高橋秀、志村拓生、馬渕久夫編：日本のオルガンⅡ （日本オルガニスト協会, 1992）
37   辻宏：風の歌　パイプオルガンと私 （日本基督教団出版局, 1988）
38   皆川達夫：バロック音楽 （講談社現代新書, 1972）
39   阪田寛夫：どれみそら （河出書房新社, 1995）
40   渡辺裕：音楽機械劇場 （新書館, 1997）
41   境久雄編：聴覚と音響心理 （コロナ社, 1978）
42   電子楽器と電気楽器 （「無線と実験」別冊, 誠文堂新光社, 1961）
43   F. K. プリーバーグ／入野義朗訳：電気技術時代の音楽 （音楽之友社, 1963）
44   H. クロッツ／藤野薫訳：オルガンのすべて （（株）パックスビジョン, 1978）
45   NHK オルガン研究会編：オルガン音楽のふるさと （1975）
46   中村とうよう：ポピュラー音楽の世紀 （岩波新書, 1999）
47   大和明：ジャズの黄金時代とアメリカの世紀 （音楽之友社, 1997）
48   金田一春彦、安西愛子編：日本の唱歌 （上・中・下） （講談社文庫, 1977）
49   長田暁二、千藤幸蔵編著：日本の民謡　西日本・東日本編 （現代教養文庫, 1998）
50   月刊ミュージックトレード （ミュージックトレード社）
51   アグネル＆ハンナ・カルミ／郡司すみ訳：奇蹟のピアノ （音楽之友社, 1984）
52   皆川達夫：楽譜の歴史 （音楽之友社, 1985）
53   茂手木潔子：日本の楽器　その素材と響き （音楽之友社, 1988）